CONFLICT AND CRISIS
IN THE
POST–COLD WAR WORLD

ALGERIA

THE FUNDAMENTALIST CHALLENGE

James Ciment

Facts On File, Inc.

To my sister

Algeria: The Fundamentalist Challenge

Copyright © 1997 by James Ciment

Facts On File, Inc.
11 Penn Plaza
New York NY 10001

Library of Congress Cataloging-in-Publication Data

Ciment, James.
    Algeria : the fundamentalist challenge / James Ciment.
      p.   cm. — (Conflict and crisis in the post-cold war world)
    Includes bibliographical references (p.   ) and index.
    ISBN 0-8160-3340-4
    1. Islam and politics—Algeria. 2. Algeria—Politics and
government.   I. Title.   II. Series.
    DT295.5.C56   1997   96-48372
    965.05′4—dc21

Facts On File books are available at special discounts when purchased in bulk quantities for businesses, associations, institutions or sales promotions. Please call our Special Sales Department in New York at 212/967-8800 or 800/322-8755.

Cover design by Robert Yaffe

Maps by Dale Williams

MP FOF 10 9 8 7 6 5 4 3 2 1

This book is printed on acid-free paper.

CONTENTS

LIST OF MAPS

PREFACE: CONFLICT AND CRISIS IN THE POST–COLD WAR WORLD

The eminent British historian E. J. Hobsbawm has recently declared the end of the "short twentieth century," delimited by the two great Russian revolutions of 1917 and 1991. If that is so, then this series might be considered among the first histories of the twenty-first century.

Whatever date we care to assign the beginning of the new century, we carry into it a lot of baggage from the past. The Cold War may be over, but just as the two global struggles of the first half of the twentieth century left a legacy of troubled peace, so has the great confrontation of the second half.

Conflict the Crisis in the Post–Cold War World explores that legacy. Each conflict described in these volumes has been a place where the Cold War turned hot.

The confrontation between East and West, however, did not ignite these conflicts. Each one has a history that stretches back to long before the atom bomb was dropped on Hiroshima or the wall was built in Berlin. Most of them, in fact, are not products of the Cold War so much as they are legacies of the European imperial order of the last several hundred years, and, in the case of Kurdistan, of a struggle that goes back a lot further than that.

Similarly, these conflicts have had important indigenous and regional components. The great delusion of the Cold War, that all conflicts were essentially superpower confrontations by proxy, has been exposed in the post–Cold War era for the myth that it was. Ethnicity, religion and the animosity between settler and indigenous societies are, in varying measures, at the root of the very different conflicts examined in this series.

But that is not to let the Cold War off the historical hook. The struggle between Washington and Moscow exacerbated, extended and exaggerated each of these conflicts, and many more. Both East and West offered support in the form of money, weaponry, intelligence and military training to their favored clients. Worst of all, they provided an ideological force-field that deflected potential negotiations and peaceful solutions.

The books in this series examine the roles of pre–Cold War history, the Cold War, and indigenous and regional factors in these conflicts.

They are intended as introductory volumes for the reader acquainted with but not versed in the stories of these wars. They are short but comprehensive and readable reference works. Each follows a similar format and contains similar chapters: an introduction and overview of the conflict;

its history; the participants, both those in power and those struggling against it; the issues, tactics and negotiations involved; and a final chapter as update and conclusion. (The volume on Israel/Palestine contains an additional chapter on the larger regional conflict between Israel and the Arab nations of the Middle East.) Each book also contains several maps, a glossary of names and terms and a bibliography.

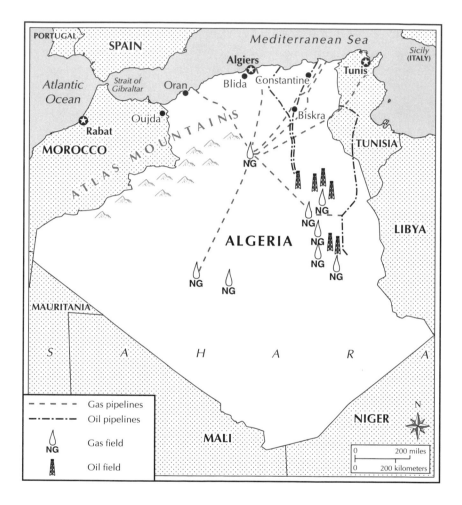

PORTUGAL

SPAIN

Mediterranean Sea

Sicily
(ITALY)

*Atlantic
Ocean*

*Strait of
Gibraltar*   Oran

Algiers   Blida   Constantine

Tunis

Oujda

Rabat

MOROCCO

A T L A S   M O U N T A I N S

Biskra

TUNISIA

NG

LIBYA

ALGERIA

NG

NG

NG

NG

NG

NG

NG

NG

NG

NG

MAURITANIA

S   A   H   A   R   A

N

NIGER

MALI

Gas pipelines

Oil pipelines

Gas field
NG

Oil field

0   200 miles

0   200 kilometers

1

INTRODUCTION[1]

Algerians are allergic to social injustice.
—Ghania Moffok, journalist

There's a national psychosis.
—Anonymous Algerian woman

Algeria is a nation at war with itself. Islamic militants battle government security forces. Secularist death squads assassinate fundamentalists. Civilians are routinely caught in the crossfire. During the height of the war in 1994 and 1995, hundreds of people are killed each week. The toll in human lives, most experts agree, now stands at over 40,000. The political system as it exists is polarized, and there has been little constructive dialogue between the government and its opponents. The Algerian economy, in precarious shape before the war began, is now a catastrophe, marked by food shortages, massive unemployment, a crumbling infrastructure and an external debt of over $25 billion. Nonpolitical Algerians feel a mix of resignation, dread and anger. "Fear is in the heart, but life goes on," explained a woman in Algiers. "Fanatics or no fanatics, this is the only country I have."[2]

What has brought Algeria to the brink—some say over the brink—of civil war? The short-term answer is obvious. In 1990 and 1991, the leadership of Algeria, in power since their victory over the nation's French colonizers in 1962, responded to popular pressure and organized the first multiparty elections in the nation's history. But when Islamic fundamentalists, represented by the Islamic Salvation Front (FIS) swept the first two elections and seemed poised to win a more than two-thirds majority in the National Popular Assembly (APN)—large enough to amend the nation's constitution—the military organized a successful coup, forced the president to resign, canceled the final round of elections, disbanded the parliament, outlawed the FIS and then jailed almost 10,000 members of the party without trial. Within days, soldiers were shooting down demonstrators. Within weeks, radical FIS members had gone underground to launch a largely urban guerrilla war against the junta. The war has escalated since.

The middle-term answer is not as easy to formulate. Clearly, the pre-coup Algerian government was extremely unpopular. Most Algerians considered it corrupt, elitist and economically incompetent. Moreover, Algeria has been a single-party state run by the National Liberation Front

(FLN) since independence. All independent political, economic and social organizations have been subordinated to the will of the party, and the party has operated in an inherently undemocratic fashion. The only independent institution in Algeria was the network of free mosques, established by fundamentalist mullahs during the 1970s and 1980s. Thus, when the political opening came, the only organization capable of taking advantage of the widespread dissatisfaction with the ruling FLN was the fundamentalists.

The long-term answer depends on one's perspective on Algerian politics. Most Algerian secularists (a term defined below) believe that the electoral appeal of the FIS is based precisely on the above-mentioned dissatisfaction. FIS spokesmen partially agree, but they say that Algerian identity is essentially Islamic, and the government's blatant effort to separate Islam from governing alienated the masses. Voters were drawn to FIS for positive reasons: they supported the party's program for the Islamicization of Algerian society.

In any case, civil strife has engulfed Algeria since early 1992. And like most civil conflicts, this one is especially vicious. Fundamentalist militants employ suicide bombs, assassinations and death threats in order to make Algeria ungovernable. They have targeted domestic opponents, including anti-fundamentalist journalists, government workers, security force personnel (and their relatives) and, most controversially, women who do not wear the veil in public. They have carried out the murders of over a hundred foreigners, hijacked planes and bombed targets overseas in order to isolate Algeria and halt the support that foreign powers, especially France, extend the government. Secularist death squads assassinate Islamic militants and women who do wear the veil. The government conducts routine sweeps through Islamist neighborhoods, arbitrarily detains tens of thousands of prisoners in camps in the Sahara Desert, tortures suspects and assassinates Islamic militants. More than one observer has noted the irony of freedom fighters from the War of Independence against France using the same methods, and sometimes the same facilities, the French government once used against them.

While a sudden breakthrough in negotiations between the government and the Islamists is always possible, events do not indicate such a breakthrough is likely. First, the ruling junta and the FIS have thoroughly demonized each other. Military leaders are convinced that if the FIS comes to power it will never relinquish it. As they continue to repeat, the fundamentalist idea of democracy is "one man, one vote, one time." For its part, the FIS refuses to recognize the legitimacy of the ruling junta and argues that it is the military that circumvented the democratic process.

Second, the political polarization of Algeria has been accompanied by a fracturing of political institutions. Although the FIS negotiated a common platform with secular opposition forces in Rome, radical fundamentalists have formed alternative organizations that continue the violence. Many in Algeria and abroad wonder if FIS leaders could persuade radical organizations like the Armed Islamic Group (GIA) to accept a negotiated peace or a gradual transition to power. Fundamentalists, their sympathizers and many uncommitted Algerians wonder if the military and domestic security forces are answerable to anyone anymore.

Adding to the confusion is the Berber question. A culturally and linguistically distinct minority representing about 25 percent of the Algerian population, the Berbers are traditionally hostile to Islamic politics, seeing it as a cover for the Arabization of Algerian society and an assault on their own cultural identity. Berbers are also traditionally more left-wing than Arabs, though since the political opening of the early 1990s, a particularly virulent and anti-Arab strain of nationalist politics has gained support in the Kabyle, the largely Berber enclave just east of the capital, Algiers.

Finally, Algeria is a country with a dual personality. The 132-year French reign and the experiences of millions of Algerians who have worked and lived in France since independence have left a definite imprint on the Algerian people, who are among the most westernized people in the Arab world. At the same time, the vast majority of Algerians are devoutly Muslim and identify deeply with the teachings of that faith. One side of that personality longs for an Algeria that is socially, politically and economically modern and Western, where faith remains important but is firmly separated from matters of state. The other seeks an Algeria that is technologically up-to-date but culturally and socially Islamicized, where faith governs all activities of state and infuses every aspect of daily life.

This book examines both visions and why many in Algeria and abroad see them as mutually exclusive. It explores the scriptural and historical roots of both Islamic and secular Algerian and Muslim thought on politics, economics and society. It lays out the various issues the parties to the conflict are fighting over. It chronicles the vicissitudes of a vicious civil war and suggests a few possible endings of the conflict.

ALGERIA IN THE MID-1990s

Since the January 11, 1992, coup, Algeria has been ruled by a joint executive body known as the High Council of State (HCE). Although the council includes several civilian members, the military runs Algeria; few have been deceived by its largely transparent efforts to hide the fact. Immediately after taking power, they brought back Mohammed Boudiaf, one of the *chefs historiques*, or historical leaders, of the revolution, to serve as president. Less than six months later, Boudiaf was assassinated, allegedly by hard-liners in the military who did not appreciate his advocacy of a negotiated settlement with the Islamic militants. Since early 1994, former defense minister Liamine Zeroual, a relative hard-liner, has been at the helm of state. The military has also established a 60-member advisory council to serve in place of the disbanded APN. He was elected to the presidency in November 1995, though the FIS was not permitted to run candidates. In May 1996, Zeroual promised elections for the national parliament to be held in early 1997.

The current wave of political violence did not begin with the coup. Algeria has experienced violent demonstrations and brutal governmental crackdowns since the nationwide riots of October 1988 and the subsequent shooting of some 1,000 demonstrators by the army. But the conflict that has emerged since the coup has involved violence on an exponentially increased level. In March 1995, for instance, the government released statistics on the previous year's carnage: 6,388 civilians killed, including 682 civil servants, 52 progovernment imams (Muslim religious leaders), 101 teachers, 61 foreigners, 21 journalists, 15 judges and 13 high-level government officials. Overall, said the president's office, some 10,000 people had died in the war, a statistic virtually every Algerian and international publication considers a gross underestimate.

The violence is qualitatively different as well. Unlike the riots of 1988, the current violence is neither spontaneous nor capable of being put down by a simple show of force. Several clandestine organizations, both fundamentalist and secularist, are conducting specifically targeted attacks on security forces, political opponents and civilians who do not conform to the social goals of these groups. This last group consists largely of women, allegedly targeted by Islamic groups for not wearing the veil in public or other acts against codes of Islamic propriety, or attacked by secularist groups for succumbing to Islamic threats and donning the veil.

In addition, the GIA has been targeting foreigners in Algeria since September 1994, when it issued an ultimatum: get out or be killed. In its communiques, the GIA said it considered the 100,000 foreigners who live and work in Algeria as invaders of the Muslim state and supporters of the government. In fact, the attacks, which began in earnest with the murder of fourteen Christian Bosnian and Croatian workers in December 1993, are designed to isolate the Algerian junta and bring the economy to a halt, since foreign technicians are crucial to the smooth operation of Algeria's critical oil and gas sector. This strategy also explains the spate of attacks on French targets, including the hijacking of an Air France airbus in December 1994 and a spate of bombings and attempted bombings in France in the summer of 1995. Given its long colonial relationship, France is the European country with the closest ties to Algeria and is rightly considered by the GIA and the FIS as the junta's leading supporter in the West.

Civilian carnage and foreign targets aside, the war is being fought largely between Islamic militants and Algeria's military, *gendarmerie* (national police) and local police. The bulk of the war's casualties, certainly over two-thirds and perhaps as many as three-quarters, involve militants, suspected or real, and members of the various security forces. There is some fighting in the Algerian *bled*, or countryside. But most of the fighting goes on in the same poor and working-class enclaves of the nation's cities, particularly the capital's, where the war of liberation against France was fought—and for much the same reason. Like the FLN revolutionaries, the GIA militants realize that attacks in the capital have a greater propaganda and morale effect.

Even though most of the fighting occurs between security forces and Islamic militant organizations like the GIA, the Algerian civil war is not a strictly bilateral affair. Since the conflict began in 1992, there has been a splintering and multiplication of forces. On the Islamic side, the FIS appears to have come apart. There is still a political leadership, though much of it is in exile or in prison. There is also an armed wing. Mostly composed of Islamic veterans of the anti-Soviet struggle in Afghanistan, these militants, known popularly in Algeria as "Afghanis," have formed groups like the GIA and the Armed Islamic Movement (MIA). Meanwhile, the government has invoked a state of emergency, which gives security forces a virtual free rein in conducting their antiterrorist activities. Known as "ninjas" because they wear black outfits and balaclava hoods to mask their identity, these forces act as a law unto themselves. In addition, secularist and Berber death squads have begun a campaign of revenge killings against GIA militants for the murders of secularist opponents.

For Algerians and outsiders alike, it is often difficult to determine who bears responsibility for a given act of violence and terror. The FIS, an undisciplined and antihierarchical structure to begin with, has issued contradictory statements concerning its position on violence. Various communiqués and statements, from underground in Algeria and exile abroad, have alternatively advocated civil disobedience only, violence limited to self-defense and all-out war. Moreover, the FIS' relationship with the militant GIA and MIA is not clear. The government asserts they are one, while the FIS usually denies responsibility for GIA actions. If there is a consensus among outside observers and nonpolitical Algerians, it is that there is some kind of relationship between the GIA and the FIS but that, in general, the cells of the militant organizations act largely independently of each other. Given the intense level of counterinsurgency tactics by the government and the numerous government infiltrators in the militant organizations, this may very well be so.

As for the government side, there is undoubtedly more accountability and cohesiveness among the various branches of the security forces. Yet there is an increasing suspicion among Algerians, and not just fundamentalist sympathizers, that many of the terrorist acts, up to and including assassinations of police officers, may be the work of elite units of the security forces themselves or their *agents provocateurs* among the Islamists. If this is indeed true, these acts are obviously designed to instill fear and revulsion in the population against the Islamic militants. The government, indeed, has a well-oiled propaganda machine aimed at both the domestic and international audiences.

The chaos in Algeria is especially hard to sort out because those who might normally provide information, that is, domestic and foreign journalist, have become targets themselves. Over a hundred journalists have thus far been killed in the war and most Western news organizations have either pulled their correspondents out of Algeria or allowed them to report on events only in the company of government security forces. Thus, objective reporting and facts about the war are hard to come by, and answers to basic questions of responsibility for the violence virtually impossible to reach.

A PROFILE OF ALGERIA

Population: 27,895,000 (July 1994 estimate)
Area: 919,591 square miles
GDP: $89 billion (1993 estimate)

GEOGRAPHY AND CLIMATE

Algeria is an immense nation, the tenth largest in the world by area, the second largest in Africa, and more than four times the size of France. It is situated between Morocco and Tunisia on the North African coast, across the Mediterranean from Spain and France. The five Muslim countries of northwest Africa—Algeria, Libya, Mauritania, Morocco and Tunisia (and, if and when it becomes a sovereign state, the Western Sahara)—form a region known as the Maghrib, an Arabic word meaning "the West" or "Land of the Setting Sun."[3] The country is geographically and climatically diverse. The coastal area consists largely of valleys, plains and low mountains. Here the climate is Mediterranean, that is, hot dry summers and relatively mild rainy winters. The western portion of the coastal zone is hillier and drier, traditional pasture land. The eastern portion, wetter and laced with valleys, supports more agriculture. Rising from the coastal valleys and plains are the Tellian Atlas Mountains, with peaks climbing to 8,000 feet. Behind these mountains lies the high plains, or *hautes plateaux*, a harsh dry landscape with seasonal extremes of temperature and devoted to sporadic pasturage. From these plains rise the Saharan Atlas Mountains, comparable in elevation to the Tellian Atlas range. Both mountain ranges include a series of passes that provide access to the Sahara Desert, which covers more than seven-eighths of the country. There is a number of inhabited oases in the Sahara; the most important are a chain known as the Tuat complex in the central part of the country.

Only 3 percent of Algeria is arable farmland, 13 percent is pasturage and 2 percent is forest. Since independence, there have been significant problems with soil erosion, deforestation, overgrazing and pollution. But the greatest limitation on Algerian agriculture is lack of water. As historian John Ruedy notes, "the availability of water has been the most important physical variable shaping Algerian history."[4] The Atlas Mountains, while substantial enough to trap moisture blowing in from the Atlantic and the Mediterranean, are not high enough to form extensive snow packs whose melting would feed permanent navigable rivers. An additional water problem is the erratic nature of rainfall from season to season. This has made it difficult for Algeria to sustain a predictable agricultural output. Much of Algerian agriculture is devoted to the production of dry-farming wheat, as well as sheep and goat-grazing. Oases in the desert support date farming.

Algeria is rich in mineral deposits, including iron, phosphates, uranium, lead and zinc. But its most important resource is fossil fuel. Algeria boasts massive natural gas reserves (fifth largest in the world) and lesser oil reserves (14th largest). Discovered by French geologists in 1956, they are located in the Sahara and connected to the Mediterranean and Europe by a network of pipelines.

DEMOGRAPHICS AND POLITICS

Algeria has experienced explosive population growth throughout the twentieth century, and especially since independence. In 1962, the nation's population was roughly ten million, a figure that included approximately one million people of European descent, known as *colons*, the vast majority of whom fled to France shortly after independence. Since that time, the population of Muslim Algerians has more than tripled. Improved medical care and education, as well as government encouragement of large families produced an annual growth rate of 3.6 percent through 1985. Since that time, the government has tried to promote family planning, which, combined with the current conflict, had brought the growth rate down to an estimated 2.3 percent in 1994. While life expectancy at birth is a relatively lengthy sixty-eight years, Algeria's population is extremely young. Approximately three-quarters are under twenty years old.

Another important demographic development of the independence period has been urbanization. In 1900, only about one in eight Algerian Muslims lived in cities. When the revolution began in 1954, the figure was roughly one in five. Today, approximately half the population is urban, with five million in the Algiers metropolitan area alone. Other important cities include the port of Oran in western Algeria and Constantine in the east. Tizi Ouzou, about 75 miles east of Algiers, is the cultural capital of the

Berber region of Kabyle. Approximately 20 to 25 percent of Algerians are Berber, though many Berbers have emigrated from the Kabyle to Algiers, where they have adopted Arabic as their primary language. Berbers and Arabs are virtually identical physically. The distinctions between them are linguistic, cultural, historical and to some extent political. There are also scattered populations of indigenous nomads in the Sahara. The most numerous of these tribal peoples are the Tuaregs, who are largely Muslim but speak their own language.

Algerians, both Berber-speaking and Arabic-speaking, are predominantly Sunni Muslim. Only about one percent of Algerians are Jewish or Christian. While most urban Algerians possess a smattering of French, and French is a common second or third language in the Kabyle, there is a small population that speaks French as its primary language. Though relatively few in number, these francophones are extremely influential and represent much of the bureaucratic, military, business and intellectual elite. It is fair to say that the class structure of Algeria roughly follows the nation's linguistic and cultural faultlines.

Politically, Algeria is divided into forty-eight provinces, known as *wilaya*. The capital is Algiers. There are three major parties: the once-ruling FLN, the Berberist FFS and the now-outlawed religious FIS. Algeria is technically a constitutional republic, with a unicameral legislature, the National Popular Assembly, a prime minister, who appoints the cabinet, an independently elected president, who is the commander-in-chief of the armed forces, and a supreme court. All of these institutions, however, have been supplanted since January 1992 by the High Council of State and an advisory body appointed by the president, the National Consultative Council. The judiciary is still functioning, but on internal security issues has largely been supplanted by military tribunals established under the state of emergency in force since February 1992.

In December 1996, a new constitution, written largely by the military and High Council of State, was approved in a national plebiscite. The new constitution offers sweeping powers to the presidency, restricts those of parliament and bans Islamist political parties.

In 1993, Algeria spent $1.35 billion, or 2.5 percent of GDP, on defense.

ECONOMY

While the conflict in Algeria has crippled the economy, it is more an effect than a primary cause of the nation's current economic woes. These include an official unemployment rate of 25 percent in 1993 (unofficial estimates put it closer to 33 percent, with urban youth experiencing unemployment levels of approximately 75 percent), a $26 billion external debt and food imports estimated at 70 percent of consumption. In 1992, Algeria exported

$11.4 billion worth of goods, 97 percent of which were oil and gas, and imported $9 billion. France is by far Algeria's largest trading partner, at about 30 percent, followed by Italy, Spain, the United States, Germany and Japan in that order.

Algeria's economic problems stem from both long-term and short-term causes. The centralized command economy in Algeria, established after independence, emphasized the development of heavy industries such as steel and petrochemicals. These "industrializing industries" were expected to be the engine of Algeria's rapid rise into the industrialized world. And indeed, Algeria made dramatic gains in industrial growth in the 1960s and early 1970s. This growth, as well as the dramatic increase in oil prices following the OPEC oil boycott in 1973–74, allowed the government to build what for the Third World was a rather impressive social welfare system, including compulsory education through high school, national health care and subsidized fuel and food prices. The country made dramatic gains in health and education, among both male and female Algerians. Infant mortality fell by a third between 1960 and 1981, life expectancy climbed by about a decade and literacy rates more than tripled, though adult women still have a literacy rate half that of men.

Beneath this facade of modernization, however, lurked two serious economic problems. First, Algeria succumbed to many of the same economic troubles bedeviling socialist regimes elsewhere in the world. Huge bureaucracies multiplied, rendering the industries inefficient, slow to adjust to economic change and uncompetitive in international markets. Corruption was rife and relations between the public and private sectors were based on personal connections and bribery. Second, the emphasis on investment in heavy industry came at the expense of consumer goods production, housing and agriculture, none of which were adequate to the demands of Algeria's rapidly growing population.

In the early 1980s, the government began to recognize these basic problems and elaborated a plan to fix them. In the climate of supply-side economics prevailing in much of the West, the Algerian government chose to liberalize its economy, with an emphasis on free trade, some privatization and the breaking up of large state monopolies into independent, competitive state firms. The government also launched an anti-corruption drive. None of these plans, however, was carefully thought out. Liberalization and free trade led to massive imports of consumer and luxury goods. The breakup of the state monopolies only increased bureaucratic overhead. And the anti-corruption campaign was limited to the prosecution of a few errant individuals, rather than the establishment of effective watchdog agencies.

These systemic problems, however, were masked by a massive new infusion of petrodollars, following price hikes in oil and gas triggered by the Iranian revolution in 1979. With oil prices expected to continue rising into the foreseeable future, Algeria was able to borrow heavily on the international money markets. This, and the increased hydrocarbon revenues, allowed the government to maintain its social welfare net, even as the country increased its imports of luxury goods.

The bottom fell out in the mid-1980s, when oil prices plunged again to pre-1973 levels (adjusted for inflation). Algeria was suddenly confronted with rapidly diminished revenues and falling productivity. Under the liberalization plan, this resulted in massive layoffs and little hiring in Algeria's now cost-conscious industries. Unemployment, already growing due to the massive influx of migrants from the impoverished countryside, exploded. Faced with diminishing revenues, the government began to scale back its social welfare programs and subsidies on food and fuel in order to meet its international debt obligations.

Hard times visited Algeria, but not all Algerians, with a vengeance. Well-connected bureaucrats, businessmen, speculators and politicians continued to prosper, thus aggravating latent class conflicts in Algerian society. In October 1988, these exploded in seven days of nationwide rioting against the regime and its elite beneficiaries. The government then proceeded to liberalize the political system in the hope that this would let off steam and get the economy back on track. But like Gorbachev's *glasnost* in the former Soviet Union, a comparison frequently made by commentators on the Algerian situation, the political opening was not accompanied by economic improvement.

Thus, when given the chance to express themselves politically for the first time in the 1990 and 1991 municipal and parliamentary elections, the vast majority of those who voted chose the FIS, the most radical and well-organized of the parties, Islamic or secularist, in contention. The ruling FLN, once the revolutionary vanguard and sole legitimate party in Algeria, fared miserably, running third in parliamentary seats after the Berberist FFS.

ISSUES

POLITICS

The immediate political dispute tearing Algeria apart concerns legitimacy. By circumventing the political process when the FIS was poised to win control of the national government, or at least its legislative branch, the Algerian military has called into question the very legitimacy of that government. FIS leaders rightfully claim that they are the duly-elected representatives of the Algerian people. The current regime, they say, is an illegitimate military junta that maintains its hold on power through its control of Algeria's internal security forces and army. Indeed, the regime used that power to ban the FIS and launch an all-out assault on the FIS and its sympathizers immediately after the coup. Only then, say the fundamentalists, did they fight back, and only because they were forced to.

This, then, is the immediate issue behind the war. Yet this explanation begs an important question. Why would those in power, including some of the very same people who agreed to the political democratization process, choose to circumvent it when it appeared the fundamentalists were about to win? There are essentially three answers to the question, two offered by the government and a third by its opponents: first, fundamentalism is incompatible with democracy; second, the FIS stole the elections through fraud; and third, the military and senior bureaucrats behind the coup did not want to relinquish power.

The first answer is the most difficult to assess, involving as it does issues dating back to the origins of the Islamic faith. As one Arabist, Peter Mansfield, has pointed out, "It is a paradox of Islam that as a social system it is at once the most democratic and the most authoritarian of religions."[5] That is to say, scriptural Islam eschews religious hierarchies of all kinds and emphasizes the rights of all believers to interpret the teachings of the Prophet Muhammad in their own way. At the same time, historical Islam has sanctified the rule of autocrats by emphasizing the importance of consensus and harmony, as well as the avoidance of social divisions. Those who would choose to rebel openly against a Muslim ruler can do so only if that ruler violates the faith in some way. By invoking God's blessing on the ruler and emphasizing consensus, historical Islam has often sanctified autocracy and social injustice.

Faced with an aggressive non-Muslim Europe, Islamic political thought underwent a dramatic renaissance in the nineteenth century. Trying to cope with the unprecedented invasion of the Muslim homeland by infidels, these political thinkers offered two solutions: one was *itjihad*, or the free interpretation (that is, modernization) of Islamic scripture; the other was a return to the roots of the faith in order to provide a conceptual framework for the adoption of new technologies and ideas from the West that would be compatible with the ethics of Islamic culture and faith.

With the decolonization of the Muslim world in the twentieth century, Islamic political thinkers took the ideas of their nineteenth-century forebears one step further. Opposed to the nationalist, secularist or socialist policies of native Muslim rulers, they began to reformulate the idea of the *jahaliyya*, that is, the anarchic and amoral order that prevailed in Arabia before the coming of Islam, and apply it to these modern regimes. The message was clear: the political system had to be Islamicized. But what exactly did that mean?

Theoretically, of course, it implied the inverse of democracy. Since only God has sovereignty, the only legitimate political activity of humans is interpreting the will of God. The will of the people, as expressed in elections, is secondary at best. And if it contradicts the will of God, as interpreted by

Islamic scholars, then it must be ignored. Thus, the essentials of democracy, that is, political pluralism, checks and balances on power, and rotation in office, are theoretically anathema to the Islamic state. As the Algerian junta reiterates: Islamic democracy is a contradiction in terms; once in power, the fundamentalists will never relinquish it.

The FIS denies this charge. Its spokesmen say the party has demonstrated its commitment to democracy by playing by the electoral rules, an assertion questioned by the junta, which cites numerous irregularities during the elections, especially in municipalities already controlled by the FIS. Second, FIS spokesmen point out that it is hypocritical for anyone in the current regime to question anyone's commitment to democracy. Finally, they say that the concept of *itjihad*, to which many in the FIS profess a commitment, means that no one has a monopoly on interpreting the kind of political order God intends for humanity. Thus, secularists have as much right to rule as political Islamists, so long as they do not violate the principles of the faith. Yet, despite these soothing assurances, numerous FIS leaders are on record saying that democracy is indeed incompatible with Islam. As Ali Belhadj, one of two top FIS officials, said after the election victory in December 1991: this is "a victory for Islam and not for democracy."[6]

SOCIETY

No one in Algeria, not the fundamentalists, the government nor the populace, denies that Algerian society was in crisis long before the 1992 coup and that social pathologies have been especially prevalent among the young. Living conditions have deteriorated for virtually every class of Algerians except the very wealthy. Housing is in such short supply that few young persons can hope to find housing and establish families of their own. A profound sense of hopelessness about the war, the economy and the country's political future engulfs the population. People dream of emigration, but even that traditional escape valve is being closed by the growing anti-immigrant politics of France. Adding to the confusion is Algeria's almost schizophrenic attitude toward the West, at once embracing its mass consumer culture and rejecting its influence as inimical to Muslim society. The government seems unable to cope, and the democratic opposition cannot find its voice. Only the fundamentalists seem to have a coherent vision of Algeria's future, an asset that has drawn millions into their ranks but alienated millions more.

The fundamentalist diagnosis of Algeria's malaise is simple. Under the rule of a secularist, pro-Western FLN, the nation drifted from its cultural and social roots. It has become, to use a term the FIS has borrowed from Iranian Islamists, "westoxicated." The government has reproduced the social order of a "weak and sick" civilization and has corrupted it further by applying it forcefully to Algeria. For many fundamentalists, the symbol of this corruption is the satellite dishes that have "sprouted like a forest of mushrooms" on Algerian rooftops, drawing in the images and ideas of French culture.[7] That Algerians willingly watch these programs is a measure of the degree to which they have lost their bearings in the world. The fundamentalists' cure is as simple as their diagnosis. Algerians must rid themselves of this "westoxification" through a renewed application of the *sharia*, or holy laws of Islam. That means Algerians must stop viewing Western TV, abstain from alcohol, practice the rituals of the faith and adhere to the patriarchal family values that once ordered Algerian society.

The simplicity of the fundamentalists' social diagnosis, certainly a major part of its appeal, is also the source of its weakness and the reason millions of Algerians who consider themselves good Muslims are repelled by the cure it offers. Islamic fundamentalism, say many scholars, lacks a realistic sociology. That is to say, it emphasizes morality and virtue to the detriment of institutions, politics and economics. Fundamentalists believe, these scholars say, that if human beings become moral and virtuous, all social, political and economic problems will solve themselves. Thus, the task of the state is to create an environment in which morality and virtue prevail; the criterion for political leadership is ethical behavior; and economic problems are caused by immoral economic agents.

The prospect of this cure instills fear in many Algerians. Would an Islamic Algeria become a puritanical state? Would the state enforce behavioral norms on its citizens? As many secularist Algerians, and even some Islamic politicians, have pointed out, the fundamentalists have things backward, believing that the strict application of the *sharia* will induce moral behavior. Instead, these critics say, the *sharia* can be applied in all its rigor only after humanity has become purely moral and ethical. Since that day is far off, the *sharia* should be only a guide, not the law. Applying the *sharia* before the moral transformation of humanity will breed only social hypocrisy, as people say one thing in public and practice another in private, and a totalitarian state. The example they offer is not Iran, but Saudi Arabia.

If there is one issue that embodies the conflict between these two views of Algeria's future, it is the role and place of women in society. Fundamentalists argue that the "westoxification" of Algerian society has denigrated Muslim women by turning them into objects of men's desire. The veil, they say, allows women to participate in public life free of that objectification. Opponents of the fundamentalists say that these arguments are pure casuistry. What the religious leaders intend, they say, is to put the Algerian women back in the home, under the iron hands of patriarchal husbands and fathers. The current violence against women who do not wear the veil in public is, they argue, a truer indication of the fundamentalists' ideology than their rhetoric. FIS leaders counter that they are not targeting women and hint that the government and its *agents provocateurs* are staging the killings and the mutilation of women for propaganda purposes.

ECONOMICS

Like many African countries, Algeria is rich in potential and poor in substance. Blessed with vast gas and oil reserves, the nation's ruling elite largely squandered these assets in the pursuit of an unfeasible model of rapid industrialization in the 1960s and 1970s, followed by an inadequately thought-out liberalization program in the 1980s. The result was a stifling command economy, a speculative and parasitic private sector and a burgeoning black market for the basic necessities of life.

In its first two decades, Algeria developed a class of bureaucratic managerial elites and a private sector of industrialists who made their fortunes through the personal connections they established with government officials in charge of the state-owned industrial sector. After a generation of this hybrid economy in which, in sociologist Marnia Lazreg's formulation, "a form of socialism" coexisted with an economy "largely determined by capitalist relations," Algeria stagnated.[8] Beginning in the early 1980s, however, a new generation of bureaucrats, educated in the latest free-market thinking of Western management schools, came to the fore. Like the young *nomenklatura* of Gorbachev's Soviet Union, they came to the realization that the model no longer worked, while at the same time they chafed at the limitations the system placed on their own earning potential.

In Algeria, they embarked on a thorough liberalization program in which individual state enterprises would act as profit-oriented centers of production. But rather than unjamming the command economy, it simply removed what checks and balances existed on profiteering by the management of state firms. Speculation increased, as firms sought short-term profits over long-term development. The lifting of restrictions on trade threw up a whole new class of import-export speculators who flaunted their new-found wealth in the purchase of luxury imports. Algeria's foreign debt ballooned, but with very little in the way of capital investment to show for it. In effect, the new liberalization program combined the worst of statist and free-market economics: socialized risk and privatized profit.

When the economic crunch came in the mid-1980s with the collapse of gas and oil prices, the government launched an austerity program and cut off the import of consumer goods. This created a massive underground economy that continues to flourish throughout the country, enriching a network of organized crime rings involved in smuggling and bribery of officials. Members of these rings, say some Algerians, include both government officials and fundamentalists. This underground economy in turn has bred resentment among ordinary families that are desperately trying to get by on the devalued earnings of the single breadwinner who has a job.

It is in this context that the government and fundamentalists offer their solutions to the profound economic crisis gripping the country. Given the depth of the crisis and the conflict it has bred, it is strange how similar both programs are to each other. Both the government and the fundamentalists are committed to a further liberalization of the Algerian economy, though there are disputes on both sides about the pace this program should take. Both sides also support free trade, privatization and continued austerity, though for different reasons. The government continues to be run by free-marketeers who came to power in the early 1980s and, like their counterparts elsewhere in the Third World, seem to possess a remarkable capacity to maintain doctrinal purity in the face of disastrous economic results.

Fundamentalists, not surprisingly, base their economic programs on the *sharia* and Koran, or at least their interpretation of these. This interpretation includes an aversion to *fitna*, or social division. Thus any appeal to class interests is considered anathema. The fundamentalists displayed their hostility to agricultural reform in the 1960s and early 1970s, when landed estates were broken up, by accusing the government of encouraging *fitna*. According to various FIS spokesmen, the party has nothing against the accumulation of wealth and sees no state role in income redistribution. The party has also made it clear that an FIS-run Algeria would be receptive to foreign investment and foreign ownership of the means of production, a message currently being broadcast by Algeria's ruling junta as well. As with their views on politics, fundamentalists emphasize virtue in their conception of an Islamic economy. As one spokesman said, under Islamic law "you have the right to become rich, but not at the expense of others," a statement that both bourgeois and socialist critics argue means nothing. "The Islamization of the economy," concludes Islamicist Olivier Roy, "is largely rhetorical."[9]

PARTICIPANTS

FUNDAMENTALISTS

Like the other great religions, Islam is not monolithic. There is the ancient rift, familiar to most Western readers, between Shiism and Sunnism, but this division is not directly relevant to Algeria since there are virtually no indigenous Shiites in the Maghrib. A more important division in Algerian Islam is that between popular and traditional Islam. The former, known as Sufism in most of the Arab world and *maraboutisme* in Algeria, is an ecstatic and mystical version of the faith that emphasizes the popular worship of Muslim saints. Finally, there is a distinct rift between what might be called "establishment" Islam and reformist or fundamentalist Islam.

These various forms of Algerian Islam have been in conflict with each other for most of this century. Fundamentalists criticize Maraboutism for its emphasis on the mystical, the afterlife and its appeal to believers to withdraw from the affairs of this world. As for establishment Islam, it represents a long tradition of cooperation between state and Islamic scholars going back to the Ottoman Empire, and before. Since independence, of course, it has meant a close working relationship between the official mosque and the Algerian state. Fundamentalists attack establishment clerics for their cooperation with an apostate regime, and radical militants have assassinated over a dozen state-appointed imams (religio-political leaders) since the coup.

The fundamentalists of Algeria represent both the latest incarnation of a trend in Islamic thought going back to the reformism of the nineteenth century, as well as a significant deviation from it. Some scholars, in fact, make a pointed distinction between those they call Islamists, best represented by the regime in Iran, and fundamentalists or neo-fundamentalists. In this conception of Islamic politics, Islamists are the modernists who see the *sharia* as a flexible general set of principles that, when appropriately modified, can be used to regulate some aspects of contemporary Islamic society. Fundamentalists, on the other hand, see the *sharia* as a fixed set of very specific rules to which all aspects of modern society can and must conform.

Algerian religious politics includes both trends, though which one is currently in ascendancy and which one will take the reins of power in any future Islamist government is difficult to assess. The two trends in Algerian political Islam include the "techno-Islamists" and the "neo-fundamentalists." As their name implies, the techno-Islamists are largely university-educated, accept modernization and believe that the Algerian state and government can be kept relatively intact, albeit with a replacement of personnel. They are also more likely to come from an earlier generation than the neo-fundamentalists. Critics say this cadre of political Islamists are simply frustrated and want to get their hands on power. But the techno-Islamists, like their neo-fundamentalist allies, believe that the virtue and morality of those who rule the system is crucial to the success of Algerian society; the change in personnel would not be purely cosmetic. The leader of this contingent is Abbassi Madani. Born in 1931, Madani has a Ph.D. in education from the University of London.

Neo-fundamentalists, largely high school graduates or self-educated mullahs (religious teachers), are hostile to the Algerian state and society in its totality. They want to turn the clock back on modernization and westernization and envision an Algerian society fully in conformity with the most rigid interpretation of the *sharia*. Ali Belhadj represents the neo-fundamentalists. Born in 1956, Belhadj was formerly a high school teacher of Arabic and Islam before becoming a political leader.

The problem with assessing the relative power of the two groups is this: those spokesmen of the FIS who have access to the Western press are largely from the former group; those doing the actual fighting in the streets come largely from the latter. Whether the war comes to a negotiated or revolutionary conclusion may very well decide which cohort will rule in any future Islamic Republic of Algeria.

GOVERNMENT

As historians of the pre-modern Maghrib point out, political authority and power was often based on clan and tribal affiliation. While the 132 years of French rule largely destroyed the clan structure of Algerian rule, by essentially destroying almost all indigenous political institutions, the clan was resurrected in a new form by the FLN during and after the revolution. Indeed, after the initial post-independence struggle between the revolutionaries of the war within Algeria and the military and bureaucratic leaders of the FLN's exterior forces, largely isolated in Tunisia and Morocco by French border defenses, Algeria was ruled by the latter group.

This cadre of leaders, often referred to as the *chefs historiques*, or historical leaders of the revolution, established a firm grip on power during the Boumédienne regime of 1965–1978. Largely French-speaking and consensus-oriented, they entrenched themselves in positions of power in the military, state-owned industries and bureaucracy, passing on their positions either to their children or to aspiring members of the lower classes who had somehow obtained the necessary "cultural capital": fluency in French and a degree from a prestigious foreign university.

In consolidating its power, the FLN clan had to confront several challenges, both within the FLN and without. Of the latter, the most important were the spontaneous peasant and worker organizations that were part of an immediate post-independence movement popularly known as *autogestion*, or self-management. In the wake of the mass flight of *colons*, large numbers of peasants took command of the farms and, to a lesser extent, the industrial enterprises that were once in European hands. Over the course of the Boumédienne administration, these independent collectives were tethered to a state bureaucracy that emphasized national development over local economic democracy.

This application of statist economic development was part and parcel of the FLN's tripartite plan for Algeria: the creation of a modern, assertive nationalism; the elaboration of a corporatist political structure; and a separation of church and state, or rather the dominance of the state over religious institutions and practices. On the first score, the FLN was largely successful. Even fundamentalists largely accept the Algerian nation as a given and see Islamicization as a national, rather than pan-Islamic, project. The second two goals, however, created problems that eventually proved the undoing of FLN rule.

The FLN's corporatist state was based on the idea of a neutral, all-encompassing revolutionary party that would be both a neutral arbiter of internal conflict and an institution that would represent all Algerians. To that end, all political parties except the FLN were outlawed. In their place, the FLN established new institutions (or yoked existing ones to the party) based on citizens' economic or social affiliation (there were organizations for workers, peasants, women, students, etc.). While these institutions were technically independent, and their leaders elected democratically, they were in fact tightly controlled by the FLN.

The result, say many scholars, was both a stifling lack of democracy within the FLN institutional framework and a near-total absence of independent political and social organizations within Algerian society. Thus when citizens became frustrated at the collapsing economy and hardships of the mid-1980s, they had nowhere to turn except to the streets.

SECULAR OPPOSITION AND BERBERS

As numerous observers of contemporary Algeria point out, the "explosion of associations and associative life after [the political opening] of 1988 [was] amazing."[10] Indeed, the number of political parties went from one to over fifty in about a year. Most of these organizations were "salon" parties representing well-connected urban liberals or rural notables and their followers. But several parties made pretensions to national leadership, including the FIS, the Berber-dominated FFS, and the now politically independent FLN.[11]

Besides these political groups, numerous independent civic organizations came into existence, including those representing working women, intellectuals and human rights activists. Some of these organizations had either existed before 1989 or inherited the mantle of previous organizations. For example, there had been organizations of working women since the late 1970s that arose when the state was considering a fundamentalist-inspired set of family codes, which, despite unprecedented public protests by urban women, eventually became law in 1984.

As for the political parties, most were swept aside in the 1990 municipal and 1991 parliamentary elections. Only the FFS, the FLN, and of course the FIS scored enough votes in any district to gain a seat in the new parliament.

But while a vast plurality of Arab Algerians voted for the FIS, the majority of Berbers voted for the FFS and the more nationalist Rally for Culture and Democracy (RCD). Indeed, the history of Berber-Arab relations has been marked by both assimilation and separation, though the kinds of conflicts that exist between Arab and non-Arab Muslim peoples of the Arab East such as the Kurds are not present in Algeria. The cultural conflict between Arabs and Berbers is ameliorated by both having the same historical roots. In terms of physical characteristics virtually all Algerians are really Berbers. The difference between them is that when the Arabs invaded

Algeria from the eighth to the eleventh centuries, lowland Algerians adopted Arab culture in its entirety, while highlanders adopted the Islamic faith but kept their indigenous culture.

The French applied a divide-and-rule policy in Algeria, elevating the Berbers to a higher status, attempting to shape them into quasi-Frenchmen and using them as intermediaries with the Arabs. The policy failed because France's modernization of Algeria brought large numbers of Berbers into contact with Arabs, thus accelerating their assimilation into the majority culture. The only lasting legacy was a higher propensity for bi- and trilingualism (that is, French, Arabic and Berber) among the Berber population, and a higher percentage of immigration to France.

Since independence, the Berbers have prospered. The Kabyle, where most Berbers live, is relatively well-off. In Algeria generally, Berbers have been largely successful, though they have achieved this through their own independent fiefdoms and clans within the Algerian bureaucracy and army. This has had two effects on Berber politics. First, as austerity is imposed on the bureaucracy and Berbers are laid off, they tend to see their predicament in cultural terms; they believe they are being laid off because they are Berbers. Second, the Berbers' disproportionate presence in the bureaucracy adds to their fears of the FIS, which intends either to replace the personnel of the Algerian bureaucracy or get rid of the bureaucracy altogether. Thus Berber politics are generally anti-fundamentalist, while ranging from left to right.

INTERNATIONAL

Given its history of colonial domination, France continues to wield more influence over Algerian politics than any other outside power. It remains Algeria's largest trading partner, and its culture continues to permeate Algeria, via television broadcasts, emigration (between one and two million Algerians live, work and go to school in France) and the deeply Gallicized Algerian elite. France has also been the Algerian government's firmest Western supporter and has spoken up for the regime in international human rights conferences and in financial circles, the latter of especially crucial importance given the level of Algeria's external debt. France also supplies the regime with much of its military hardware and provides technical assistance and intelligence for the Algerian army and security forces.

Because of this close relationship, France has been targeted by GIA militants, who have hijacked a French jet and planted bombs in Paris and elsewhere in France. FIS leaders routinely assert that France did not give up control over Algeria with the revolution, but has maintained its influence through the FLN and the military who are largely puppets of Paris.

This assessment is rather strange given the vehemence with which the FLN fought the French in the 1950s and the government's largely successful efforts to diversify Algeria's trading relationships. Beginning with the nationalization of the gas and oil industry in 1971, Algeria has established significant trading partnerships with the United States, Japan, Italy and Spain, the last two countries directly connected to Algerian gas fields by pipelines under the Mediterranean. Many international observers say that the diversification of Algerian trade and financial borrowing has been one of the few economic success stories of FLN rule.

Nevertheless, French support for the regime is still significant. The irony of Parisian support for the very people it once fought so hard to defeat is actually quite easy to explain. The French government fears that an Islamic takeover of Algeria will send hundreds of thousands of refugees across the Mediterranean and, given the recent anti-immigrant backlash in France, no administration, neither the Socialists under François Mitterrand in the early 1990s nor the conservatives of Jacques Chirac in the mid-1990s, wants to be seen as responsible for that.

This French fear has put Paris and Washington at loggerheads. For a variety of reasons, not least of which is the Iranian legacy, the Clinton administration does not want to antagonize any future Islamic regime in Algeria, and thus has taken a decidedly neutral stance in the conflict. Washington's approach may also be influenced by the fact that FIS leaders have made a point of cozying up to the United States. They insist that American corporate investment will be very welcome in an FIS-ruled Algeria. This friendliness seems to run through the ranks of the fundamentalists. Despite the FIS ultimatum to foreigners, no American has been killed in the Algerian conflict as of this writing, a fact that some French leaders, particularly those within the nationalist/Gaullist tradition, have found significant.

TACTICS

GOVERNMENT

As the FLN regime always asserted, the FLN was not anti-Islamic. This argument is echoed by the current military rulers as well. There is some truth in these assertions, at least from the perspective of secular politicians. The Algerian revolution against France was conducted partially in the name of Islam, and, since independence, the government has tried to encourage a form of Islam that jibes with FLN ideology, a kind of socialist Islam and Islamicized socialism.

This, of course, has not satisfied religious purists in Algeria who want a thorough Islamicization of state and society. As these individuals began to recruit followers and assert their political muscle in the 1970s and 1980s, the FLN in characteristic fashion tried to subsume the new politics into the party's structure. While scholars continue to argue whether or not the government actively encouraged fundamentalists in the 1970s and early 1980s as a counterforce to the radical Marxists of the universities, it was clear that the fundamentalists' anti-socialist ideology was in accord with the prevailing sentiment of Algerian elite politics.

When the political opening came, the government continued to believe that it could control the fundamentalists. Thus it legalized the FIS despite constitutional prohibitions on religious parties. As a hedge, the government also began to encourage, or according to Islamists secretly establish, government-controlled religious parties. Whatever the case, the FIS's overwhelming victory in the municipal elections of 1990 shocked the ruling elite, who then embarked on a new policy toward the fundamentalists. The government's propaganda machine began to denounce the efforts of the fundamentalist councils, saying they were incompetent and puritanical. Whether this was wishful thinking or not, national leaders tried to make it fact by cutting off funds to the councils and hemming them in with new regulations and limitations on their jurisdiction. As parliamentary elections approached in June 1991, the government tried to gerrymander districts to assure an FLN victory. The attempt was so brazen it produced FIS-sponsored demonstrations throughout the country. The government crushed these protests and called off the elections, but backed off by modifying the rules and announcing elections for December.

The overwhelming victory of the FIS in those elections forced the government to alter its tactics once again. This time it took the gloves off and banned the FIS, detained thousands of its supporters, imprisoned its leaders and canceled all elections for several years. The intensity of the resulting conflict, however, forced the government to offer new elections, but on terms very much its own. Only independent candidates with no party affiliation may run.

FUNDAMENTALISTS

The modern tradition of Islamic politics asserts that the current secularist regimes of the Muslim world have created a kind of modern-day *jahaliyya*, or pre-Islamic state of anarchy and iniquity. Given this assessment, good Muslims have but two choices: either they can withdraw from society and create Islamicized spaces, such as mosques and mosque-affiliated institutions, or they can overthrow the government and establish an Islamist state. Iranian militants chose the latter course. Until the 1980s, Algeria's fundamentalists had chosen the former.

These Islamicized spaces served a dual function. First, they provided a refuge for Muslims to conduct their lives in accordance with scripture. Second, they were meant to provide a model of an Islamicized order that would influence the rest of Muslim society. Beginning in the 1980s, and corresponding to the collapse of the Algerian economy, these Islamicized spaces became centers of radical indoctrination and agitation. Increasingly, the self-appointed mullahs of these "free mosques," that is, mosques not officially sanctioned by the government and situated largely in the unserviced working-class neighborhoods and *bidonvilles*, or shantytowns, of Algeria's cities, began to insist upon a larger role in the political affairs of the country. Their first great success was the enactment of the Islam-inspired Family Code of 1984.

While fundamentalists were not directly responsible for the largely spontaneous riots of October 1988, they took effective advantage of them, using the unrest among the large urban population of unemployed rural migrants to force both political change and an Islamic agenda on the ruling FLN. While secularist opponents also played a role in the political opening of 1989, the fundamentalists benefited most from the change. No other organization in Algeria had the kind of infrastructure and influence that the fundamentalists had. Thus, when the FIS was born, it was a ready-made political power.

But the transition from sect to party took its toll on the fundamentalist movement. Like any other political force with an absolutist agenda but seeking electoral validation, the FIS was forced to ameliorate some of its positions in order to appeal to a majority of Algerians. Thus, the party produced no coherent platform and no fixed program to achieve its goal for the Islamicization of Algeria. While this helped bring in voters disgusted with the ruling FLN, it alienated hardliners within the party.

After the coup of 1992, the vagueness of the political platform and the rifts with hardliners came out into the open. The government and secular opponents of the FIS have effectively argued that the party is neither prepared to run Algeria nor capable of ending the war. Meanwhile, the fundamentalists pursue two seemingly contradictory policies. On the one hand, they have successfully worked with secular opposition parties to fashion an anti-junta front (see "Negotiations" below). On the other hand, militants within the organization and without have launched a campaign of terror against Algeria's security forces and, says the government, against anyone in Algerian society who disagrees with their politics, their methods or their agenda.

NEGOTIATIONS

Negotiations between the military regime and the FIS can generally be described as fitful, desultory and fraught with distrust. In a sense, nothing has really changed since the coup of January 1992. The government says the FIS cannot be trusted with state power and will not relinquish that power once it gets it. The FIS maintains that the current regime represents an illegitimate usurpation of power. One side points to a potential threat to democratization; the other points to a very real assault on that process.

Not surprisingly, negotiations between Belhadj and Madani, both imprisoned since the June 1991 anti-gerrymandering demonstrations, and President Liamine Zeroual have produced no effective results. The government claims that the FIS has not negotiated in good faith. It says FIS leaders talk of peace but at the same time issue secret orders to continue the war. The FIS claims the government will never negotiate in good faith because, behind its talk of preserving democratization, it is interested only in maintaining its grip on power by whatever means necessary, including the cooptation of FIS leaders.

Meanwhile, both sides have issued programs for ending the war. Early in 1995, the regime offered a program for a gradualist return to democracy, beginning with a presidential election. This was held in November; Zeroual won handily with 61 percent of the vote. Opposition parties, including the banned FIS, had denounced the election, which permitted only individual candidacies with no party affiliations, and organized a boycott. With 75 percent of the electorate participating, the election was seen as a solid victory for the regime and a significant setback to the FIS and its secular allies, as well as hard-liners within the military and the administration who had opposed the election as a capitulation to terrorists. Afterward, both sides called for a new dialogue, though this has yet to start. In May 1996, Zeroual announced a referendum on a new constitution toward the end of 1996 and a new round of legislative elections for the first half of 1997, though it was unclear if the FIS, or indeed any party, would be permitted to participate. In September 1996, the government hosted a national conference to end the violence, but the major opposition parties either boycotted or were banned from attending. Meanwhile, the government maintains the upper hand, and the violence continues. In May, GIA militants assassinated a former interior minister and set off a bomb at a bus station in Tizi Ouzou that left two people dead.

On the other side, the FIS has achieved better results. In January, virtually all the opposition parties, both secularist and religious, met in Rome where they signed "a platform for a political and peaceful solution to the Algerian crisis."[12] The platform included a renunciation of violence, respect for human rights, equality of gender, as well as the end of the dictatorship and a demand for free and full elections. It also set a list of conditions that would have to precede negotiations with the government. These included the freedom of all jailed FIS leaders, the ending of the ban on the FIS, the cancellation of the state of emergency and the establishment of an independent commission to investigate acts of violence and human rights violations committed by all sides in the war. The regime, which declined an invitation to attend from the Sant'Edigio Catholic community that sponsored the talks, says the Rome platform is nothing more than blackmail, demanding that the government surrender its sovereignty before opponents would negotiate. The regime does not, however, have a monopoly on obstructivism. In August 1995, the Rome signatories unanimously agreed to boycott the regime's presidential elections.

NOTES

[1] A brief note on labels and terms for the players and issues in the Algerian conflict is necessary here, for the sake of consistency and since they are often used haphazardly in the Western press. Muslim, in this book, refers to people who practice the Islamic faith. *Islamist* and *fundamentalist* (or, *integriste*, in French) are terms denoting Muslims who believe in a political, social and economic order based on Islamic teaching. There is a distinction between Islamists and fundamentalists, which will be explored in Chapter 3. *Secularist* is used to denote those Muslims who, in general, advocate a separation of church and state. *Islamicist* refers to scholars, both Muslim and non-Muslim, who study Islam sociologically and historically. *Islamic scholars* refers to those Muslims who interpret the faith scripturally.

In addition, the term *Arab* refers to those who speak Arabic as their primary language. Berbers, also known as *Kabyles* after their regional homeland Kabyle, are those who speak Berber as their primary language. The cultural and historical differences between these two peoples are discussed in Chapter 4. Finally, the names of all Algerian institutions and organizations are rendered in English, followed by their French acronyms since that is how they are referred to in most international publications.

[2] *New York Times*, June 6, 1995, p. A8.

[3] The eastern half of the Arab world is referred to as the Mashriq, which means the East, or Land of the Rising Sun.

[4] Ruedy, John, *Modern Algeria: The Origins and Development of a Nation*, Bloomington: Indiana University Press, p. 7.

[5] Mansfield, Peter, *The Arabs*, New York: Penguin, 1992, p. 69.

[6] Burgat, Francois and Dowell, William, *The Islamic Movement in North Africa*, Austin: Center for Middle Eastern Studies at the University of Texas, 1993, p. 125.

[7] Hakem, Tewfik, "La parabole de la démocratie" in *Reporters sans frontières, Le drame algérien: un peuple en otage*, Paris: Éditions la découverte, 1994, pp. 42–47.

[8] Lazreg, Marnia, "Bureaucracy and Class: The Algerian Case Dialectic" in *Dialectical Anthropology*, vol. 4, 1976, p. 295.

[9] Roy, Olivier, *The Failure of Political Islam*, Cambridge, Mass.: Harvard University Press, 1994, p. 144.

[10] Lazreg, Marnia, interview with author, June 1, 1995.

[11] The 1989 constitution formally detached the party from the government.

[12] Haddam, Anwar, "The Algerian Crisis: FIS Viewpoint," unpublished manuscript, 1995, after p. 14.

HISTORY

This Algerian . . . nation is not France;
it is not possible that it be France;
it does not want to become France; and even if it wished,
it could not be France.
> —Abd al-Hamad Ben Badis, Association
> of Algerian Muslim Ulema

We have rid ourselves of the past with a fever
that we suffer from still.
> —Salah Eddine Jourchi, Islamist historian

BEFORE THE FRENCH (TO 1830)

During their 132-year occupation of Algeria, the French elaborated a complex set of rationales for their presence there and for the political incorporation of Algeria into metropolitan France, rationales that it repeated at increasing volume as the Muslim population began to speak and act against its colonial masters in the mid-twentieth century. Of these rationales, perhaps the most compelling, as far as the French were concerned, was nationalism. There was not, and had never been, a nation of people on the North African coast between Tunisia and Morocco. In short, the French colonists and government said, there were Algerians, but no Algeria, at least not until the French made it so.

Just as the implication of their argument, that one million Frenchmen had the right to rule nine million Muslims, was out of step with mid-twentieth-century North African history, so their premise of a people without a nationality was flawed. People have inhabited the region since at least the mid-Paleolithic era, and have experienced, in historical time, several important periods of indigenous rule. There was a century or so of self-rule before the coming of the Romans at the end of the second century B.C., through the exploits of the semi-legendary Jugurtha, the "first Berber nationalist," and a series of Berber kingdoms for several centuries before the arrival of the Ottomans in the sixteenth century A.D. And even under Ottoman rule the country had been self-ruling in all but name.[1]

On the other hand, Algerian history reads like a who's who of Mediterranean powers: the Phoenicians/Carthaginians settled the region

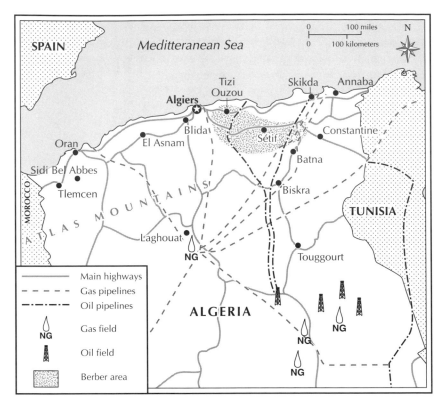

from approximately 800 B.C. to 200 B.C.; the Romans ruled it from 100 B.C. to 400 A.D.; there was a Vandal invasion in 429 A.D.; nominal Byzantine rule for three centuries; Arab invasions in the eighth century; Ottoman rule from the early 1500s to 1830; and French rule until 1962. Of these myriad peoples, the two most important occupiers of Algeria were the Arabs and the French. The former established much of the social and virtually all of the religious content of subsequent Algerian life; the French deeply influenced independent Algeria's political and economic structures.

ARAB INVASIONS

Algerians were nominally a Christian people when the Arabs first invaded in the late seventh century. But under the Romans and Byzantines, Algeria had been racked by religious controversy. The official Christian church was resisted by Berbers because of its association with a Roman rule that included slavery, resource exploitation and large Roman *latifundia*, or plantations. Instead, the mountain Berbers of the Kabyle region in central Algeria embraced the Donatist heresy, which emphasized the communalist and egalitarian strains of early Christian thought. This Berber resistance to state-established religion would not be confined to Christianity, however. During the first centuries of Arab rule, and arguably down to the present, the Berbers have maintained distinctive religious practices and, more important, a distinctive reading of Islamic thought and faith that emphasizes ethnic and tribal identity. When Roman rule was succeeded by the weaker Byzantine Empire, the Berbers largely dispensed with the imported culture and reestablished the tribe as the dominant political and social unit of Algerian life. The importation of camels or, more precisely, the introduction of new saddles that permitted the use of camels as beasts of burden added a new factor, trans-Saharan trade, to the largely pastoral economy of the Berbers. Meanwhile, Latin culture and rule clung precariously to a few coastal cities.

The Arab invasions of North Africa, which began in the late seventh century and continued until the eleventh, took two different forms and produced two different results. The first invasion was largely military and was determinedly resisted by the Berber tribes. While Tunisia and Morocco succumbed relatively easily to the invaders, the Berbers of Algeria, says historian John Ruedy, "mounted the fiercest and longest-lived opposition to the Arab conquerors of the seventh century met anywhere in the world."[2] Conversely, the Maghrib generally and Algeria specifically converted to Islam rather quickly, within a generation, as opposed to the centuries this process took in the Arab East. Accepting Islam, however, did not mean acquiescing to Arab rule. Embracing "the most egalitarian and democratic" of Islamic sects, Khariji Islam, the Berbers, under charismatic tribal leaders including the semi-legendary priestess El Kahina, effectively resisted and then threw back Arab armies by 740, leaving the Maghrib free to develop its own independent kingdoms. Three of these, the kingdoms of the Rustamids (759–910), the Hammadids (1011–1151) and the Abd al Wadids (1235–1545), were based in Algeria and prospered on trans-Saharan and Mediterranean trade.

While Arab armies introduced Islam as a religion of state, it was the invasion of Arab tribes in the eleventh century that brought Islam to the people. As Islamicist scholar Peter Knauss writes, "The gradual Islamicization of the Berber peoples took place in a social context that was tribal."[3] Through conquest and assimilation, the Arab tribes brought with them the Sufi brotherhoods (*marabouts* in the Maghrib), or holy men of popular Islam. With their worship of holy places and saints, and their emphasis on ecstatic worship, the brotherhoods were thoroughly embraced by the Berber masses. Along with the *shurama*, or descendants of the Prophet, the brotherhoods produced the leaders and ruling lineages of subsequent Arab-Berber tribes in a process that gradually Arabized the land of the Berbers. "Together [the brothers and *shurama*]," says historian Charles-Robert Ageron, "gave [their] strongly oriental character to Algeria, a country long dedicated socially and culturally to its religion."[4] In addition, the majority of Berbers were linguistically as well as religiously converted by these nomadic tribes from the east. The gradual spread of Arabic arguably did as much to Arabize the native Algerians as Islam.

While it has been argued that the invasion of the Arab tribes had a destructive effect on the political and economic power of the Maghrib, reverting the countryside to pastoralism and disrupting trans-Saharan trade, the lifeblood of the coastal cities, the eminent Arab historian Albert Hourani argues, "The process was not simple as this." In fact, he says, trade was disrupted by competition from kingdoms to the east and west. While the cause of Algeria's political fracturing was not due to the "spread of Arab tribes so much as the assimilation of Berbers into them."[5] In either case, the growing chaos of the middle Maghrib in the late fifteenth and early sixteenth centuries was further exacerbated by events on the other side of the Mediterranean.

THE OTTOMAN REGENCY (EARLY 1500s TO 1830)

In 1492, the twin monarchy of Aragon and Castile drove the last Moorish kingdom, Granada in southern Iberia, from Western Europe. But the newly united Spanish government did not stop there, pushing eastward along the North African coast and occupying several Maghribi cities in the early sixteenth century.[6] Defenseless against this assault by Christian forces, the Muslims of North Africa appealed for help to their co-believers in the East. But, says Ruedy, "It was not mainly out of altruism that the Arab privateers Aruj and Khayr al-Din . . . responded to the pleas from the notables of Algiers in 1516." They wanted bases for their depredations on shipping in the western Mediterranean and set about consolidating their hold on coastal Algeria, raising opposition among the Berbers there. In 1519, Khayr al-Din turned to the Ottoman sultan for support. His offer of submission to Constantinople was accepted and imperial contingents of infantry and artillery were dispatched, thus beginning three centuries of Ottoman rule.

While Turkish rule had a significant impact on the social and economic structure of Algerian society, particularly in urban areas, its most lasting legacy was political. "These semi-Europeans [Ottomans]," writes Ageron, "brought to Africa the idea of frontiers and territorial sovereignty; they gave Algeria its basic shape." But, he adds, "The Turks of this Ottoman regency, distant vassals of the Sultan at Istanbul, scarcely dreamed of making their mark on the country."[7]

In fact, Ottoman rule was largely one of not-so-benign neglect. Technically, Algeria was a regency of the Turkish state, its deys, or governors, answerable to the Sublime Porte in Constantinople. In reality, however, "they ruled as absolute monarchs," but only in limited sections of the country.[8] Algeria was divided into four provinces, three of which were ruled by sub-governors. Only Algiers and its immediate environs came under the direct control of the dey. The rest of the country was only nominally under Ottoman rule; tribal leaders largely controlled the countryside, offering a minimum of revenue and submission to the local Ottoman governors. As the French colonial historian L. Rinn wrote,

> Neither the fiscal authority nor the magistrature, nor the metropolitan administrations wanted to admit that certain groups of the Algerian population had remained, until 1830, independent from the [governor] and his lieutenants and had never submitted themselves to obligations like taxation which we [French] intend to extend throughout and maintain for our own profit.[9]

Meanwhile political power in Algiers was roughly divided in an uneasy alliance between the officers of the local imperial garrisons, who handpicked the governor, and a "guild" of corsair captains who, says historian John Entelis, "were the main financial source of support for the state."[10]

This fractured political landscape had important implications for the subsequent development of Algerian society and economy. The urban elite, comprising perhaps 5 percent of Algeria's population, saw itself as a race apart from the tribesmen of the interior who, for their part, "loathed" this class and considered the cities occupied territory, a fundamental cleft in the Algerian psyche that persists to this day. The two groups diverged economically as well. Dependent on piracy for their goods and revenue, Algerian cities never developed as customers of the Algerian *bled*, or hinterland, while the tribes turned inward and became largely self-sufficient. "Ottoman penetration," says historian Rachid Tlemcani, "pushed mightily forward the twin processes of the separation of powers and the economic disintegration and social stratification of society."[11]

Renewed European penetration of Algeria predated the French invasion of 1830 by at least a century. In order to expand revenues, the Turkish governors began offering European companies the right to import and export goods. The revenues from these concessions were not, however, invested in the economic infrastructure of the country but, rather, went to support the import of perishable luxury goods for the bureaucratic elite and the court. As elsewhere in the ailing Ottoman Empire, the indigenous merchant class "remained without high positions, excluded from all juridical or honorific privilege and was in fact despised, as it is in general in a precapitalist context."[12] The penetration of cheap European goods undermined native crafts and increased Algeria's foreign debt, a situation aggravated by a series of crop failures and epidemics in the late eighteenth and early nineteenth centuries. To compensate, the governor devalued the coinage, thereby upping the tax burden on tribesmen. This produced unrest throughout the countryside still under Turkish control. As the state strove to suppress dissident unrest, social conflicts increased. "On the eve of French aggression," writes Tlemcani, "the Turkish state [in Algeria] was bankrupt financially [and] disintegrated politically . . . No wonder the

Turkish power was unable to provide military resistance to the French invasion."[13]

ALGÉRIE FRANÇAISE (1830–1962)

INVASION (1830–37)

France's initial invasion of Algeria had as much to do with internal French politics as it did with international affairs. A collapsing Bourbon monarchy, under Charles X, was eager to quiet its critics with a foreign venture. Maintaining France's privileged trading position in Algeria seemed the perfect issue, especially after the dey of Algiers, claiming French diplomats had insulted Islam and the sultan during negotiations over a debt, struck the French consul, "two or three light blows with the fly-whisk which I was holding in my humble hand."[14] The French dispatched 37,000 troops under the pretext of suppressing Algerian piracy, but, as historian Peter Mansfield points out, "This had long ceased to be a serious menace."[15]

To the Algerians, the French claimed they came in friendship. "We French . . ." a leaflet distributed in Algiers read,

> are going to drive out your tyrants, the Turks, who persecute you, who steal your goods, and never cease menacing your lives . . . Abandon your pasha [governor]; follow our advice; it is good advice and can only make you happy.[16]

In fact, the French committed atrocities and depredations in the first days of the invasion that no Turkish force had ever dared. Of the French looting of 100 million francs from the casbah on the first day of the invasion, Ruedy writes, the "rampage and the uncontrolled pillaging of private properties in and around Algiers were early signs of the great importance the pursuit of personal gain would have in the calculus of France's Algeria policy."[17] Due to the political divisions of Algeria, however, there was virtually no Turkish resistance and "no general rising against the Christian invaders."[18]

CONQUEST AND RESISTANCE (1837–71)

Despite the enthusiasm with which French merchants, both in Algiers and in Marseilles, greeted the invasion, Paris's attitude toward conquest remained ambivalent during the first ten years of occupation. On the one hand, the army's goal was restricted: "limited occupation" of the immediate territory around Algiers and indirect rule elsewhere. On the other hand, the government encouraged colonial settlement. While only 37,000 settlers had appropriated 50,000 acres of land by 1841, a figure that would be dwarfed in the decades to come, their political impact was disproportionate to their numbers. Facts were being created on the ground and a powerful constituency was being established for continued French occupation and expansion. "The physical violence and usurpation of property with which the era began continued for many years," notes Ruedy, "gradually giving way to institutionalized forms of violent usurpation which even in the later years could be reinforced by the former means when the colonials felt threatened."[19]

This institutional violence represented an assault on every aspect of Algerian life: economic, social, political and religious. Driving the French military and government before it was a colonial hunger for land that was, in turn, institutionally facilitated. Soldiers were encouraged to buy land and settlers from France, Corsica, Spain, Italy and Malta were advertised for. Some of the land was reclaimed from unsettled swamp, but most was confiscated from Muslim owners. Sometimes it was sequestered for defensive purposes, but usually it was obtained by "legal chicanery" whereby French authorities seized land when traditional owners could not provide the appropriate documentation. During the first decades of occupation, historian John Entelis writes, "The French had [taken] . . . the most productive lands around the coastal cities, leaving the Muslims with the less-fruitful areas inland."[20]

The French also assaulted Algerian tribal life, beginning early on. As did the United States government in its relations with Native Americans, the French passed laws that cantonized tribes onto lands the French deemed adequate for their support. In addition, tribes were allocated more or less land depending on their "hostility to the French presence."[21] The natives, said Marshal Bugeaud, in charge of French military activity in the 1830s, "must be prevented from sowing, from harvesting, and from pasturing flocks."[22] Again, laws and institutions had a more devastating effect on tribal life than did the military. By the 1860s, French law had converted tribal holdings to personal property, making the land a "freely circulating commodity and thereby facilitat[ing] its sale by individuals to settlers."

Though driven by colonial economics, the French elaborated several rationales for their presence in Algeria. After driving the Turks out, the French began to develop their idea of a *mission civilizatrice*, or civilizing mission, based on the notion of the universality of French civilization. But, where metropolitan France envisioned the assimilation of the Muslims, the *colons*, or European colonials, sought a two-tiered state, based on race, in which Europeans would become "supercitizens" and Algerians a "servile class." In both scenarios, Muslim culture was relegated to gradual extinction. The keystone of this policy, in both versions, was of course the substitution of Christianity for Islam. Shortly after the occupation of Algiers, the French converted the Grand Mosque to the cathedral of Saint-Phillipe, an act that the archbishop of Algiers hoped would begin the process by which Arabs were steered from "the vices of their original religion generative of sloth, divorce, polygamy, theft, agrarian communism, fanaticism, and even cannibalism."[23]

Though initial resistance to the French assault was minimal, it quickly grew in the face of such social, political and economic affronts. While several limited uprisings emerged throughout the country, including one led by a female Berber chieftain named Fatma N'Soumert, resistance to French rule soon coalesced around Abd al-Qadir, an Arab emir, or tribal leader, from the western part of the country and Algeria's "greatest national hero." Deeply religious and politically pragmatic, al-Qadir sought to create an Islamic state in the Algerian interior while acquiescing to French occupation of the coast. Al-Qadir negotiated several peace treaties with the French in the 1830s and 1840s, and lived up to them to the letter, even to the point where he stood by as the Europeans subdued a separate independent Muslim emirate around Constantine in the east.

But the conquest of Constantine, though separated by several hundred miles from al-Qadir's territory, spelled his doom. No single action by the French, says Ruedy, did more to change their policy from one of limited occupation to direct rule over all Algeria. When al-Qadir moved east and occupied territory the French needed to establish communications between Algiers and Constantine, the two sides went to war. Defeated in 1847, the emir was exiled to France, became a close friend of Napoleon III, and was soon being manipulated by the French, who spread rumors that al-Qadir now accepted the premises of the *mission civilizatrice*.

The continued expropriation of Muslim land and decrees vastly extending direct *colon* control, as well as France's defeat by the Prussians in 1870, convinced Algerians that the time was again ripe for driving the French out of the country. Following a shootout between French troops and native police who refused to be transferred to France in January 1871, rebellion spread from tribe to tribe throughout Kabyle. It took the French almost a year and a half and the lives of over 2,500 European settlers and troops (the number of Algerians who died was never determined but, says Ruedy, "was clearly many times greater")[24] to finally suppress the rebellion.

COLONIAL CONSOLIDATION (1871–1914)

Retribution against the rebels was furious, "an orgy of vengeance," says Ruedy, "compounded with a pell-mell rush for economic gain." The people of Kabyle were punished through the seizure of no fewer than 1.4 million acres of land (unwanted land was eventually sold back to the locals for 63 million francs), dragged in front of *colon* juries bent on vengeance rather than justice, and burdened with 36.5 million francs in reparations, imposed on rebellious and unrebellious tribes alike. The crushing defeat ended Algerian armed resistance for three-quarters of a century.

Economically, the Muslim population of Algeria was besieged on all sides. By the beginning of the First World War, the population of *colons* had increased to three-quarters of a million, and while the majority lived in the cities, by 1914 three-quarters of Algerian land was European. The so-called *grands colons*, or great European landholders, had seized approximately one-third of Algeria's arable land, the one-third that was most productive and closest to transportation. The impact of the land squeeze was exacerbated by the practices of traditional Muslim agriculture, which depended on land-intensive pasturage and fallow field farming. The result was that per capita livestock figures were cut in half for Muslims between 1865 and 1900. By the latter year, almost half the Muslim population was either sharecropping and renting land from colonial landholders or working as agricultural laborers on their estates. The late nineteenth century also witnessed the elimination through restrictive laws and *colon* competition, of whole sectors of urban Muslim society, including the former court elite, the educated mercantile class and artisans.

Meanwhile, the French were hemming in the Muslims with a series of statutes and political reforms designed to turn Algeria into a kind of apartheid state. The 1881 Code de l'Indigénat, or Native Code, the most notorious of such statutes, was in fact a collection of forty-one laws applying exclusively to Muslims, which made it an offense, among other things, to criticize the French government, travel without a pass, teach children without state authorization or hold unauthorized gatherings of more than twenty people. During the same years, the network of Islamic social services and judiciary was systematically dismantled and outlawed. Both local judges, or *cadis*, and the Upper Council of Islamic law were eliminated in 1874 and 1875. Muslim education was strictly regulated and confined to a handful of schools.

The French assault on Muslim institutions was supplemented by efforts to control those that remained. Although Sunni Islam is a faith largely devoid of a formal priesthood, France "took it upon itself to create and maintain an official Muslim clergy paid by the state and responsible for the conduct of worship in the mosques" (Ruedy). Unlike the British in many of their colonies, the French made very little effort to cultivate an indigenous class of administrators, since lower-class *colons* filled the numerous posts of the colonial bureaucracy. Nevertheless, the French established a few French-speaking elites, derisively labeled *beni-oui-ouis*, or sons of yes-men, by the Muslims, who served as spokesmen and facilitators between the two largely separate and unequal peoples. Predictably, some of these French-nurtured *evolués*, or evolved ones, would form the nucleus of early Algerian nationalist organizations.

THE RISE OF ALGERIAN NATIONALISM (1914–54)

While French control of the Maghrib in the immediate post–World War I era, says Hourani, was "stronger than ever before," there were two forces undermining this hegemony, both of which would gradually emerge in the 1930s and threaten French control after World War II. One problem was the lack of a cultivated Algerian elite that the French could use as *interlocuteurs valables*, or useful interceders, with the Muslim masses. The other was the growing intransigence of the *colon* population toward any kind of legal reform, an intransigence made all the worse by the weakness of Third and Fourth Republic governments in Paris.

Secular Algerian nationalism followed a predictable trajectory over the course of the twentieth century and can be divided into five periods (though the following dates should, of course, be taken as approximate): first a crusade for equality based on assimilation (1900–WWI); next, a drive for equality based on cultural distinctiveness (1920s); then a political campaign for autonomy (1930s); then a movement for negotiated separation (1945–54); and finally armed resistance (1954–62). The Young Algerian movement of French-educated Muslim intellectuals, professionals and businessmen dominated the first period, while the more radical North African Star (ENA) emerged in the 1920s, based largely among the Algerian emigré working-class population in France (numbering approximately 100,000), who brought their new political ideas back with them to Algeria. When the French government banned the ENA in 1937, its leader, Messali Hadj, founded the Algerian People's Party (PPA), whose motto was "neither assimilation nor separation, but emancipation."

The 1940 Nazi defeat of France and the Anglo-American liberation of Algeria in 1942 had a profound effect on Algerian nationalists in the postwar era. After the spontaneous 1945 uprisings in Setif and Guelma in eastern Algeria, in which between 1,500 and 45,000 *colons* and Muslims died (estimates depend upon sources), the secular Algerian nationalist movement split into two branches. Ferhat Abbas formed the moderate Algerian Manifesto for a Democratic Union (UDMA), while Hadj and his increasingly separatist PPA, now outlawed, re-formed as the Movement for the Triumph of Democratic Liberty (MTLD). Frustrated by the latter party's inability to decide between electoral activism (approximately 500,000 Muslims had been enfranchised to vote in a separate Muslim assembly under the Jonnert Law of 1919) and armed resistance, several militants, including future Algerian president Ahmed Ben Bella, organized the Special Organization (OS) and began recruiting guerrilla fighters. Some of the members of the OS would provide the nucleus of the Revolutionary Committee of Unity and Action (CRUA), which launched the Algerian war of liberation in 1954 and would soon emerge as the National Liberation Front (FLN).

Meanwhile, another nationalist movement had emerged after World War I under the aegis of the Algerian *ulemas*, or Islamic scholars. Under the undisputed leadership of Abd Ben Badis, the so-called Islamic Reform movement emphasized both a return to the roots of Islam and the embrace of modern civilization. By insisting on the essentially Islamic nature of Algerian culture and society, its motto being "Islam is my religion; Arabic is my language; Algeria is my fatherland," the movement both challenged French rule and repudiated the official, French-instituted Islamic clergy. According to Ruedy, the impact of the reformist *ulema* movement on Algerian nationalism was mixed. While it inspired a renewal of Algerian Islam, it never attracted a broad following. Many Algerians were repelled by the fierce infighting between the reformers and the traditional clergy and popular *marabouts*, whom the reformers criticized as lackeys of the *colons*.

Spurring on all these groups were the continued repression and exploitation of the Algerian people by the *colon* minority and the latter's obstructionist resistance to political reform. In 1930, for example, the *colons* celebrated 100 years of French rule in Algeria with a "grotesque" display of racist and ethnocentric "breast-beating" that deeply offended both French liberals and Algerian Muslims. Then, in 1937, the left-wing Popular Front government of Léon Blum proposed the Blum-Violette bill, which would have created a common legislature for Algeria, but confined the Muslim electorate to about 20,000 elite officers and *évolués*. Even this rather modest reform was shot down by *colon* parliamentarians in Paris, confirming, in many Algerian Muslim minds, the impossibility of changing the system from within.

THE ALGERIAN WAR OF INDEPENDENCE (1954–62)

The Algerian War of Independence, one of the great twentieth-century liberation struggles, has been written about extensively. This brief discussion will focus on those aspects of the struggle that portended developments in post-independence Algerian history.

"The more one studies the Algerian revolution," writes Alistair Horne, author of the definitive English-language history of the war, "the more one comes to realise how well the F.L.N. leadership succeeded in spinning an impenetrable cocoon of secrecy around the incessant rifts and dissents at the top."[25] Horne's observation is worth noting for two reasons. First, it hints at the discipline of the FLN's leadership, which never moderated or altered its determination to achieve total independence from France despite numerous (often self-inflicted) setbacks. Second, it reveals how the FLN was never an institutionally unified or ideologically consistent organization.

Because the French had effectively isolated the FLN's National Liberation Army (ALN) in independent Tunisia and Morocco from the guerrilla forces within the country, a deep rift developed between the emerging leaders of the exterior and the radical independents of the interior, a rift that would eventually be settled in the former's favor, particularly after the accession to power in 1965 of Houari Boumédienne, the secretive and

effective leader of ALN forces in Morocco.[26] And, as its name indicates, the
FLN was a front, not an ideologically driven political organization. While
most of its members were secular nationalists, and a few were Marxists, the
FLN leadership included both political moderates like Ferhat Abbas and
radicals like Ben Bella who embraced radically different visions of postwar
Algeria, as the intense struggle for power during the country's first few years
of independence would reveal.

The war itself, which began on November 1, 1954, with a coordinated
FLN assault on French military positions throughout the country, was
among the most brutal anticolonial struggles of the twentieth century.
Estimates range between 200,000 and 1,000,000 dead on the Algerian side.
It was also a highly political war, fought as much on the ideological front
as on the battlefield. While the FLN gradually gained the allegiance and
support of the vast majority of the Muslim population, in part because of
France's brutal attacks on the civilian population, two aspects of the struggle
for the hearts and minds of the Algerian people are worth noting here,
because they came to play such an important role in today's struggle in
Algeria: Islam and women.

Historians disagree about the FLN leadership's use of Islam as a
weapon against the French. Some, like Knauss, argue that the appeal to
Islam as a path to resistance was genuine. Knauss quotes Ben Bella to that
effect: "The peasants," Ben Bella remarked in 1981,

> have always been very attached to Islam. It was they who gave us the
> combatants of the liberation struggle, not the workers. And not in the name
> of national union, but in the name of Islam. It's an error to believe that our
> nationalism is the nationalism of the French Revolution. Ours is a nationalism
> fertilized by Islam . . . All of our political formulation is a Koranic formulation.
> Thus Algerian nationalism and Arab nationalism is a cultural nationalism
> essentially based on Islam.[27]

Others like political scientist Hugh Roberts disagree, seeing in the FLN's
appeal to Islamic unity a mere tactical concession by the leadership. The
arguments are, he writes,

> that the historic FLN of 1954–1962 was the artisan of, above all, a jihad, that
> the revolution was first and foremost an Islamic affair, and that Islam was not
> only the basis on which the people were mobilized for the war but funda-
> mental to the FLN's purpose. This axiom is false. It willfully denies that the
> real purpose of constituting Algeria into a sovereign nation-state and the
> Algerian people into a nation, and that the attitude of the leaders of the FLN
> was an essentially instrumental one.[28]

As for women and the revolution, the ground is less contested, but
equally crucial to an understanding of the current struggle. As sociologist
Marnia Lazreg has written, women became the most important symbolic
object of the struggle between Algerian nationalism and continued French
rule. The disintegrating fabric of the *mission civilizatrice* was re-stitched during

the war as the *colons* and the French government tried to define the war as a struggle for the liberation of Algerian women. Portraying them as veiled and virtual slaves of Algerian men, French propagandists argued that only through the continuing liberating influence of French culture and law would Algerian women become truly free. On the other hand, the FLN, through its most effective theorist, Frantz Fanon, presented the liberation of women through their participation in the revolution. "Behind the [revolutionary] girl," he wrote, "the whole family—even the Algerian father, the authority for all things, the founder of every value—following in her footsteps, becomes committed to the new Algeria."[29] As Lazreg concludes,

> The French fought the Algerians through women. The Algerians fought the French through women. It's a tragic thing, but it's continuing to the present [i.e., the 1990s struggle between the FLN and military governments and the fundamentalists].[30]

What didn't continue, however, was French rule in Algeria. Even more than the Americans in Vietnam, it could be said of the French that they prevailed on the battlefield, but lost on the streets back home. By 1962, the war in Algeria had cost the lives of almost 25,000 French soldiers and 3,000 *colons*, drained 55 billion francs (roughly $10 billion 1960 dollars) from the French treasury, polarized French politics and brought down the Fourth Republic. Charles de Gaulle, brought out of retirement in 1958 to form the Fifth Republic and find a way out of the Algerian quagmire, began tortured negotiations with the FLN that would last from 1960 to 1962 and end in the Evian agreements of March 1962, whereby France granted Algeria independence in exchange for military bases and concessions in the newly discovered gas and oil fields of the Algerian Sahara. Despite the signing of these agreements, however, the war had a final painful and significant chapter left to be written. Unrepentant and vengeful, a hard-core contingent of *colon* militants formed the Secret Armed Organization (OAS) and conducted a campaign of terror during 1961 and early 1962, destroying key parts of the economic infrastructure built by the French, killing almost 3,000 Muslim civilians, and thoroughly poisoning whatever goodwill remained between the one million *colons* and the nine million Muslims of Algeria. The former fled en masse to France within weeks of the new nation's independence.

INDEPENDENT ALGERIA (TO 1992)

INDEPENDENCE AND THE BEN BELLA ERA (1962–65)

The ecstatic celebrations that greeted the Algerians' historic victory over the French in the summer of 1962 were shadowed by some sobering facts.

Because France had dismantled virtually all independent native political, social and economic structures in the nineteenth century, the new nation was faced with a monumental task of reconstruction made worse because the fleeing *colons*, who constituted the vast majority of the technical and professional personnel of the country, "acted out their despair by wantonly destroying hospitals, schools, libraries, communication facilities, factories, and other valuable infrastructure."[31]

The French occupation and the war of liberation had left two other important legacies. First, most of the remaining bureaucratic, professional, technocratic and business elite owed their positions to the very colonial power that had just been overthrown. As Amilcar Cabral, the anticolonial leader and theorist from Guinea-Bissau, noted:

> Some independent African states preserved the structures of the colonial state. In some countries they only replaced a white man with a black man, but for the people it is the same. You have to realize that it is very difficult for the people to make a distinction between [one white] administrator and one black administrator . . . if [he] is living in the same house . . . with the same car . . . what is the difference? The problem of the nature of the state created after independence is perhaps the secret of the failure of independence.[32]

In the case of Algeria, over three-quarters of those holding managerial positions in the government bureaucracy, and nearly half of those in senior decision-making offices, owed their appointments to the French administration. As Ben Bella wondered, "How could the people have confidence in such persons?"[33] And while accusations of collaboration were frequently leveled against such administrators, the government conducted few purges and made no effort at political reeducation, as was the case in the roughly contemporary Cuban revolution.

On the other hand, the war of liberation and the general political climate in the newly decolonized Third World led to an embrace of radical economic and social programs, though not without a struggle. As the FLN had included a variety of people with different ideological positions, united only in their common struggle against the French, so the defeat of that opponent permitted long-hidden conflicts to emerge. During the summer of 1962, various factions of the FLN literally battled for control of the government, leaving upwards of 15,000 dead in the process, until the radical Ben Bella, a revolutionary FLN leader who had been jailed in France for most of the revolution, emerged triumphant. Thus, the Ben Bella regime was marked by talk of socializing the economy and radicalizing the political and social structures of the country—by means of a bureaucracy created by and committed to the old order, *sans* the French. "Despite much revolutionary, socialist, and populist rhetoric," notes Ruedy, "Ben Bella . . . [was] primarily occupied with the painful process of consolidating [his] political power."[34]

What this meant was essentially the imposition of a one-party FLN state, not the FLN of the revolution, but the FLN of the bureaucratic-military hierarchy of the exterior who had imposed their program at the last pre-independence FLN congress in Tripoli, Libya, in May 1962. All other parties were quickly outlawed, including the communists, the Party of Socialist Revolution (PRS) of Mohammed Boudiaf, and the Berber-dominated Socialist Forces Front (FFS) of Hocine Ait Ahmed, while the FLN was declared "the one and only party of progress."[35] Trade unions and other independent organizations were harnessed to the FLN as well. The National Constituent Assembly, or provisional parliament, was bypassed in the writing of the first Algerian constitution, which, according to Ageron, was "presidential and authoritarian in character and revolutionary in style."[36] The constitution was confirmed and Ben Bella elected president in two up-or-down plebiscites in 1963. Both won by margins of about fifty to one.

By inclination and by circumstance, the peasant-born Ben Bella turned his attention to the countryside. In the wake of the *colon* exodus, agricultural laborers and tenants had seized huge tracts of farmland, vineyards and pasturage. (Of course, much of this property was also occupied by better-off Algerian landowners who took advantage of desperate colonists and picked up land, housing and equipment for a song.) These groups established management committees in a process known as *autogestion*, or self-management. As Tlemcani writes, nobody in power had predicted this phenomenon, and none had envisioned "autogestion as a system of economic and social organization in an independent Algeria."[37] The *autogestion* movement was not, however, confined to the agricultural sector. Over 1,000 industrial and commercial enterprises were occupied by workers as well.

While Ben Bella spoke favorably of this spontaneous movement, particularly in the radical Charter of Algiers in 1963, the bureaucracy, steeped in the attitudes of statist control inherited from the French and influenced by the centralized command structure of the Soviets and their Third World emulators, immediately set about taking control of these new local structures in the name of political and economic nation-building. As the Algerian political scientist Ali el-Kenz writes, the political order in Algiers sought "a *command function* to the detriment of the *leadership function* and, within the former, upon the function of public order to the function of politics, properly speaking."[38] (Emphasis in original.)

Socially, the Ben Bella years witnessed a somewhat different struggle between interest groups. Focusing on the key issues of women, family and faith, the early post-independence period witnessed conflicts between a generally conservative populace, particularly in the countryside, and a progressive westernized elite. According to Ruedy, the true reconstructive dynamism among peasants was dedicated to rebuilding the religious infrastructure, so thoroughly dismantled by the French, rather than building the "various infrastructural and other community projects for which local government and party officials tried to mobilize them."[39]

As for women and family, the government made a point of emphasizing women's contribution to the revolutionary cause and the importance of liberating them from the oppressive strictures of the patriarchal Algerian family. In fact, Ben Bella went so far as to threaten men who harassed women in public with forced labor in the Sahara. Unfortunately, writes Lazreg, the government saw women as an objective problem to be rectified rather than as a potential ally and cohort of revolutionary change. Moreover, the government expressed itself in alien modernistic terms, referring to traditional gender relations as an example of the "low cultural level" that Algerians must transcend. This approach was, of course, patronizing, and it ran against the grain of revolutionary and post-revolutionary rhetoric, which emphasized pride in the distinctiveness of Algerian culture and the key role of the peasantry and workers in building a new Algerian nationalism.

Still, it was none of these specific programs and proposals that led to Ben Bella's downfall but rather the general method by which they were promoted. His erratic policy shifts disturbed important sectors of the Algerian bourgeoisie while his authoritarian method alienated constituencies that might have sympathized with his radical agenda. These factors, along with his efforts to weave a personality cult around himself, an effort deeply offensive to FLN and military leaders who preferred collegial rule and decision by consensus, led to the military coup of June 1965, a takeover, according to Entelis, that "hardly caused a ripple in Algerian society."[40]

STATE SOCIALISM AND THE BOUMÉDIENNE YEARS (1965–78)

One of the reasons for the lack of turmoil in Algerian society at this abrupt change in power was that it didn't represent much of a change. Certainly the background and ideology of Houari Boumédienne was not much different from that of his predecessor, who was arrested and imprisoned until after Boumédienne's death in 1978. Both were of peasant origin and both embraced statist economics, one-party politics, an anti-imperialist foreign policy and social modernization. The difference was more one of personal and administrative style: Ben Bella was flamboyant and autocratic; Boumediénne secretive, reserved and consensus-oriented, which made him a more congenial leader as far as the FLN *nomenklatura* and military were concerned.

Under the Boumédienne regime whatever remained of independent institutions and worker self-management were eventually eliminated, coopted or placed under bureaucratic control. However, despite the new leader's efforts to rule by consensus, an opposition began to crystallize around left-wing ministers, independent elements of the General Union of Algerian

Workers (UGTA), student organizations and some sections of the army. Loyal to the dying principle of *autogestion*, Colonel Tahar Zbiri, the army chief of staff, launched an uprising in the Aures and Kabyle regions of the country at the end of 1967.

The quick suppression of the rebellion and the failure of an attempt to assassinate Boumédienne the following year resulted in the complete victory of the new government's bureaucratic agenda. Unions, including the UGTA, the National Union of Algerian Peasants (UNPA) and others, were incorporated into the FLN, while communal and syndicalist economic enterprises, whether agricultural, industrial or commercial, were taken over by state managers whose decision making was yoked to the interests of the state.

Writing about the countryside in the period following Boumédienne's accession to power, Entelis says that "collective ownership and management [*autogestion*] was ultimately bureaucratized and subordinated to the all-powerful control of state technocrats who put agricultural profitability ahead of political mobilization of the peasantry."[41] Only student organizations were left independent. They proved a great nuisance to the regime in the early and mid-1970s when they became increasingly radicalized and attempted not only to reestablish *autogestion* in the schools but also to spread their political program to factories, farms and urban working-class districts throughout the nation.

The FLN had largely stabilized the political scene in the country by the late 1960s, and the military had increasingly become the final arbiter of internal FLN conflicts. With the political situation under control, the Boumédienne regime moved decisively on its economic program. The first of several multiyear economic plans was inaugurated in 1968. Patterned on the model elaborated by French economist Destane de Bernis that was widely adopted in the newly independent Third World (particularly its francophone parts), the plan emphasized rapid industrialization. The idea was to emulate the developmental history of the industrialized world, but at a pace greatly accelerated through rational, statist planning. New technology and capital were to be lavished on key sectors of the economy, especially the so-called "industrializing industries." By increasing productivity in these areas, national income would rise, thus creating increased demands for import-substitution industries. One key industry was supposed to be farm machinery and chemicals, which would in turn have a similar effect on the agricultural sector. As Boumédienne declared, "Heavy industry will be the locomotive which will draw behind it agriculture, light industry, and other carriages [on the railroad] of our economic life."[42]

While the model was encouraged by Western intellectuals and Third World elites with the best of intentions, that is, breaking the grip of poverty in the developing world and freeing the people there from Western economic domination, it also had several unfortunate and deleterious effects on the economies and politics of Third World nations like Algeria. As Tlemcani notes,

> The model contains a fundamental contradiction in the relationship between labour productivity in industry and agriculture, on the one hand, and the eradication of high unemployment . . . on the other. The crucial question to be asked is, how is unemployment to be resolved when the importing of sophisticated technology is perceived to be the *sine qua non* condition upon which the model rests?[43]

Unfortunately, the question was begged by the Boumédienne regime. "We have decided that our equipment has to be ultra-modern, because it is more profitable in the middle term," the president declared. "We cannot accept machines dating from the 1940s, even if their use would provide jobs for a greater number of workers."[44] This, say critics of the model, strengthened an elite group of skilled workers at the expense of the rest of the working class and the peasantry for, in the case of the latter, development funds were siphoned away from their sector and into the creation of modern industry. In short, full employment and economic justice were sacrificed in the name of productivity and national prestige. During the period of centralized economic planning of the 1960s and 1970s, Algeria had one of the highest rates of capital accumulation in either the industrialized or the developing world. Nearly 40 percent of output was reinvested to expand production, largely in the industrial sector. Yet for all of that, gains in the gross domestic product lagged. Taking into account Algeria's explosive population growth of some 3 percent a year between 1965 and 1980, the gross domestic product (GDP) rose by barely 2 percent annually.

The most important element in Algeria's industrialization plan was the hydrocarbon industry. In 1956, huge reserves of natural gas, and smaller ones of oil, were discovered by French geologists in the Sahara Desert. This key "industrializing industry" was expected not only to provide the capital necessary to fuel Algeria's economic development, but also to generate new technologies as well as produce the petrochemicals needed for agricultural modernization. The nationalization of Algeria's hydrocarbon industry in 1971, an aspect of the Boumédienne administration's disdain for direct foreign investment, and the quadrupling of oil prices in 1973–74 only enhanced the importance of this industry, but it still failed to fulfill the economic planners' goals.

Investment in agriculture and consumption-oriented industry steadily declined throughout the 1970s, and even in the heavy industrial sector there were serious problems during these years. The growth of huge monopolistic state enterprises and the vast bureaucracies needed to run them created problems of their own. According to the National Charter of 1976, which rationalized the policies of the Boumédienne regime largely after the fact, the rapid creation of a socialist society required a "solid and ever strengthened state." According to Tlemcani, this included "hierarchy in power structure, pyramidal institutions, mass organizations, efficiency, rational relationship between supervisors and agents and honesty between official-dom and governed." But, he adds, it also carried

> ineluctably the permanent risk of engendering the bureaucratic phenome-non . . . red-tape and slowness; rudeness and delays; proliferation of paper work and rigidities; buck-passing and rubber-stamps; incompetence and inefficiency; and corruption and nepotism.[45]

All of these things Boumédienne's Algeria had in abundance. John Nellis, an expert on administrative development, wrote of Algeria in 1976 that "in an increasingly inefficient world, the Algerian bureaucracy maintains its standing as one of the most difficult with which to deal and one of the least productive in terms of output."[46]

Lastly, there were serious social implications with the model as it was implemented. Under the French, economic development in the country had been extremely uneven, with the bulk of investment concentrated in several industrial and commercial agricultural zones, largely around the main coastal cities. The Boumédienne economic program exacerbated this uneven growth. Those same cities became centers of heavy industry, drawing hundreds of thousands of peasants from the increasingly depressed countryside into already overcrowded urban areas. And since the priority was on the establishment of an infrastructure designed to support heavy industry rather than human needs, services and utilities became increasingly overtaxed and inadequate.

Not that the Boumédienne regime and its modernization program were without successes. There was, in fact, much to boast of in the progress made in several key indices of social development. Life expectancy increased by a decade for both men and women between 1965 and 1984, while the infant mortality rate fell by a third between 1961 and 1980. Education was a government priority and the effects were telling. Primary school enroll-ment doubled for both boys and girls between 1960 and 1980, secondary school enrollment tripled, and literacy rates for men and women jumped 100 percent during these same years. Algeria had no universities when the French abandoned the country in 1962; there were ten by 1980. And for all the problems with Algeria's economy, the gross national product (GNP) more than doubled between 1965 and 1985, though much of this was due to the increase in oil and gas prices, and unevenly distributed.

By the time of Boumédienne's sudden and unexpected death from a rare blood disease in December 1978, Algeria was a semi-industrialized economy with a high dependency on hydrocarbon revenues, which, even before the current unrest began in 1992, still generated well over 90 percent of the country's foreign earnings. In terms of social indicators, Algeria was in the upper 50 percent of the developing world in literacy, life expectancy and infant mortality and in the top tenth percentile for Africa.

Algeria's industry, however, was highly inefficient and its agricultural sector was, in the words of one economist, a "basket case." While Algeria had an agricultural foreign exchange surplus under the French, largely due to high-value crops like wine and fruit (it imported grain and other basic foodstuffs), it barely produced 40 percent of its grain requirements by 1981, even though the agricultural population had grown during these years (outmigration was more than compensated for by a high birthrate). While this shortfall was partly due to Algeria's geography—only some 3 percent of the land is arable—much had to do with economic policy. Between 1970 and 1984, capital earmarked for the agricultural sector never amounted to more than 12 percent of overall investment.

Given Algeria's tremendous oil and gas resources, however, these relative positions indicated that something was clearly wrong. In June of 1975, on the tenth anniversary of his accession to power, Boumédienne announced plans for the drafting of a new National Charter, which was drawn up and presented for public debate in 1976. The president intended this event to initiate the opening up of the political process. "With a degree of freedom unparalleled in Algerian political life since the first year of independence," writes Ruedy, "Algerians discussed and criticized the document over a period of months."[47] Nevertheless, the amended National Charter was largely unchanged when it was put before the people for ratification. It passed overwhelmingly.

The new Algerian constitution, largely modeled after the charter, was a reaffirmation of the principles that had guided Algeria since the coup of 1965. It declared Islam the religion of the state, though it maintained the government's right to control religious institutions and clergy; it reasserted the socialist orientation of the economy, including severe restrictions on foreign investment and the use of private property "to exploit the labor of others"; and it guaranteed women the full right to participate in every facet of Algerian life. Politically, the document was a model of republican form and the guarantor of full civil liberties. But it maintained the government's near-total control of the country's social and political institutions. "Ultimately," comments Ruedy,

> the great political restructuring of 1976, trumpeted as the vehicle for read-mitting the Algerian people to the political process, served to reinforce Boumédienne's powers in the same way the constitution of 1963 and the Algiers Charter of 1964 had reinforced Ben Bella's.[48]

In fact, the National Charter of 1976 can be seen as the last great document and affirmation of the Algerian revolution. After Boumédienne's death and the accession of Chadli Benjedid to the presidency, and especially after the drop in oil prices in the early 1980s, Algeria moved away from its efforts at socialist planning and embraced economic liberalization. It came to abandon its emphasis on secularism, by encouraging fundamentalist leaders in an attempt to combat the radicalism of the left, and surrendered its role as protector of women's rights. In the process, it unleashed forces that challenged and eventually destroyed the FLN's monopoly on political organizing and expression.

LIBERALIZATION AND BENJEDID'S FIRST DECADE (1979–88)

Though he had been a minor player in the war of independence, Chadli Benjedid was the quintessential bureaucratic insider when he was appointed to succeed Boumédienne. Military commander of the Oran district in western Algeria and member of the Council of the Revolution, the chief advisory body to the president, Benjedid had a reputation as a serious and competent administrator in the Boumédienne mold, and a loyal defender of the president, even if, as later events proved, he was not an absolute believer in *Boumédiennisme*. Nevertheless, says Ruedy, "As a candidate of the establishment, Benjedid's election [in 1979] naturally connoted continuity rather than abrupt change, and such was the rhetoric of the new regime."[49]

Behind the scenes, however, Benjedid began quietly to install his own men in power, gradually centralizing power around himself as Boumédienne had done. "Under this process, which is similar to that practiced in the [former] Soviet Union," wrote political scientist I. William Zartman, "a single leader emerges out of the collectivity; his competitors and their followers as well as the followers of his predecessor are removed; and even the custodians of power during the collective interregnum are disbanded and dispersed."[50] The Algerian populace has a more laconic way of expressing this backroom wheeling and dealing: *boulitique*, an Arabization of the French word for politics.

Benjedid inherited a host of serious economic and social problems from the Boumédienne years. Economic stagnation, bureaucratic inertia and shortages in housing and water were severely aggravated by a population explosion that required the construction of a million new units of housing annually just to keep pace. The emphasis in the Boumédienne era, of course, had been on developing heavy industry. This left the countryside in a severely depressed state and cities crowded well beyond capacity with workers frustrated at the lack of consumer goods and the inadequate public services and utilities. Even though they were part of the problem, Algeria's bureaucratic elite recognized that serious structural economic and perhaps even political change was necessary if the country was not to slide into social turmoil. Benjedid made "for a better life" the motto of his administration, in notable contrast to that of the Boumédienne regime's "to build an Algerian socialism."

The new president was given precious little time to act on this goal before a series of crises engulfed the country. During the 1979–80 school year, the first of these crises emerged at the University of Algiers. The immediate conflict was over language (whether classes would be in French or Arabic), but that issue represented economic and social rifts that had been deepening in Algerian society since independence. No country in the Arab world was occupied by a European power as thoroughly or as lengthily as Algeria. And no other country on the globe has found itself the inheritor of two such profoundly different and universalist cultures and languages as French and Arabic. Since independence the government had effectively ignored the problems inherent in this cultural and linguistic duality, preferring instead, reasonably enough, to view it as a national asset.

Unfortunately, the duality was and is not only cultural, but economic and social as well. Throughout Algerian society, the francophone population occupies positions of power. They are also noticeably better-educated and wealthier than their arabophone neighbors. In the winter of 1979, Arab-speaking students at the university launched a two-month strike "to protest the favoritism shown the francophone students and the better career opportunities open to them."[51] Fearing that radical leftists or the emerging fundamentalist movement might take advantage of the strike to push for more universal reforms, the government responded to the students' demands quickly and favorably. The process of Arabization of the educational system was accelerated. Within five years, nearly two-thirds of all high school students and one-third of all undergraduates were receiving an Arabic-language education. While critics complained that this policy had lowered academic standards, the new policy clearly indicated that the balance of power between Arabized and Gallicized students, and citizens, was shifting.

Having defused this crisis, the government was almost immediately confronted with another, a second conflict over culture triggered by the solution applied to the first. In March 1980, a student strike at the University Center of Tizi Ouzou quickly spread to nearby high schools and then to the population at large when a general strike was called in mid-April. Tizi Ouzou is both the political capital of Tizi Ouzou province and the cultural and economic hub of the Kabyle region, the heartland of Algeria's Berber population. While the history of Berber-Arab relations and the major issues between these two peoples will be explored more thoroughly in Chapter 4, a few of the most important points about Arab-Berber relations should be made here.

First, the two peoples, despite a common origin, differ ethnically. During the Arab invasions of the Middle Ages, virtually all Algerians converted to Islam, but not all fully adopted Arab culture. The more isolated tribes in the mountains retained their indigenous Berber culture and language. The French exploited this difference as part of their policy of maintaining control over the majority Arabs, usually by recruiting the Berbers as native troops and building more schools in the Kabyle region than elsewhere. Thus French policy produced both a more francophone Kabyle population and mutual resentment between Arabs and Berbers.

When the Benjedid administration caved in to Arab-speaking students' demands, it produced an immediate reaction in the Kabyle. In contrast to the soft approach it had taken in Algiers, the government was fierce and unbending in Tizi Ouzou. When the *gendarmerie*, or national police, were sent in, the worst rioting in post-independence Algerian history up to that time erupted, leaving scores of Kabyles dead or injured. "The protesters," says Ruedy, "promptly baptized the events 'le printemps de Tizi Ouzou' [the Tizi Ouzou spring] in explicit recollection of the infamous Prague spring twelve years earlier [when Soviet tanks crushed the Czechoslovak rebellion]."[52] While the government did make a few minor concessions to the Kabyles, it nevertheless stuck to its commitment to rapid and thorough Arabization of education and the state.

While Arabization might be interpreted as a logical development of Algerian nationalism—an attempt to unify a dualistic culture—the policy in fact represented a much deeper shift in the political and social landscape, a shift that became more readily apparent in the next few years with the drafting of new legislation concerning the place and role of women and the family in Algerian society, as well as in reforms in the nation's economic policies. That is to say, Arabization in Algeria is often associated with Islamicization.

Since 1975, when all colonial-era family laws were repealed, Algeria had lacked a comprehensive code concerning marriage, spousal rights, divorce and other issues of special concern to women. The *sharia*, or body of Islamic law, remained, but it was clearly inadequate for modern-day Algeria, as even the *cadis* who administered it admitted. There had been talk since the revolution of developing such a code, but nothing serious was attempted until the Benjedid era. The process of drafting the code was conducted in typical FLN fashion, that is, by a secret committee largely made up of government officials, and without any input from the public. While members of the officially backed General Union of Algerian Women (UNFA) were included in the process, none of them was female. Nevertheless, from the time the process began in 1979, a small group of university women known as the Women's Collective began to organize in an attempt to influence the process. When a government official leaked a copy of the draft proposal to the group, the women went public, going to the then unheard of extreme of public demonstrations in front of the National Assembly. Seeking to embarrass the government, the women recruited renowned heroines of the revolution. The strategy worked, and the Family Code of 1981 was sent back for revision.

The activism of this group of women had defeated the proposal, but it had been the growing fundamentalist movement that had influenced the initial drafting of the code. And of the two forces, the latter was both more powerful and more in tune with the drift of Algerian society. As in the issue of Arabization, the government feared the growing fundamentalist movement, even as it sought to exploit it as a weapon against leftists. It hoped to placate the fundamentalists by making concessions on those social issues it perceived as dearest to them and their agenda. In its search for national consensus, it was trying to make room for this new movement under the umbrella of FLN leadership.

But as the fundamentalists increased their numbers and power, they began to shove aside more vulnerable groups, like working women. Thus in 1984 the National Assembly ignored renewed women's protests and passed a family code modeled after, but even more conservative than, the original of 1981. Under the 1984 code, women were explicitly forbidden from marrying non-Muslim men (though the inverse was permitted), polygamy was condoned and divorce was declared "the exclusive faculty of the husband" (meaning that only men could unilaterally demand a divorce; women had to ask permission of the husband or the state). Implicit in the code were rules that required a wife to seek permission from her husband (or her eldest son if she was widowed) to work or to travel out of the country. "The Family Code," concludes Knauss, "revived many of the traditional features of the patrilineal and patrilocal family and relegated women to the legal status of minors in the society."[53]

While the FLN was giving in to fundamentalist demands in the area of social legislation (though one could argue that many in the party leaned in that direction to begin with), this did not mean the party was willing to sacrifice its monopolistic control over Algerian politics. While the government sought to improve economic efficiency by breaking up the gigantic and monopolistic state-owned firms that dominated virtually all heavy industry, as well as many light industries and the service sector, and achieve greater accountability by insisting on the profitability of individual firms, this Algerian *perestroika*, or *intifah* in Arabic, was not accompanied by a *glasnost*-style opening up of the political system, not at least at first. For example, under Boumédienne, the government had established workers' councils in most state-owned industrial and agricultural enterprises. But this had been largely a sham exercise, as the opposition newspaper *El Moudjahid* (*The Warrior*) had noted.

> The managers of firms have ignored the deliberations of the assemblies, failed to provide them the data on which they can base reasoned decisions, and have used the disciplinary committees in rubber-stamp fashion.[54]

Still, the intent to democratize the factories had been there. Not so under the Benjedid regime, which did away with the councils altogether in 1985, through an agreement with the largely FLN-controlled UGTA. "The pro- and anti-liberalization factions within the Central Committee, the Politburo, and the National Assembly were unified on only one issue," writes political scientist Dirk Vandewalle, "preventing the dispersal of power outside the party."[55]

While political reform in the first decade of the Benjedid administration was minimal and largely for show, the liberalization of the economy was quite real. Besides dismantling superministries and huge economic enterprises like Sonatrach,[56] the national oil and gas corporation, which was broken up into thirteen parts, the regime embarked on a high-profile anti-corruption and anti-bureaucracy campaign. This effort culminated in the prosecution of Boumédienne's foreign minister on charges of embezzlement and the establishment of the Audit Court, the Algerian counterpart to the U.S. General Accounting Office, though it proved largely powerless. But as Tlemcani argues, the effort to streamline the economy was largely an old FLN strategy, purging new administrations of holdovers from the previous regime, in a new, politically correct guise. And as for the corruption campaign, it was, he says, doomed to failure even before it was conceived.

> In a nutshell, corruption, mismanagement, racketeering and embezzlement are not accidental contingencies of the [Algerian] state. On the contrary, this sociological phenomenon is a structural element characteristic of the BSC [Bureaucratic State Capitalism]. For instance, the privileges in which corruption and misgovernment are associated, aims ultimately at owning people and making sure they stay owned.[57]

Moreover, the breaking-up of large firms and the new emphasis on productivity and profit, under the slogan "Discipline and Hard Work to Guarantee the Future" did not necessarily guarantee either. Since the firms were broken up with little attention paid to their specific mission, they each expanded haphazardly and reestablished monopolies over their sectors of the economy, albeit on a smaller scale. Moreover, as the heads of independent economic units, the managers of restructured state-owned enterprises were in fact responsible to no one but themselves. In short, the restructuring may have achieved the worst of both market and state-planned economies: anarchic growth, continuing corruption and increasing bureaucracy, since the number of managers grew as firms multiplied.

The Benjedid administration was slightly more successful in its agricultural reforms. During the years of the Boumédienne administration's so-called "agrarian revolution," state marketing agencies were responsible for setting the prices paid to cooperatives and most private farmers. Needless to say, with the emphasis on industrialization, prices were kept down to lower the urban working-class food bill, which would, in turn, allow state-owned industrial enterprises to lower their payroll costs. Under

Benjedid, private farmers were permitted to market their crops independently, and, while this mainly benefited the better-off farmers, since most of the poorer agriculturists worked on state cooperatives that continued to be subject to price controls set by the marketing agencies, it did increase overall agricultural output. At the same time, about one million acres of state-owned farm land were privatized. Still, the problem of food importation did not go away. After three years of reforms, food imports and subsidies on domestic food prices still consumed one-quarter of Algeria's export earnings.

These complex economic problems with the *intifah* went largely unnoticed by the urban populace except indirectly, in that the increasing inefficiency and anarchy of the system were steadily lowering the standard of living. The sources of this decline, of course, were not new in the 1980s; they had been part of the Algerian system since the mid-1960s, but they had been hidden from the masses. Revenues from Algeria's extensive natural gas and oil reserves allowed the government to maintain food subsidies, universal health care, expanded educational facilities and employment, even if that often meant workers doing pointless tasks on the payrolls of bloated state-owned firms.

But the rapid collapse of oil and natural gas prices in the mid-1980s destroyed this cozy system. Over the course of just two years, 1985 and 1986, Algeria's foreign income, 95 percent of which came from hydrocarbon revenues, fell from $13 billion to $8 billion, making the nearly $4 billion in annual service on the $23 billion foreign debt even more difficult to bear. Indebtedness to international lenders was seen by the revolutionary-era generation that governed Algeria as a virtual return to colonialism. Determined to pay off the debt, the government cut imports drastically and limited capital investment to finishing projects already begun. This in turn increased unemployment, which had officially reached 25 percent in the latter year, though most experts agreed the true rate was significantly higher. Food subsidies for everything but semolina (wheat for pasta and couscous) and cooking oil were slashed, and, while food from private farms was readily available, its high cost put it out of reach of many Algerian families. Free health care was suspended, though Medicaid-type subsidies were offered in its place to the poorest citizens.

In short, all the economic ingredients for a social explosion were evident by 1986, though the explosion might have been avoided if there had been a feeling that the burden of austerity was being shared equally by all classes. That, however, was not the case. The hostility to the private sector, though evident in virtually every government and FLN proclamation issued in the pre-Benjedid era, was largely rhetorical. A significant private sector had always existed in Algeria and had in fact been heavily subsidized, albeit indirectly, by the policies that kept prices down. To take two examples, steel, which was produced at a loss by state-owned mills, was bought up by, say, private food-canning firms at lower-than-market prices, while subsidized sugar was far more of a bargain to private bakeries that bought it by the ton than it was to individual consumers who purchased it by the kilo.

The liberalization of the early Benjedid years, however, added a new and more troubling element to the general corruption and profiteering inherent in the system. The economic boom following the second major hike in oil prices after the Iranian Revolution of 1979 included several years of industrial expansion and income growth. But this growth had not been distributed equally. The newly autonomous managers in the bureaucracies of state-owned industries paid themselves handsomely. Their new power, as well as the Benjedid administration's increasing reliance on letting the market dictate its economic decision making, helped shift spending on imports from the capital sector to consumer goods. Algeria witnessed a spurt in luxury goods purchases by this new elite, as evidenced by the designer boutiques that lined the better boulevards and the fancy cars that clogged them. Later, an ex prime minister asserted that FLN officials had stolen some $26 billion from the public treasury since independence. This figure, most outside observers say, was grossly exaggerated— an opinion supported by the figure's convenient correspondence to Algeria's foreign debt—but the point was well taken by Algerian citizens who, even if they hesitated to believe the extent of the claim, were sure of its substance.

The increasing discrepancies between the standard of living of the elite and that of the populace, exacerbated by the austerity policies of the post-oil-boom era, quickly took on political significance. "The FLN's claim to pursue equity and economic justice for all Algerians was increasingly becoming tarnished," writes Vandewalle.

> The growing gap between those who had no access to FLN patronage and the elite of public sector managers, party apparatchiks, and allied ALN officers, exposed the true nature of the party. It was no longer considered neutral.[58]

That is to say, a party that claimed to represent all Algerians, and had created a one-party state based on that claim, really represented the few, and the majority knew it.

Moreover, the growing income gap was made even more painful by the sense of disappointment that gripped many ordinary Algerians. For much of their lives (or all of their lives for the two-thirds of the population born since 1962), Algerians had been promised that the gap between the promise of the revolution and the reality of everyday life was soon to be bridged by means of FLN policies. But that promise, if it ever rang true, was so patently false by the late 1980s that few outside or inside the party believed it anymore. Adding to the frustration was the fact that the FLN, in its search for national consensus and revolutionary unity, had eliminated, usurped or coopted virtually every political and social institution that might have served to channel opposition and discontent. "The FLN claim that it represented an indispensable political intermediary had vanished," says Vandewalle, "[and] all belief in the political, ideological, and cultural value of the party had dissipated."[59]

How and where was this discontent to express itself? In 1986, riots broke out in the eastern cities of Constantine and Setif. When several hundred fundamentalist protesters were arrested and brought to trial, nationwide student strikes ensued. By September 1988, labor unrest had spread through the industrial belt around Algiers and to public service companies in the capital itself. Rumors began to spread that a national general strike to protest official corruption, unemployment, stagnant wages, lack of housing and inflation had been called for October 5. But before it could materialize, rioting erupted among unemployed youth, who were soon joined by fundamentalist organizers. The violence spread quickly across the country.

After two days, the government declared a "state of siege" and sent in the army. The soldiers were ordered to fire point-blank into the crowds, in an episode subsequently referred to as Black October, killing over 200 (by official count; opposition spokespersons have quoted figures as high as 1,500) and injuring thousands. That ended the violence, and also closed a chapter in Algeria's history. As Vandewalle notes, "The symbolic value [the FLN] once shared with the ALN, as guarantor of national independence and egalitarianism was in question even before the October 1988 riots." The riots, he says, ended "once and for all [such] pretensions of the country's single party."[60] The Algerian revolution, which had begun thirty-four years earlier on November 1, 1954, was over.

DEMOCRATIZATION (1988–90)

While much of the country was in shock, both because of the extent of the violence and the government's harsh response, Benjedid quickly acted to defuse the tension by calling together 5,000 delegates for the long-postponed Sixth Congress of the FLN, which took place at the end of November. The unprecedented vigor and acrimony of the debate revealed the changes that had been germinating for years, but were spurred to life by the riots. The military hierarchy and a portion of the old civilian leadership maintained the old party line: continued FLN monopoly of political and social life; hostility to expanding economic reforms; and a continued crackdown against militants of all stripes, including fundamentalists.

But the FLN bureaucracy and leadership had never been as ideologically uniform as its outward show of solidarity made it seem. Many of the leaders of the revolutionary generation, who were still largely in control of party machinery, as well as some of the new generation in middle administration, supported the president in his calls for expanding economic reform, including a radical rewriting of the prohibitions on foreign investment, and offering a potentially historic break from the past on the political front. Several measures to detach the FLN from the government were passed, but the idea of establishing a multiparty system was postponed. Presidential deputy Abdelhamid Mehri, Benjedid's choice to succeed the hard-line Cherif Messaadia, fired after the October riots, explained the reason for this hesitancy. "We first want to give the idea of returning to the broad front [a more inclusive but monopolistic FLN] every chance of success . . . a multiparty system would have to be approved by popular referendum."[61] Benjedid's subsequent election to a third five-year term with 81 percent of the popular vote gave him a mandate to act on the reformist program outlined at the Congress.

In February, Benjedid put a new constitution to a public referendum, and it was approved overwhelmingly. The new document dropped all references to Algeria as a socialist state, and changed its emphasis of language from the rights of the people to the rights of individual citizens, or at least male citizens, since all references to women's rights contained in the 1976 constitution were omitted. On the other hand, guarantees on freedom of expression, association and assembly represented a momentous victory for the liberal wing of the FLN.

Throughout 1989, the National Popular Assembly (APN) passed a series of political reforms, filling in the framework provided by the new constitution. The State Security Court, the judicial arm responsible for political crimes, was abolished. Press restrictions were lifted, making the Algerian press (not including the still officially controlled electronic media) "the most free and politically varied in the Arab world."[62] But perhaps most important, the APN approved radical new laws on political associations and elections. Almost immediately, Algerians began to organize dozens of parties of every political stripe and, by early 1991, over fifty had obtained official recognition, including the largest of all, the Islamic Salvation Front (FIS).[63]

Technically, the government should not have authorized this last party, since the 1989 law of associations explicitly prohibited parties based on religious and ethnic affiliation. Algerian ambassador to the United Nations Ramtane Lamamra explained the decision.

> It was felt that the Islamic movement exists in the society, and whether the reference to Islam appears in the title or not can be alleviated by the kind of political program adopted. You have in European countries parties with Christian in the name, but it doesn't mean they are really going to Christianize the government. We thought our own Islamic parties would evolve in this way.

Perhaps, but the decision also followed in the FLN tradition of using fundamentalist groups as a foil against radical left-wing parties. As Roberts notes, Benjedid, Mehri and the new prime minister, Mouloud Hamrouche, "play[ed] this Islamist card in their own interests."[64]

Nonetheless, while the new constitution was presented in typical FLN fashion, that is, to use Roberts' description, "like a rabbit out of a hat . . . imposed with minimal public discussion," the rebirth of associative life it produced was nothing short of extraordinary.[65] "Once the ruling 'bargain' became unstuck," writes Entelis, "civil society, institutional life, and associational activity [re]asserted themselves in ways never before imagined."[66] Liberal FLN leaders applauded these developments, expecting their party, with its vast organizational apparatus, control of the electronic media and association with the heroics of the Algerian revolution, to compete successfully in the new political environment.

They were wrong. Like Mikhail Gorbachev in the former Soviet Union, Benjedid freed up the political system, promising that this move would produce benefits in people's everyday lives. But the Algerian economy continued to deteriorate. Instead of identifying the FLN with the revolution, an irrelevant fact to the majority of voters who came of age after the French departure, the party and its policies of economic liberalization were linked in the popular mind to economic hard times.

In September, Ben Bella returned to the country from his exile in Morocco to found the unlicensed Algerian Democratic Movement (MDA), though the party, along with Ait Ahmed's Berber-dominated FFS, would boycott the coming municipal elections. But as the new political order began to emerge, there were really only two parties in national contention: the FLN and the FIS. While the rise of the FIS will be more thoroughly discussed in Chapter 3, several factors are useful to consider here. First, for all the professed secularism of the FLN, Algeria was a deeply Islamic society. The FLN had, in fact, appealed to religious solidarity in its struggle with the French and had readily agreed to the fundamentalist agenda when redrafting family law in the early 1980s. Second, while social and political associations burst onto the scene with the new constitution and new legislation of 1989, the fundamentalists had always had a network of institutions in the form of mosques, religious schools and social services facilities. Third, as the only real party of nationwide dimensions—the FFS was concentrated in the Kabyle, Ben Bella was an anachronism and the other fifty or so parties were either local in origin or vehicles of traditional local leaders, the so-called "salon" parties—the FIS was the only place most Algerian citizens could turn to profess their profound disgust with the ruling FLN.

There is also the FLN's rhetorical tradition to consider. For decades, Algerians had been exhorted to think in terms of revolution, radicalism and militancy as their distinctive national patrimony. They had also been taught to believe that the profound problems confronting Algeria could be blamed on the machinations of either international imperialists or internal reactionaries, a conspiratorial political conceptualization that matched perfectly the ideas and rhetoric of the Islamic fundamentalists, who, like fundamentalists everywhere, also tend toward such explanations of political events. The growing maldistribution of wealth and displays of conspicuous consumption by members or supporters of the FLN provided an objective foundation for this kind of political thinking, which FIS leaders exploited in sermons, speeches and pamphlets.

ELECTIONS AND THE COUP (1990–92)

The first set of elections, for municipal office, were scheduled for June 1990. As in France, Algerian municipalities carry more political weight than they do in the United States. Not only do they have a greater impact on people's everyday lives, they also serve as the political base and organizing platform for national politics and national politicians. Thus, the FIS's overwhelming victory in these elections—they garnered 54 percent of the popular vote to the FLN's 28 percent and control of 850 of 1,500 municipal councils, including the country's four largest cities, to the FLN's 480—represented not just a takeover of local government but also a very real potential for national leadership.

Not surprisingly, the two parties reacted very differently to the elections, choosing to find in them very different messages. The FLN issued a series of *mea culpae* blaming itself for the FIS victories and promising to do better by the people in the future, while secretly hoping and expecting that the largely amateur politicians of the FIS would so bungle their administration of municipalities that they would be rejected in the coming parliamentary elections. "Hardly a few weeks had passed [since the elections] before news stories began appearing in the national and international press," says Islamicist scholar Francois Burgat,

> reporting signs of the FIS' presumed inability to keep its "fabulous promises" to the voters . . . in this flood of rumors in the form of accusations, it was for a long time difficult to determine what was really going on. [But] week after week, it became clear, in fact, that the balance sheet for the Islamists was far from the catastrophe predicted by the media on both sides of the Mediterranean.[67]

Moreover, FLN leaders hoped that when the Algerian people got a taste of the kinds of social restrictions envisioned by the FIS, they would return to the FLN in droves. But, as Burgat argues, this did not turn out to be the case either.

> In [many] cases the [Islamic] measures had already been taken by FLN communal officials much earlier, and had not aroused any opposition at the time (this was the case notably in the ban on wearing shorts outside beaches, and the closing of certain places serving alcohol.)[68]

But, he adds, the FIS achieved no miracles in turning local economies around. "There was evidence of technical and political errors . . . especially the war on Raï [Algerian rock and roll] music . . . [and] there was sometimes a chilly retreat to symbolic measures that were easier to carry out because they did not demand money."[69]

Whatever the assessment, FIS leaders felt that their party was in the ascendant and immediately began making demands for early parliamentary elections. In this they were assisted by two events that occurred outside Algeria. First, there was French foreign policy. Fearing an Islamist victory and the flood of trans-Mediterranean refugees it would produce, the Mitterrand government quickly made clear its support for the government and the FLN. This proved a grave tactical error for both Paris and Algiers. If the latter government's attack on rioters during Black October had not destroyed the last remnants of the FLN's revolutionary credibility, then this heavy-handed support from its ancient foe surely did. Second, there were the events in the Persian Gulf. Unlike most Arab societies, Algeria did not experience a deep rift between a government that supported Desert Shield and Desert Storm and a population sympathetic to Saddam Hussein. The government stayed largely neutral for both ideological and tactical reasons. Anti-Western sentiment was still strong among the FLN leadership, and most in the government feared what would happen if they openly supported the presence of American and European troops on Arab territory. Nevertheless, the FIS made a point of associating FLN neutrality with anti-Islamicism. On January 18, during one of the largest demonstrations in Algerian history, FIS leader Ali Belhadj pointedly stood in front of the defense ministry and proposed sending volunteers to assist Iraq.

Meanwhile, the government tried to damage the FIS by making its job of running municipalities even more difficult by imposing new regulations and withholding revenues. The FLN also resorted to older tactics. In the hope of coopting the Islamist movement or, at least, splitting its constituency, it encouraged several moderate Islamist parties. Then in early April 1991, Hamrouche pushed through a new electoral law for the upcoming June parliamentary elections that, says Ruedy, "subdivided and flagrantly gerrymandered electoral districts to the advantage of FLN candidates . . . and established a runoff procedure most observers also thought favored the FLN."[70]

The FIS was temporarily caught off guard by these complicated new electoral laws, but, once it understood their implications, it loudly protested, calling for their repeal and for presidential elections to accompany the legislative ones. It called a general strike for May 25, which largely failed, and then mobilized its supporters in violent confrontations with security forces. Interpreting this violence as an assault on state authority, the government canceled the elections and declared martial law. This decision, most observers agree, was largely made at the instigation of military leaders who, in the face of social chaos, were reemerging from their self-imposed political isolation following the outrage that greeted the events of Black October.

Nevertheless, the Benjedid administration acted in characteristic form by offering a carrot to its opponents, as well as a stick. A new government was organized under a long-term critic of the FLN, Sid Ahmed Ghozali, who promised "free and clean" elections by December. The appointment and promises temporarily cooled the situation and satisfied FIS leaders, but, as Ruedy writes, "The momentum of the mass movement they had created soon impelled it forward again." As Ghozali struggled to achieve a parliamentary and FLN consensus on a new electoral law, Belhadj and FIS co-leader Abbassi Madani began to call for an openly Islamic government, threatening a jihad, or holy struggle, to achieve it. Despite this inflammatory rhetoric and hard-line FLN obstructionism in the assembly, things began to improve by autumn. Street violence largely disappeared, the state of emergency was lifted and Ghozali finally got a more equitable electoral law through the assembly. It called for elections on December 26, with runoffs on January 16 in districts where no candidate received a majority of the votes.

Like the municipal elections, the parliamentary elections were largely violence-free and an overwhelming victory for the FIS. Of the 430 districts, the FIS received an absolute majority in 188, while the FLN took just 15, even running behind the FFS, which won 26 seats. Ironically, the electoral law designed by the FLN worked against the party. While the FLN received almost 25 percent of the popular vote, it won only 7 percent of the new parliament's seats. The FFS, which took a smaller percentage of the vote, won almost twice as many seats because its support was concentrated in Kabyle districts. More disturbing, as far as the government was concerned, it looked like the FIS was headed to win an equally large portion of the still undecided districts. In fact, it was likely to achieve a more than two-thirds majority in the APN and, under Algerian law, this would allow it to amend the constitution. As Ruedy concludes, "The results of the December 26 elections were a shock to the mostly westernized elites who had ruled Algeria since independence."[71] They were shocked, perhaps, but not immobilized.

Benjedid liberals intent on pursuing the three-year-old Algerian *glasnost* to its culmination and arguing that the president could always veto extreme legislation emerging out of an FIS-dominated assembly confronted hard-liners, including the heads of internal security and defense, who believed that there was no effective legal safeguard against the inevitable implementation of an Islamist state. By the second week of January, the latter group had come to a decision and confronted Benjedid with it. They ordered him to dissolve parliament and, in so doing, the position of speaker, the constitutionally mandated successor to the president. Then on January 11, they forced Benjedid to resign, which he did over national TV, implying that he had not done so voluntarily.

Three days later, the High Security Council, the Algerian equivalent of the U.S. Joint Chiefs of Staff, announced the formation of a collective presidency, under the rubric of a new body known as the High State Council (HCE). The first acts of the council were to recall Mohammed Boudiaf, one of the *chefs historiques*, or founders, of the FLN from his twenty-eight-year exile in Morocco, void the December balloting and cancel the upcoming runoff elections scheduled for later that week.

There were at least three reasons for these moves by FLN hard-liners, two publicly acknowledged and one offered by the FIS and many outside observers. First, the new leaders of Algeria said that the FIS was an antidemocratic force that merely used democratic means to achieve theocratic ends. In other words, once it had achieved power, it would not surrender it—"one man, one vote, one time" was the HCE's description of Islamist politics. While this was a rather hypocritical statement given what the HCE had just done, there was some truth in it. On learning of the election results that December, Belhadj was heard to say they represented "a victory for Islam and not for democracy."[72]

The second rationale for the cancellation of the elections was the accusation of FIS-organized fraud. "Chicago-style" election practices, say the government and many outside observers, such as listing 900,000 dead on the voter rolls and failing to send registration cards to known FIS opponents, were employed. This was made possible by the fact that the municipalities, which the FIS largely controlled, were in charge of election logistics. These practices, as well as the abnormally low election turnout (61 percent compared to turnouts of 80-plus percent in the FLN-controlled elections of the 1960s and 1970s), said the HCE, made the elections useless as an indicator of the democratic will of the Algerian people. Needless to say, the FIS has routinely denied the charges of fraud and forcefully challenged the implications the government has drawn from them.

But there is a third reason, many outside the government say, for the hard-liners' decision to cancel the elections and seize power. As Ruedy notes, "A FIS victory would also mean, of course, [the FLN leaders'] own displacement and that of most of the secularized elites who still dominated Algerian national life."[73] Whatever the reasons, the coup was a disappointing setback for those in the Middle East who had hoped that Algeria would once again be a model for other Arab countries to follow. As it had served as a revolutionary beacon to many Arabs in the 1960s, so they had hoped it would be a democratic example for the Arab world in the 1990s. For Algerians, the coup represented more than just a disappointment. November 1, 1954, marked the commencement of Algeria's heroic struggle for national sovereignty; January 11, 1992, signaled the beginning of the nation's descent into civil war.

NOTES

[1] Entelis, John, *Algeria: The Revolution Institutionalized*, Boulder, Colo.: Westview Press, 1986, p. 9.

[2] Ruedy, John, *Modern Algeria: The Origins and Development of a Nation*, Bloomington: Indiana University Press, 1992, p. 12.

[3] Knauss, Peter, *The Persistence of Patriarchy: Class, Gender, and Ideology in Twentieth Century Algeria*, New York: Praeger, 1987, p. 4.

[4] Ageron, Charles-Robert, *Modern Algeria: A History from 1830 to the Present*, Trenton, N.J.: Africa World Press, 1991, p. 2.

[5] Hourani, Albert, *A History of the Arab Peoples*, New York: Warner Books, 1991, p. 104.

[6] Two of these first European colonies on the African mainland, Ceuta and Melilla, are today the last European holdings on the continent.

[7] Ageron, *Modern Algeria: A History*, p. 2.

[8] *Ibid.*, p. 3.

[9] Cited in E. Hermassi, *Leadership and National Development in North Africa*, Berkeley: University of California Press, 1972, p. 46.

[10] Entelis, *Revolution Institutionalized*, p. 21.

[11] Tlemcani, Rachid, *State and Revolution in Algeria*, Boulder, Colo.: Westview Press, 1986, p. 26.

[12] Gaillisot, R., "Pre Colonial Algeria" in *Economy and Society*, November 1975, p. 432.

[13] Tlemcani, *State and Revolution*, p. 29.

[14] Mansfield, Peter, *The Arabs*, New York: Penguin, 1992, p. 115.

[15] In an early military intervention in the Middle East, the United States sent a largely ineffective expedition of Marines against the corsairs in 1815. *Ibid.*, p. 115.

[16] *Ibid.*

[17] Ruedy, *Modern Algeria*, p. 52.

[18] Ageron, *Modern Algeria: A History*, p. 9.

[19] Ruedy, *Modern Algeria*, p. 50.

[20] Entelis, *Revolution Institutionalized*, p. 27.

[21] *Ibid.*

[22] Laroui, A., *The History of the Maghrib: An Interpretative Essay*, Princeton N.J.: Princeton, University Press, 1977, p. 301.

[23] Goldschmidt, Arthur, Jr., *A Concise History of the Middle East* (third edition), Boulder, Colo.: Westview Press, 1988, pp. 204–5.

[24] Ruedy, *Modern Algeria*, p. 78.

[25] Horne, Alistair, *A Savage War of Peace: Algeria, 1954–1962*, New York: Penguin, 1987, p. 408.

[26] Both Tunisia and Morocco, because they lacked a large colonial population, achieved their independence from France relatively peacefully in 1956.

[27] Knauss, *Persistence of Patriarchy*, p. 74.

[28] Roberts, Hugh, "Doctrinaire Economics and Political Opportunism in the Strategy of Algerian Islamism" in Ruedy, John, *Islamism and Secularism in North Africa*, New York: St. Martin's Press, 1994, p. 143.

[29] Fanon, Frantz, *A Dying Colonialism*, New York: Grove Press, 1965, p. 60.

[30] Lazreg, Marnia, interview with author, June 1, 1995.

[31] Ruedy, *Modern Algeria*, p. 195.

[32] Tlemcani, *State and Revolution*, p. 91.

[33] *Ibid.*

[34] Ruedy, *Modern Algeria*, p. 196.

[35] Ageron, *Modern Algeria: A History*, p. 132.

[36] *Ibid.*

[37] Tlemcani, *State and Revolution*, p. 97.

[38] El-Kenz, Ali, *Algerian Reflections on Arab Crises*, Austin, Tex.: Center for Middle Eastern Studies, 1991, p. xi.

[39] Ruedy, John, "Continuities and Discontinuities in the Algerian Confrontation with Europe" in Ruedy, *Islamism and Secularism*, p. 79.

[40] Entelis, *Revolution Institutionalized*, p. 59.

[41] *Ibid.*, p. 141.

[42] Tlemcani, *State and Revolution*, p. 113.

[43] *Ibid.*

[44] *Ibid.*

[45] *Ibid.*, p. 156.

[46] Nellis, John, "Maladministration" in *The National Charter*, Algiers: El Moujahid, 1976, p. 409.

[47] Ruedy, *Modern Algeria*, p. 209.

[48] *Ibid.*, p. 210.

[49] *Ibid.*, p. 233.

[50] Zartman, I. William, "The Military in the Politics of Succession: Algeria" in Harbeson, John (ed.), *The Military in African Politics*, New York: Praeger, 1987, p. 29.

[51] Ruedy, *Modern Algeria*, p. 240.

[52] *Ibid.*

[53] Knauss, *Persistence of Patriarchy*, p. 125.

[54] Tlemcani, *State and Revolution*, p. 162.

[55] Vandewalle, Dirk, "At the Brink: Chaos in Algeria" in *World Policy Journal*, 1992, p. 707.

[56] SONATRACH is the French acronym for the National Society for Research, Production, Transport, Transformation, and Commercialization of Hydrocarbons.

[57] Tlemcani, *State and Revolution*, p. 160.

[58] Vandewalle, "At the Brink," p. 707.

[59] *Ibid.*

[60] *Ibid.*

[61] "Chadli pushes ahead with party reforms in Algeria" in *Africa Report*, January–February 1989, p. 8.

[62] Ruedy, *Modern Algeria*, p. 251.

[63] Two other explicitly but more moderate fundamentalist parties, the Islamic Society Movement, or *Hamas* (no relation to the party of the Israeli-occupied territories), and the Islamic Renaissance Movement, were also authorized.

[64] Roberts, Hugh, "Doctrinaire Economics and Political Opportunism in the Strategy of Algerian Islamism" in Ruedy, *Islamism and Secularism*, p. 137.

[65] *Ibid.*

[66] Entelis, John "Islam, Democracy, and the State: The Reemergence of Authoritarian Politics in Algeria" in Ruedy, *Islamism and Secularism*, p. 246.

[67] Burgat, *Islamic Movement*, pp. 284 85.

[68] *Ibid.*, p. 284.

[69] *Ibid.*, pp. 284–85.

[70] Ruedy, *Modern Algeria*, p. 253.

[71] *Ibid.*, p. 254.

[72] Burgat, *Islamic Movement*, p. 125.

[73] Ruedy, *Modern Algeria*, p. 255.

3

THE FUNDAMENTALISTS

There is no progress in using the name of the holy book.
　　　—Fatiha Younsi, human rights activist

Islamism is the rocket of decolonization's third stage.
　　　—Francois Burgat, Islamicist sociologist

TRADITIONAL ISLAMIC THOUGHT

Most discussions of political Islam begin with a discussion of terms. That's because fundamentalism is a problematic concept when applied to Islam as a religion and Islamism as a political ideology. The term, of course, was first coined in reference to certain trends in twentieth-century Christianity, and applied cross-culturally to a religion that shares much with, and differs much from, Christianity. As with language itself, nuances are often lost in such cultural translations. But at the same time, the basic essence of the word usually comes through relatively intact. And so it is with Christian and Islamic fundamentalism once they are shorn of their specific sociopolitical connotations. They both represent an effort to return faith, and the actions based on that faith, to their scriptural roots. While this is not a study of Islam per se, an understanding of Islamic fundamentalist politics requires an understanding of the sources of Islamic politics, economics, society and ideology since, by definition, fundamentalism implies a return to Islamic roots, which, in some cases, means a challenge to centuries of scholarly interpretation of those sources.

　　Islam, like Christianity, is a religion based on the revealed word of God. But while the two faiths share a body of scripture, the collection of writings we know as the Old Testament, they differ radically in the emphases they place on God's word. Like Judaism, to which it is theologically more closely akin, Islam places a greater emphasis on the ways of right living in this world, rather than on the ways of achieving grace. That, of course, is not to say that either religion ignores issues of greater concern to the other. Muslims are concerned with heaven, and Christians are concerned with the doings of this world. But Islam possesses an elaborate historical body of religion-inspired law and state theory, and a tradition of applying them, that has no precise counterpart in the development of Christianity. Islam was also less affected by the (European)

Enlightenment, and in Arab and Islamic culture the social dislocations of industrialization and modern state-building are phenomena of the present day.

POLITICAL THOUGHT

With the death of the fourth caliph, Ali ibn Ali Talib, in 661 A.D., the era of "right-thinking" leaders of the Islamic community came to an end. According to Sunni thought, all caliphs since that date are neither "prophets . . . nor infallible interpreters of the faith."[1] This distinction between what is called "prophetic time" and "normal time" is critical when discussing Islamist politics because it goes to the heart of the question of the legitimacy of Muslim leaders' authority, and hence the right to rebel against them. In general, Sunni tradition says a leader should "uphold peace and justice in the community [and] for this he should possess adequate virtues and a knowledge of religious law."[2]

But this assumption leaves more questions begged than answered. For instance, is peace more important than justice? What if preserving peace means preserving an unjust political, social and economic order? The highest ideal of Islamic society is the *umma*, or Islamic community. In fact, Muslims conceptualize humanity in two parts, the house of peace (the Islamic world) and the house of war (the non-Islamic world). An Islamic leader's most important duty, aside from defending the House of Peace, is to fight against *fitna*, or social unrest. Based on that priority, it is easy to see the potential for authoritarian or aristocratic rule, and an exploitative economic order. But, like all political theorists, Islamic scholars have elaborated a system of checks and balances on authority over the centuries.

As Islamicist Peter Mansfield writes, "It is a paradox of Islam that as a social system it is at once the most democratic and the most authoritarian of religions."[3] On the one hand, Islam has no established church hierarchy. Theoretically, he says, all (male) Muslims are their own priests and in religious matters the humblest worshiper is on a par with the most learned *cadi*, or judge. Thus, *ijma*, or consensus of the people, should in theory be as important a consideration in the ruler's decision making as the Koran and the *sharia*, the sacred body of law established over the centuries through the scholarly debate and interpretation of the sayings and actions of the Prophet Muhammad.

The *ijma*, however, can be easily misinterpreted by Western observers. It does not mean polling and electioneering on the question of who rules, how they rule and what they rule upon. Rather, it is based upon "the slow accumulating pressure of opinion over time."[4] In abstract terms, the *ijma* was democratic in that it was an expression of popular will, and as such was suspected by Islamic elites who tried to limit its influence in the same way that the elites of Western Europe and even early America tried to limit suffrage to the propertied and well-educated.[5]

Still, it is easy to see the limitations of the *ijma*. First of all, it leaves little room for minority opinion and, in Alexis de Tocqueville's noted phrase about democracy, permits "the tyranny of popular opinion." As Mansfield notes, "when a consensus had been reached on any given point it was irrevocable,"[6] especially when it met the triple criteria of conformity with the Koran, the *sharia* and the *ijma*. Yet Islamic tradition offers a potential challenge to this despotism of consensus as well. It is known as *itjihad*, or the right of individual interpretation of the components of political and social consensus. It is also easy to misread the meaning of *itjihad*. It is not free-thinking in the sense John Stuart Mill might give it but, rather, in Mansfield's words, "a zealous attempt to discover the proper application of the Koran and the tradition to a particular situation," and it should be part of any attempt to interpret the *ijma*.[7]

While the *ijma*, of course, is subject to change, the Koran and *sharia* are not. In the sixteenth century, nearly a thousand years of scholarly interpretation and debate over the meaning of the Koran and the *sharia* officially came to an end when Ottoman jurists counseled the caliph to declare that "the Gate of Interpretation has been closed." This declaration and its acceptance over the centuries would seem to point to a kind of monolithic and unchanging Islamic law. But that is far from the case. Like the medieval papal bull against the eclipse, the closing of the "Gate of Interpretation" could not stop the inevitable. The world has continued to evolve since the 1500s and Islamic jurists have had to rule upon and counsel leaders to make decisions based upon technological, political, economic and social innovations. And because there are several legitimate schools of Islamic law, there are many potential decisions concerning the legality, permissibility or desirability of one change or another.

Secondly, there is the issue of the *ijma*. Since the nineteenth century, Islamic reformers have tried to open the "Gate of Interpretation" and they have cited a changing *ijma* as the source of legitimacy for that challenge. The contemporary fundamentalists of Algeria are wont to dismiss the many centuries of interpretation elaborated after the death of the fourth caliph, especially that interpretation that has provided the foundation for the spiritual legitimation of secular authority. Ironically, they cite election tallies, something no traditional Islamic scholar would consider, as giving them the *ijma* for their challenge.

Finally, we need to consider what is actually contained within the Koran and *sharia* concerning legitimate authority and the right to rebel against that authority. Islam literally means "submission," that is, to God's will. On the one hand, that definition connotes an acquiescence to the world as it is. "God wills it" are words as frequently offered to the Muslim bereaved as to the Christian. But like Christianity, Islam requires personal action to effect change—God helps those who help themselves. Specifically, the Koran says God "never changes the condition of a people until they change themselves." Muslims in general, and Arabic-speaking people in particular (since God last revealed His word in their language), feel a duty to show the world the path to right living. (What that means exactly is open to interpretation and will be discussed under the headings of "Family, Society and Nation" and "Class and Economics" below.) In short, the Muslim is called upon by God to do good and fight for good—that is, carry out the jihad, the holy struggle. Muhammad's life and sayings, of course, provide the best and most concrete examples of this. And while Islam is an evangelical religion, seeking to convert the world to its doctrine, it also emphasizes that the struggle begins at home. Jihad, a multifarious word in Arabic, can mean anything from a struggle within one's own soul to a collective worldwide confrontation with infidels.

Islam also places specific and clearly defined limitations on jihad in the form of righteous war. Muhammad, of course, launched expansive wars to spread Islam in his lifetime, always offering his new subjects the choice between conversion or, if they were "people of the book," that is, Christians or Jews, the status of *dhimmi*, or tributary submission to their Islamic rulers. While the Koran and the *sharia* offer very specific rules for which Muslim should and which Muslim must fight in this kind of war (the Koran and *sharia* are filled with this kind of specific legislation), war to expand the House of Peace was largely a voluntary affair. But in defense of Islam against invaders, the Muslim had no choice. Obviously, the French invasion of Algeria presented such a situation, and it is not surprising that much of the early resistance to it, and even many of the appeals to the populace by the largely secularist FLN, were couched in such terms.

But what of the Muslim ruler at home? What if he (or she, as in the case of Pakistan and formerly Turkey) is perceived as a threat to or even foe of Islam? What then are the duties of a believer? Here, another useful Arabic term, much employed by Algeria's fundamentalists, needs to be introduced. *Jahaliyya* means the state of war or chaos that existed either in the Arab homeland before the Prophet Muhammad, exists today in the non-Islamic world and, more controversially, in the Muslim world under rulers that are deemed apostate. When is rebellion against such rule justified? According to Islamic history and Islamic tradition, almost never.

Muslims are not permitted to rebel against a leader whom they simply dislike. Moreover, they are not permitted to rebel even if all other avenues of expressing their grievances have been closed off, as is the case in contemporary Algeria when the High Council of State nullified the elections won by the FIS. Obedience is prescribed, and the faithful are implored in the Koran to let God judge unjust rulers, as He judges other men: "God will question them about what He asked them to guard." As Islamicist John Kelsay notes,

> To depose rulers, to engage in active insurrection, is to arrogate to oneself the role of God. There is, in short, a heavy burden of proof upon Muslims who would engage in "just rebellion."[8]

God also commands that those who rule in His name listen to the people, provide them redress and not seek to punish those who have made known their legitimate grievances. But that's another question. As far as rebellion against authority is concerned, the dictum is clear: the only legitimate reason for disobeying a Muslim ruler is his command to disobey God. Of course, what constitutes disobedience to God is often in the eyes of the believer. That is why Islamic jurists have been explicit about the methods and steps by which grievances can be placed before the ruler and acted upon by the ruled. To avoid being treated as common criminals, rebellious Muslims must meet three conditions.

Rebels must act upon their grievances, as oratory alone does not adequately meet the first condition of legitimate rebellion. Rebels must engage in what we might call acts of civil disobedience, such as not paying taxes or, to take the unusual Algerian example, campaigning for votes. Secondly, the rebels must be able to cite Islamic sources for their grievances. If they do not, they are simply apostates and can be punished as such. But what if, rather than expressing apostasy, the rebels or the leader are merely guilty of a well-intentioned misreading of those sources? That, of course, would create a scenario in which the ruler and the rebels would try to line up jurists and present their own interpretations. That, in fact, has been the case in Algeria where government-sponsored religious jurists and FIS-influenced jurists have engaged in a heated war of words, parallel to the war of bullets in the streets, over the Islamic rightness of the two sides in the civil war. In general, however, Islamic tradition is clear about only two things: first, that appeals to Islamic sources be serious and that rebels be conscientious in their interpretation; and second, that the authorities be lenient if such is the case. Arguably, both dicta are being grossly violated in contemporary Algeria.

Finally, and perhaps most important, is that the rebels show they have a sizable following and that they are organized. These rules, of course, are imposed to prevent anarchy, the ultimate form of *fitna*. But they also imply other conditions. By organizing and gaining a following, the rebels prove the legitimacy of their grievances by illustrating that they have the *ijma* behind them and that they have conceptualized their rebellion in terms of an Islamic tradition widely shared by the people. More anti-authoritarian Islamicist jurors recognized what liberal Western political thinkers like Thomas Jefferson later came to understand: that the people will accept misrule for a long time before they rise up and declare they have had enough. As Jefferson and these Islamic scholars imply, the people's resort to open rebellion often indicates in and of itself that their cause is just. But where Jefferson encouraged periodic rebellions, even the most anti-authoritarian Islamic jurists, and they are rare in the Sunni tradition, do not. Organizing a rebellion takes a lot of time and effort, and so it should, they "say," if society is not to descend into constant anarchy.

To conclude, a general point should be made about the Islamic tradition and politics. For all the traditional Islamic literature on governing, there is surprisingly little on the political process as such. In the case of rebellion against unjust rule, for example, there is surprisingly little discussion of the nature and uses of power, the means and ends of organizing the populace, and the methods by which social justice and harmony can be renewed between rulers and ruled. "Classical Islamic thought," writes Islamicist Olivier Roy,

> is overflowing with treatises on governing, advice to the sovereign, and didactic tales. They do not reflect on the nature of politics, but on the nature of the good ruler and of good government (advice, techniques, paradigms, anecdotes). The issue of ethics is at the heart of classical Muslim political philosophy.[9]

In short, says Roy, the justice of the ruler was the critical element in the traditional Muslim state, not the liberty of the ruled.

FAMILY, SOCIETY AND NATION

Before the government of Algeria canceled the parliamentary elections in January 1992, the issues in contention between the FIS and the FLN were largely social ones. True, the fundamentalists profited from and exploited the economic grievances of the Algerian people, as was the case during the riots of October 1988, but their agenda was not primarily concerned with economic issues or even governmental corruption. Instead, the leaders of the FIS contended that it was the breakdown of and disregard for the precepts and rules of right living that had created the sorry state of Algerian society. Their answer to the nation's problems, then, was not a specific economic or political agenda per se, but a return to an Islamic society ruled by the *sharia* and Koran. By healing the internal spirit of the Algerian people and building an Islamic state, the economic and political problems that seemed insoluble to many Algerians would take care of themselves.

As utopian and irrelevant as this position may seem to secular or non-Muslim readers, and to many of the secularized francophone Muslim elite of Algeria, it was obviously put forth quite seriously by the Islamic leaders (as similar positions have been by Christian and Jewish fundamentalists elsewhere). In Algeria, at least, it was welcomed by a solid majority of Algerian voters, thus satisfying one of the most important conditions for challenging the rule of the self-professed Muslim rulers of the FLN. While the specific ways and means by which they hoped to achieve this transformation will be discussed in Chapter 5, it is useful here to analyze the Koranic and *sharia*-based sources of their agenda for social change. In addition, an understanding of Arab and Maghribi tradition is equally important for an understanding of the fundamentalists' social agenda, since Islamic and Arab traditions are often meshed both in the rhetoric of the leaders and in the popular imagination.

The two forces of Islamic and Arab tradition come together over the family, both in terms of its internal dynamics and its place in society. As Albert Hourani notes, the *sharia* "is most precise on questions of personal status" and the family, including marriage, divorce and inheritance. The Koran, for example, is explicit on the equality of rights between men and women concerning marriage and divorce. As Mansfield notes, "It is true that the same *sura* [verse] of the Koran [concerning that equality] says that 'men are a degree above them [women],' but this merely acknowledges the fact that the man is head of the household—something that has hardly been disputed in any civilized society until the present day." But, he adds, "Scholars and casuists of Islam in later centuries . . . succeeded in interpreting or misinterpreting the Koran in such a way as to place women in subjection."[10] In fact, part of the disintegration of women's place was due to the absence of clergy since it left each man as religious interpreter for his own household, allowing him fully to exercise his will. This, say scholars, led to the formulation of rules and traditions that permit a man the right of uncontested divorce but deny it to women. It also led to the transformation of the veil from a means of protection for women to a sign of ownership by men.

As for traditions of the Arab family, several features should be noted, for they play an important role in the political sphere as well. As Arabist Halim Barakat notes, "The family is the basic unit of social organization in traditional and contemporary Arab society."[11] Traditionally, the Arab family has been not only a center of social and economic life, but also the main source of a person's identity; hence the Arab world's idea of the "crime of honor" whereby a man, or more likely a woman, who does harm to the family name may be punished. Secondly, Arab families resemble Arab society in microcosm. Strictly patriarchal, the traditional family gives a father absolute authority over his wife and children, and Arab fathers have exercised this authority rigorously. In his Cairo Trilogy, Egyptian novelist Naguib Mahfouz movingly describes the "brutal and terrifying style of treatment" of the head of the al-Jawad household.[12]

Because a father is often absent from home, working all day and socializing with peers in the evenings, authority over the children is usually exercised by the wife. But women are clearly subordinate to men, even grown sons, for several reasons. Men largely control property, and Islamic law, despite Koranic edicts, largely favors men in marriage, divorce and inheritance. This was apparent in the Algerian Family Code of 1984 passed by a mixed secular-Muslim FLN government. Algerian sociologist Marnia Lazreg reports a conversation between a young woman and her mother on the subject. The daughter begins:

> "A husband's authorization will be required to travel . . . "
> My mother said: "Well, the husband must be asked, it is normal . . ." I replied: "O.K., now you are a widow, and if you want to visit your daughter

in Paris, what will you do? You will need to ask your son's authorization."
   She said: "Me! How could it be! My son's authorization? But *I* brought him into this world, *I* married him off, and now *I* take care of his children, and you say I need *his* authorization! This is a topsy-turvy world!"[13] (emphasis in original)

To the fundamentalists who pressured for this restriction on women's travel (it was later rescinded in the face of women's protests), the edict did not represent a topsy-turvy world but a world returned to its normal order. The point is not so much these differing concepts of normative order in family relations, but that they are a matter of such political import. It is a truism to say that the modern world, as represented by Western cultural imports, has intruded upon and threatened the traditional order within the Arab family, with great psychological, sociological and political effects. But this explanation both flatters the West, and misses the more important element of cultural transformation: the Algerian government.

By building a modern welfare state, and by Third World standards the Algerian welfare system was quite comprehensive, the state intruded upon prerogatives normally assigned to the family, such as education, welfare, health, among other things. There was, of course, nothing wrong with expanding these services from the sorry state in which the French had left them. But the FLN government, complain fundamentalists, used these services to impose individualist and universalist ideas. That is to say, the implementation of these services emphasized the individual over the family, women's equality with men, and children's rights to challenge their parents. Women, for example, were expected to go to male doctors and encouraged to take part in public life, while children were taught to think in terms of individual achievement rather than fulfilling family duties.

These individual and family issues, which are so much a part of the fundamentalist political agenda, will be discussed more thoroughly in Chapter 5. They are brought up here to provide the context for a discussion of the critical issue of the family's place in society, according to Arab tradition and Islamic law. As noted above, Algerian fundamentalists largely assign the nation's profound economic, political and social crises to a breakdown in the moral order both public and private, the result of the failure to impose the *sharia*. And, also noted above, the *sharia* is very specific in issues concerning individual behavior and family life.

In traditional Islamic states, religious jurists had the power of advise and consent over the ruler, at least in theory. In practice, however, they generally restricted themselves to matters of individual behavior and family both because they had a more solid body of law to work from and because the Koran and *sharia* gave them legitimacy to do so. Conversely, the ruler was expected to defer to them on such issues. Excessive interference by the state in matters of individual morality and family life, as the fundamentalists argue is the case with the FLN, is a violation of the *sharia* and of right rule.

Above all else, says Roy, there is an expectation that the state have a "respect for privacy, for the family space, the home, honor (*namus*) . . . Liberty is demanded in the sphere of the family, in the private sphere . . ."[14]

Two implications arise from this demand. First, that in the public domain questions of justice for and welfare of the family, as well as the maintenance of individual morality, should be ruled by the *sharia*, which in practice means returning these questions to the control of the *cadis*. "The political demand of the fundamentalist clergy," notes Roy, "is that the [state's] law conform to the sharia."[15] Second, that in the absence of extraordinary domestic disturbances that might require the *cadi*'s judgment, the family should be left at liberty to decide family matters for itself. Not liberty in the sense that wives and children have the freedom to decide or participate directly in decision making, but the liberty to return to Islamic precedents and norms—in short, the (state-enforced) return to the patriarchal family, something the fundamentalists believe the vast majority of Algerians want. Patriarchy should not be understood, of course, either by outsiders or Algerian men, as an invitation to abuse and exploitation by the father. That would violate the many Islamic precepts concerning just rule that apply as much to the family as to the larger society.

This paradigmatic division of society, into the public sphere where justice is prioritized over liberty and the private sphere where the opposite applies, seems orderly enough at first glance. And it seems to give the ruler clear guidelines on how to rule and what to rule on. The basic precept of the fundamentalists is clear: "The fundamentalist clergy want the sovereign to apply the *sharia* and to defend the Muslim community."[16] But, as Roy points out, there are two important issues concerning application of the *sharia* that muddy the formulation. First, the *sharia* is autonomous. It

> does not depend on any state, on any actual, positive law, on any political decision. It thereby creates a space that is parallel to the political space, to power, which, it is true, can circumvent the sharia or manipulate it (hence the strong theme of the corruption of the judge), but which cannot make it into something other than what it is: an autonomous, infinite commentary.[17]

In other words, the *sharia* exists independent of the state. But it also makes claims upon the state. Thus, the *sharia* is both a guide to how a ruler should govern as well as "an ensemble of precepts" that he cannot violate without violating the faith and thereby surrendering his authority. Like English common law, the *sharia* exists independent of the authority of the state and covers a wide range of human activity. "The work of the [Islamic] judge," says Roy, "is not to apply a principle or a concept, but to bring the case before him back into the realm of what is already known."[18] Unlike common law, however, the sharia includes precepts that cover the relationship between ruler and governed.

There is an obvious contradiction here. The fundamentalists rail against the state's destructive intrusion in matters of the family and individual behavior, but they lack a replacement model. And the *sharia* offers little guidance on the two extremely important questions of political and judicial authority and restraint. What is the source of legitimate authority for those implementing the *sharia* and how far does it go? In this regard, it is interesting to recall some recent Algerian history. In 1984, under pressure from fundamentalist politicians and clergy, the FLN government replaced the secular, socialist concept of the people's rights enshrined in the Charter of 1976 with a more traditional Arab and Islamic law on the Algerian family. A conflict then emerged over the public domain, that is, how behavior outside the home and family should be regulated.

Finally, there is the question of the legitimacy of the state in and of itself. The ideal society, according to the Koran and Islamic tradition, is the *umma*, or community of all believers. It knows no national boundaries or internal divisions. By idealizing the *umma*, fundamentalists elide the question of class, an issue to be discussed below. And by formulating a higher political entity than the state, they call into question the legitimacy of modern government as it has existed in North Africa since the 1950s.

By reminding ourselves of these three issues—the "space [created by the *sharia*] that is parallel to the political space," the potential expansiveness of the *sharia* and the underlying illegitimacy of the state itself—we can glimpse an understanding of the profound political confusion and social dynamism of the fundamentalists that so many observers of the current crisis in Algeria have commented upon.

CLASS AND ECONOMICS

As in the West, economics as a study of a distinct aspect of activity is largely a modern creation in the world of Islam. Just as there is no real body of economic theory in traditional Islam, neither is there a body of commercial law, though there are precepts and rules in the *sharia* about specific activities. There is the *zakat*, or tax, permitted on certain goods for revenues that are to be earmarked for the sustenance of the poor. The *gharar* is an interdiction of chance in economic relations. It is not aimed at gambling per se, but at things like insurance or loans where the creditor does not participate in the risks. There is the precept, well-known to non-Muslims, of *riba*, or the prohibition on usury. And there are other isolated rules on inheritance, property, usufruct, piracy and so on.

"As always in Islamic law," says Roy, "these concepts are constructed on the basis of isolated prescriptions, anecdotes, examples, words of the Prophet, all gathered together and systematized by commentators according to an inductive, casuistic method."[19] There is no overarching Islamic theory of economics. Instead, economics is subject to ethics: man is a material being, therefore man strives for the goods of the earth. From this logic, two ethical considerations arise. He must not violate the *sharia* in pursuit of these goods, and he must not let that pursuit, or those goods, turn him from worship of God, which includes right living and making moral decisions.

Even here, there are limits, however. Excessive accumulation and excessive consumption, even if they fall within the allowable parameters of the *sharia*, have been traditionally frowned upon in Islamic thought. Inheritance law in the *sharia* encourages disaccumulation by requiring an equal distribution to one's heirs depending on their degree of kinship to the deceased and their sex (women receive half shares). Indeed, ownership of property itself has a severe restriction placed upon it: the world and everything in it ultimately belong to God; man has only usufruct of them—the right to use them. The Koran prohibits the appropriation of "primary goods" like water, mines, pasturage and combustibles. Furthermore, that usufruct is a graduated one. Priority is to the *umma*, then the state or tribe, and finally the individual family. "It was understood," writes Lazreg,

> that all land belongs to God and that a Muslim can only have a usufruct on it. At the same time, however, the right to usufruct is obtained through work, so that if a tribesman started cultivating a plot that was previously fallow, it became his and was passed on to his heirs.[20]

In the general restrictions on accumulation, the *sharia* is reinforced by the exemplary character of the Prophet's actions, that is, moderation, humility and simplicity. Thus, Abolhassan Bani-Sadr, the first prime minister of Islamic Iran, pronounced: "to produce according to one's capacities, to consume according to virtue." The logic is clear. By restraining consumption, we create a surplus. Overconsumption or hoarding is the absence of virtue, as is scarcity. For Bani-Sadr adds, "Material self-sufficiency is an opportunity to advance toward virtue."[21] In other words, a hungry stomach is as likely to turn the Muslim from a worship of God as is the indulgence of the senses with material things. But how this redistribution is to be realized has been open to great debate. Some say it is purely up to the virtue of the individual property owner. Others have argued that it is infeasible to expect imperfect men to be perfectly virtuous. Thus, institutions are needed to accomplish the precepts of redistribution. That has been interpreted to mean anything from appeals by charitable institutions (or, to use a term from American history, "moral suasion") to progressive income taxes, to state control of production for the purposes of sharing the collective wealth of a society.

Of course, if we are to interpret Islamic precepts as constructs of human society rather than divine will (and as students of social science we must), then it is critical to follow the course of the emerging economic order of the Muslim world. Early Islamic class formation was a result of military victories. As the Arabian tribes expanded their rule, a system was developed for the distribution of wealth attained by conquest. Since that conquest was conducted in the name of God, Islamic criteria were applied, including the *nasab*, or relationship to the Prophet, and the length of time since one had converted to Islam. Eventually an aristocracy based on land and trade developed. And with the emergence of classes emerged a set of rules defining property rights. Three categories of land developed in the Maghrib: *arsh*, communal land of the tribe that could not be sold; *melk*, private land that could be sold under certain conditions (usually including vetoes by family members who would inherit the property); and *habus* or *waqf*, land donated to religious and charitable foundations.

In urban areas, like the coastal cities of Algeria, mercantile elites dominated economic and political life. These elites gradually formed an alliance with Islamic jurists, or *ulemas*. Sons were sent to be educated by *ulemas*, and they served more or less as lawyers, settling commercial and legal disputes among merchants. In fact, alliances often overlapped through marriage and in those cases where *ulemas* became merchants and vice versa. In addition, the schools, mosques and charitable foundations controlled by the *ulemas* provided a *sharia*-approved means of passing on wealth from one generation to another. This is where the *habus* came in. A merchant or landowner could stipulate that his heirs be granted a stipend as "administrators" of the land in perpetuity. Naturally, this led to abuses since it provided a way around Koranic precepts on inheritance, *zakat*, and usufruct.

Along with class formation, and a legal code to reinforce it, arose an ideology of class rule. But this process has followed a different trajectory in the Islamic world than it has in the West. In Algeria and much of the Muslim world, it has usually been power, both secular and spiritual, that has led to wealth, and not the other way around. Thus bureaucratic position and court connections often served as the path to the upper class of Muslim society. This factor, along with the intimacy of the aristocracy and urban Islamist jurists, created a powerful ideology that both justified social stratification based on wealth and power and frowned upon rabble-rousing appeals to class conflict as the worst source of *fitna* within the Islamic community. Struggle based on class was likened to banditry and was given little encouragement by religious jurists until very recent times. Moreover, since power generated wealth, rather than vice versa, there was little room for the development of an ideology of class conflict based on the oppositional roles of classes. The wealthy were conceptualized as rulers, just or unjust, but not as exploiters of workers or tenants.

In addition, there is the powerful locus of the Arab family to consider. Family rank and honor, independent of wealth, was traditionally an important consideration in precapitalist Arab society. This factor was reinforced by the role of Arab families as the center of economic production. That families produced independently "without supervision or external control contributed to the development and perpetuation of the illusion of equality among unequal families."[22] Only later did developments generate the formation of classes in a form familiar to the West. "The mechanization of agriculture; improved communications, which facilitated a market orientation; wage labor; and the acquisition of land by foreigners," says anthropologist Nicholas Hopkins, "led to the emergence of a [Western] class system [in the Maghrib]."[23]

ORTHODOX AND POPULAR ISLAM

Finally, it is important to recognize that there are several Islamic traditions. Most Westerners are acquainted with the schism between Shiism and Sunnism. Since there are virtually no Shiite Muslims in Algeria, the differences between these traditions can be ignored except where events in revolutionary Shiite Iran have played a role in Algeria. But there is another variant in Islamic practice that is largely unfamiliar to Western readers. That is the split between the Islam of scholars, state and—to the extent that it even exists in nonclerical Sunni Islam—the religious hierarchy, and popular Islam. For lack of a better English reference, we might call them high and low Islam, not as value judgments but as simple terms of reference borrowed from the more familiar context of Western European Protestantism. Arabist Halim Barakat lists the differences between the two. The former, he says,

> stresses religious texts, the shari'a (Islamic law), absolute monotheism, the literal interpretation of religious teachings, ritualism, the absence of intermediaries between believers and God . . . [the latter] personifies sacred forces, emphasizes existential and spiritual inner experiences, seeks intermediaries between believers and God, and interprets texts symbolically.

In Algeria, as in much of the Arab world, popular Islam is often associated with Sufism, known in the Maghrib as Maraboutism. Sufi mystical orders began as groups of adherents of an ecstatic and emotional form of worship roughly 700 years ago and came to Algeria in the migration of tribal Arabs after the beginning of the eleventh century. Great *marabouts* established centers of religious worship based on their idiosyncratic interpretations and practices of Islam. Their charismatic leadership attracted followers and disciples who flocked to learn and worship from these men, who were believed to have the power of intercession with God. Eventually, as in the somewhat similar development within the Catholic tradition, the greatest of these *marabouts* were worshiped as saints and had shrines built to them by believers. Worshipers came to these shrines for spiritual and even physical healing. In his study of Tunisian villagers in the 1960s, anthropologist Jean Duvignaud notes how a pregnant woman came to the village he

was studying because the *marabout* saint there was "so much more effica-
cious" than the one in her own village.[24]

Marabouts and Maraboutism have played an important role in Algerian political and social history. They have served as loci of both resistance
and accommodation to French and FLN rule. Al-Qadir associated with
marabouts and used their influence in his early struggle with the French.
Later, during the rise of Algerian nationalism in the twentieth century,
Maraboutism was attacked as antimodern, anti-Islam, and antinationalist.
Since the rise of fundamentalism, Maraboutism has been attacked as a
reactionary force hostile to Islamist politics as well as an obstacle to the
realization of an Islamist Algeria. Finally, it is safe to say that Maraboutism
is a largely rural affair; its urban influence is confined mostly to elderly
migrants from the countryside.

SOURCES OF MODERN
ISLAMIC FUNDAMENTALISM

One of the West's most significant misconceptions about Islamic thought
and culture is that it is somehow timeless and unchanging. In addition,
many assume that any innovation in the Muslim world has come from
without: capitalism from Western Europe, liberalism from the values of the
French Revolution and Marxist ideas from the Soviet bloc. Like many
sociological and historical misconceptions, these are based on a kernel of
truth. It is true that the Ottoman religious establishment attempted to close
the "Gate of Interpretation" almost 500 years ago; that the expansion of
European imperialism into the Muslim world in the nineteenth century laid
the foundations for market economies; and that Western and Soviet ideas
of nationalism and socialism have permeated various Muslim regimes since
the end of World War II. But most Westerners are unaware of an Islamic
tradition of political, sociological and economic thought that is almost as
old as the European Enlightenment.

It is, of course, true that much of this new Islamic thinking was
formulated in response to European ideas introduced by imperialism, and
some of it borrowed substantially from European thought. However,
Islamic jurists and scholars have formulated their response in their distinctive idiom and have given their European inheritance a distinctly Islamic
cast. "As with any of the sociopolitical currents that have defined the history
of the planet," notes Islamicist François Burgat, "Islamism is also criss-
crossed by internal dynamics which keep it in constant evolution."[25] This
modern Islamic thought is critical for an understanding of Algeria's fundamentalist movement since, say most scholars, it has largely borrowed from

Islamic thinkers outside the Maghrib. If the Koran and *sharia* provide the substance of today's fundamentalist ideas, it is a substance molded by this tradition of Islamic thinking, most of which is unfamiliar to Western readers.

Modern Islamist thought originated in the early nineteenth century, at least a half century before secular nationalism emerged in the Arab world. The catalyst was European imperialism. Ottoman complacency and Muslim convictions of the superiority of their own civilization over that of the West, based on the glories of the Arab Middle Ages, left many Islamic thinkers and rulers unprepared for the sudden intrusion of European power into their world. The early and middle nineteenth century was indeed a traumatic period for the Muslim world. The French had invaded North Africa, the Russians were encroaching on the Caucasus, and the British had destroyed the Mughal Empire of India. Islamic scholars began seeking Islam-based answers for the questions of the sources of European wealth and power, the reasons for renewed conflict between West and East, and which European political, economic and technological innovations, if any, should be adopted by Muslim peoples, as well as how this was to be done.[26]

Other issues and problems were indigenous to the Muslim world, though they were brought under new scrutiny by Western expansion. What were the sources of the East's weakness in the face of the Western onslaught? How much were the rulers to blame and how much was due to Muslim traditions? What should be the nature and role of the Islamic state? How could that be integrated with the ideal of the pan-Islamic *umma*? And how was the decline of Muslim power to be reversed? During the course of the nineteenth century, answers to these questions were being offered in both secular and religious terms. Of the latter, the most important school of thinking concerned the *nahda*, or renaissance of Islamic civilization, based on a revivalist movement known as the *salafiyya,* which invoked the "apparently authentic and indigenous classical Arab-Islamic culture" in the name of modernization.[27]

Predictably, Islamic response divided into two camps: traditionalists and reformers. The former were largely the official *ulemas* who enjoyed the perquisites of their position, not least of which was access to the corridors of power. But their response, a renewed invigoration and devotion to the caliphate of the Ottomans, seemed grossly inadequate and self-serving to the reformers. These latter thinkers were not in opposition to the caliphate per se—that would be too great a challenge to legitimate Muslim author-ity—but they did want the source of the caliphate's authority and legitimacy returned "to the original sources and purity of early Islam." Western imperialism must be pushed back, they agreed, but that could only be done by adopting the better products of the West's science, politics and culture.[28] This seemingly contradictory program, the revival of early Islamic principles and the adoption of the latest in Western technology and political forms, has characterized Islamic fundamentalism ever since. Egyptian reformer Jamal Eddin al-Afghani wrote to the Ottoman viceroy of his country:

> Allow me, Your Highness, to say with freedom and sincerity that . . . if you accept of a sincere man like myself and hasten to let the nation . . . partak[e] in ruling the country . . . by arranging for the election of national representatives . . . this procedure will add more stability to your throne.[29]

But the apparent contradiction was resolved in the minds of Islamic reformers who believed a return to Islamic roots would allow Muslims to sort through the innovations coming from the West and properly integrate them into a revitalized Muslim culture and society.

More powerful than democracy in the early currents of the *salafiyya* was nationalism, a defense of the Islamic *umma* in a given locale that was made easier by the fact that the invaders were infidels. The struggle, however, was not just against the European invaders, but against the countervailing *assabiyya*, or tribal loyalties, that hampered collective efforts at defense. Many of these protonationalist struggles were associated with local charismatic religious leaders, the *marabouts* or *sufis* of the countryside like those around al-Qadir. Despite some early notable victories, these religio-nationalist leaders, including al-Qadir, were soundly defeated by the Europeans. Eventually, Maraboutism would descend into introspection, parochialism, mysticism and fatalism. According to later fundamentalist thinkers, *marabouts* either directly served their colonial masters by keeping the masses quiescent in exchange for financial support and official encouragement, or indirectly served the colonial cause by offering adherents the opiate of false faith and the promise of salvation.

Thus, much of reformist thinking in the late nineteenth century was directed not just at the oppression of European invaders but also at the complicity of popular religious leaders and at the reinvigorated tribalism that they and their European benefactors encouraged in the wake of failed uprisings like that of al-Qadir. Fueling the reformers' hostility toward the *marabouts* was their belief that the latter practiced a faith that was a mishmash of Islamic beliefs, local tribal customs, occultism and other things that deviated from the purity of early Islam's principles and practices that the reformers were trying to revive. This hostility to popular forms of religion continues to animate fundamentalists in Algeria today.

But the more important target of the reformers' ire was the *ulemas* and other traditionalists. Beginning in the late nineteenth century, reformers began to insist on a revival of *itjihad*, or free interpretation of the ancient texts of Islam. The importance of this demand on subsequent Islamic politics cannot be overestimated. "The reopening of the right to itjihad," says Roy, "marked a significant rupture with ten centuries of orthodoxy."[30] Although, in its original formulation, the call for *itjihad* was not a political statement but was aimed rather at an internal spiritual revival by which

Muslim peoples could gain the strength and direction for challenging imperialist power. Sheikh Ibn Badis, an early Algerian religio-nationalist, began his crusade against the French by attacking the official *ulemas* and the *madrasas*, or official religious schools, that they ran.

On the other hand, the *salafiyya* movement was not interested in overthrowing Muslim rulers, where they still existed, insisting instead that they reform their regimes by applying the *sharia* judiciously. Resurrecting the *umma*, and the caliphate it depended on, was their main concern, at least until the 1924 abolition of the caliphate by the new leader of the Turkish Republic, Kemal Mustapha (Kamal Ataturk). The ending of the caliphate began a new trend in religious reform, emphasizing nation-based solutions to the problems of underdevelopment and imperialism, rather than the immediate resurrection of the pan-Islamic *umma*. It also provided the catalyst for a new militancy against Muslim rulers and regimes that the inheritors of the reformers, the Islamists of the mid- and late-twentieth century, considered, and still consider, apostate supporters of the modern *jahaliyya*.

While modern political Islam, or Islamism, is usually associated with Iran, and hence Shiism, its roots lie in the Sunni Muslim world.[31] Islamism, which traces its origins to the Muslim Brotherhoods of Egypt and Pakistan of the 1920s (the Brotherhoods continue to operate in numerous Muslim countries, though they are not significant in Algeria), offered both an explicitly political critique of Muslim regimes and a revolutionary solution to the problems plaguing Muslim societies whether they were ruled by Europeans, as was the case of Pakistan and Algeria, or where they were nominally under self-rule, as was the case in Egypt.

The greatest exponent of Islamism was an Egyptian named Sayyid Qutb, a radical Muslim thinker whose major opus, *In the Shadow of the Koran*, has often been called the Islamist equivalent of Lenin's revolutionary tract *What Is to Be Done?* His writings, which did not garner a wide readership until nearly a decade after his execution by Egyptian president Gamel Abdel Nasser in 1966, borrowed from earlier reformist thought in calling for a return to the authenticity of early Islam. But Qutb took the idea further, saying that there had been and continues to be an alternative model for the Muslim to appropriate. The whole world, whether under Muslim or non-Muslim rule, was in a state of *jahaliyya* and therefore had to be rejected in its entirety. Muslims of all political stripes, he said, had descended into modern forms of idolatry: democracy, or the belief in the ultimate sovereignty of the people; nationalism, and the "worship" of nationalist leaders like Nasser; and socialism, with its ideas of social perfectibility based on "scientific principles." In short, Islam was facing the danger of extinction and the leaders and masses of Muslims were allowing this threat to go unchallenged.

An immediate and radical break, said Qutb, was essential. In this belief, he went beyond even the Brotherhood, who argued that there could be no legitimate way to overthrow even an imperfect Islamic regime. Qutb and other Islamists, whose Iranian Shiite successors deposed the shah and took power in 1979, believed that society would be Islamicized through political action and revolution and that proponents of that goal had to move beyond the mosque and into the streets. The key to this political transformation was "a systematic and severe criticism" of the apostate regime and the *jahaliyya* of modern Muslim states, as well as mass consciousness-raising, aimed especially at youth, to liberate Muslim societies from "westoxification." "However," writes Islamicist Emmanuel Sivan,

> systematic criticism alone stands no chance of inducing the regimes in power to change from within because of the authoritarian, ruthless nature of these regimes and their deep commitment to the modern jahaliyya. Radicals, therefore, should not shrink from drawing the unavoidable conclusion: the existing regimes must be delegitimized . . . Delegitimation of such powerful regimes will necessitate, after a preparation stage, an armed uprising and seizing the governments by the avant-garde of Islam: only this will enable the establishment of a state in which the shari'a is applied.[32]

They also opposed the established religious jurists for their nitpicking, legalistic approach to the texts, which ignored the current social and political situation, for their slavish devotion to existing apostate regimes and for their acceptance of Western concepts like the separation of church and state, that violated the spirit of the *sharia*. Criticizing *ulemas* simultaneously for their close adherence to the *sharia* and their violation of its intent is not a contradiction to this way of thinking. Islamists see the *sharia* as a set of general principles for the Islamicization of society rather than a fixed set of laws that merely need to be enacted in order to realize that goal. In short, says Roy,

> The Islamists pose the question of politics starting from the principle that Islam is a global and synthesizing system of thought. It is not enough for society to be composed of Muslims; it must be Islamic in its foundation and its structure: a distinction is therefore introduced between what is "Muslim" and what is "Islamic" . . . From there it follows, but only for the most radical of the Islamists (disciples of Qutb and of Khomeini . . .) that one has a duty to revolt against a Muslim state judged to be corrupt.[33]

Islamism, while seemingly a return to Islamic roots, is, in fact, inherently modern in its outlook. Instead of trying to return modern society to some ancient ideal, it instead tries to modernize authentic Islamic sources. Thus there is a large body of Islamist literature concerning the application of religious principles to such modern social issues as economics, party politics, technology and other social problems.

Despite the seeming revival of Islamic political militancy through much of the Middle East in recent years, the Islamist ideals of revolutionary

Iran have never really spread beyond the Persian homeland, except for a few pockets of Shiism heavily supported by Tehran in Lebanon and Iraq. "Islamism," says Roy, "was a moment, a fragile synthesis between Islam and political modernity, which ultimately never took root."[34]

What has taken Iranian-style Islamism's place in Algeria is the subject of great debate among scholars. Islamicists like Burgat insist that the FIS is inherently Islamist, as evidenced by its commitment to democratic ideals and forms and its use of the latest technology to convey its message. Others, like Roy and Gilles Kepel, maintain that the Algerian religious politicians are not Islamist but, to use Roy's term, "neo-fundamentalist." FIS leaders are returning to the roots of Islamic fundamentalism of the nineteenth century, they say, insisting on an internal spiritual revival rather than an overt political revolution to bring about the ideal of the Islamicized state. These neo-fundamentalists have not given up the goal of taking state power, and they remain as critical of the conservative religious establishment as the Islamists. But they follow a different program: rather than modernizing authentic Islam, they seek to return modern society to an "impossible" past within the present. "Today's Islamism," says Roy,

> focuses all its action on filling daily life with morality and establishing the sharia. It replaces a discourse on the state with a discourse on society. This is the model of the Algerian FIS, which, if it takes power, will alter mores, but not the economy or the functioning of politics.[35]

The causes of this subordination of political action to reformation of morality are several: first and foremost has been the failure of the Iranian revolution due to war, inept management and, by neo-fundamentalist accounts, deviation from pure Islamicization; second, the failure of efforts by Iran to foment Islamism elsewhere, to overthrow other corrupt regimes and force the West out of the Middle East, through revolutionary terror; third, the partially successful cooptation by nationalist regimes of Islamic rhetoric, symbols and social law; and finally, through the financial support offered to political Islamist groups by the conservative Saudi regime, which emphasizes moral regeneration rather than political revolution.

Ironically, the Islamism of Iran, while arguably more threatening to the West than the FIS, is in fact more Western, in that it accepts modernity. Political Islam in Iran has promoted a political and ideological transformation of the Muslim masses, a transformation involving a serious critique of the means, methods and aims of Western imperialism, as personified by the "great satan," the United States. By seeking an internal transformation of people's ethics and morality, rather than external transformation of power, politics and economics, the FIS is at once more alien to the modern Western political tradition and yet less threatening to the unequal order of world power and wealth upon which it rests.

EVOLUTION OF POLITICAL ISLAM IN ALGERIA

"To speak today of the expansion of Islam may appear an obvious phenomenon that numerous events and the works reporting them have by now largely exhausted," Algerian sociologist Ali el-Kenz wrote in chastising Western interpreters of events in the Islamic world.

> The obvious, however, is a paradox because, to take a closer look, what would such an expansion mean in societies that have never ceased being Muslim even in the hardest moments of their history, which coincided with the deepest penetration of the Western colonization enterprise.[36]

El-Kenz was speaking of the Islamic world in general, although his own country provided the model.

Under the Ottomans, religious thought and religious activism in Algeria was largely divided into two spheres: popular Maraboutism in the countryside and an official *ulema* that essentially advised the ruling governor and elites in the capital and other main cities. The first was concerned largely with the spiritual life of the peasants and their concerns with salvation, while the second was largely an apologist for the ruling order. In neither case did Islamic jurists or thinkers contemplate or act upon reformist or revivalist principles.

And while *marabout* leaders were involved in early resistance to the French, most soon turned to local concerns and activities. As historian John Entelis writes, "French colonialism . . . by pacifying and incorporating the countryside within its colonial administration, undercut the numerous broker, social, and political functions performed by the marabouts."[37] As for establishment Islamic jurists, the record was mixed during most of French rule. Some allowed themselves to be coopted. Others, says historian Kenneth Perkins, "engaged in low-intensity obstructionism to slow down, if they could not block, French attempts to secularize the legal system, Gallicize education . . . and impose various statutes which the 'ulama regarded as inimical to Islam or their own socioeconomic interests, or both."[38]

Gradually during the first several decades of the twentieth century, many of the *ulemas* began to embrace a moderate brand of reformism, aimed not at confronting the French but at ameliorating some of the worst effects of colonialism on the Algerian people. In this they were supported by those groups most severely affected by the colonization of Algeria: the *petit bourgeoisie* of countryside and city. Squeezed between *colons* and the *grand bourgeoisie* of Muslim Algerians, they remained connected to the *ulemas*, just as the peasantry remained loyal to the *marabouts*.

Unlike the small Algerian elite, which began to prosper by cooperating with the French, these people were unable to take advantage of the limited opportunities offered to Algerians by the French colonizers, including French education. They supported the Muslim schools and social organizations founded by reformist *ulemas* who, in turn, advocated what is known in Algeria as the "little [Islamic] tradition" of honesty, hard work and the rightful share of all Muslims in the fruits of their own labor. "The social teaching at the Sidi-Safa *medersa* [*ulema*-run school]," writes anthropologist Michel Launay,

> corresponded precisely to the "sharing" and egalitarian demands of the small peasantry; at his sermon on Friday the sheikh said plainly: "God created us to live as equals. Why does one person starve at dawn, and another travels in a plane or a car? God believes it is good that everyone demand a fair share of the goods of the world."[39]

The French tolerated the Association of Ulemas and its founder Sheikh Ibn Badis largely because it seemed to offer this class of Algerians a safe and nonmilitant outlet for its frustrations and aspirations. "We do not want assimilation, nor do we want independence," declared one of the association members in the 1930s.[40] In turn, says historian Peter Knauss, "An Algerian could endorse their cultural program for the revitalization of Islam without risking prison."[41] After all, the reformers encouraged habits of thrift and hard work as the remedy to the "decline" of moral values among the Muslim population. Furthermore, the "puritanical" *ulemas'* first target was not the *colons* but the "superstitions and magical excrescences" of the *marabout* brotherhoods. What the French didn't see was that the attack was over not just religious matters, but political ones as well. The reformers were convinced that the *marabouts'* emphasis on miracles and magic was an obstacle to the formation of a rational, Islam-based Algerian nationalism.

Nevertheless, there is not a great deal of continuity between the reformist tradition of pre–World War II Algeria and the fundamentalist movement today. While both preached a return to Islamic values, today's fundamentalists have largely absorbed their tactics and ideas from external sources like the Muslim Brotherhood and, to a lesser extent, the Iranian revolution. Two developments broke the continuity in the Algerian Islamic tradition. One was the revolution and war of liberation against the French. Led mainly by secular nationalists and socialists, this momentous event in the creation of the modern Algerian identity proceeded largely without the participation of the *ulemas*. Many of the FLN leaders were devoutly religious, like Houari Boumédienne, as, more important, were the Algerian masses who rallied to the revolutionary cause; but for the most part the religious establishment in Algeria was seen as irrelevant to the creation of the Algerian state.

Those who did participate, and were rewarded by the new Algerian government with financial support and official tutelage, "strove to expand and strengthen the Islamic components of government programs and to move toward that authentically Arab and Islamic society for which the war had nominally been fought."[42] In that, says historian John Ruedy, they were partially successful. Presidents Ben Bella and Boumédienne both instituted religious education in public schools and sponsored the building of official mosques. But in so doing, they coopted the *ulemas* who, increasingly dependent on government largesse, functioned effectively as apologists for the regime.

Outside this quasi-official religious establishment were the Islamist radicals inspired by their brethren in Egypt and elsewhere. As the government lost popularity and as the economy went into a tailspin in the 1980s, the influence of these outsiders rose in direct proportion to the decline in the legitimacy of the religious establishment. As their criticism of the secular and religious leadership of Algeria gained a following, the unofficial and sometimes illegal mosques they built in the poorer neighborhoods of Algeria's rapidly expanding cities became centers of political activity. Having gained the ear of the millions of Algerians suffering from economic stagnation and political suffocation, they could begin promoting a more positive message—a spiritual revivalism that would uplift Algerian society as it Islamicized it.

THE FUNDAMENTALIST RANKS

LEADERS AND CADRES

The leadership and organizational cadres of Algerian fundamentalism have come primarily from three sectors: the alternative and unofficial mosques erected in the poorer neighborhoods and *bidonvilles*, or shantytowns (literally "phony-towns" in French); from the largely Arab-speaking science and technology departments of the country's colleges and universities; and from the semi-educated graduates of secondary schools who found access to colleges increasingly shut off as the Algerian economy went into decline in the 1970s and 1980s.

The first group traces its origins to the compromise reached between the country's official *ulemas* and the FLN government under the regime of Ben Bella in the early 1960s whereby the religious establishment agreed to an "Islamic secularism" of the state, while promoting an "Islamic socialism" in the officially sanctioned and supported mosques. The compromise failed to establish harmony between the government and some of the more radical mullahs who believed the FLN leadership was betraying the essentially Islamic ideals of the Algerian revolution. Publishing scathing critiques of the socialist policies of Ben Bella's successor Boumédienne, these mullahs, many of them educated in Egypt under the aegis of the Muslim

Brotherhoods, began to establish their unofficial mosques and religious schools in the 1960s and 1970s. They were also joined by teachers and mullahs imported by the government from Egypt and other Arabic countries, when the government's program to emphasize Arabic over French created a shortage of qualified Algerian personnel to carry it out.

The second cadre of fundamentalist leaders, the university students and graduates, emerged out of the economic frustrations that plagued many college graduates in the 1970s and 1980s. As liberalization proceeded, the guarantee of a government sinecure based on an Arabic-language university degree in the sciences began to evaporate. Those who did get jobs found their salaries eaten away by inflation; many were forced to moonlight. Meanwhile, Algerians with entrepreneurial instincts but little formal education formed a nouveaux riche class that gained increasing access to power and influence, while the children of the traditional bourgeoisie and the FLN elite, who pursued French-language education in social sciences, continued to get the more prestigious and well-paid jobs in the government's shrinking bureaucracy through their familial connections. Frustration and resentment among the Arabic-speaking students grew. "A graduate sees himself as a member of a caste," writes Roy, putting the situation in psychological terms:

> He assumes that he should no longer be subjected to physical labor, or even to physical contact; he strives to mark his difference on his physical person, in his clothing for instance. He is therefore not receptive to his new proletarian status, to which he responds by ideologizing his condition and dreaming of a revolution and a new, strong, centralized state.[43]

The existence of the third group, the secondary school students closed off from advancement by economic recession, was the consequence of the government's post-revolutionary educational efforts that offered a secondary education to unprecedented numbers of young Algerians, but so lowered the standards of that education that the graduates were unemployable in jobs that required professional competence and a command of French. The fundamentalist cadres of the 1970s were largely recruited among the graduates of university science departments and teachers' colleges; by the 1980s recruitments were largely among secondary school graduates.

Both groups of students were led to embrace the new fundamentalist politics in part by the lack of alternatives. Not only had the government usurped control over virtually all associative and political life in the country, but it also represented what was perceived as a failing ideology. Arab nationalism as the unifying goal of intellectuals and the educated classes had been losing ground since the debacle of the Six-Day (Arab-Israeli) War in 1967, a process accelerated by new rifts in the Muslim world, like that between Iraq and Iran, as well as the international debt crisis, the discrepancy between rich and poor Arab countries and the ultimate insult, to fundamentalists, of infidel troops (i.e., the UN coalition in the Persian Gulf War) being brought in by the Saudis to defend the holy land of Islam. Arab nationalism, and to a lesser extent Soviet Marxism (discredited by the slow collapse of the Soviet Union and many of the Third World regimes in its orbit), had once provided an ideological connectedness for frustrated and idealistic youth. Now they turned to the ideal of the *umma*, as formulated through political Islam. Many of the leaders of university Marxist and Arab nationalist groups in the 1960s and 1970s, says one scholar, are leaders of the fundamentalist movement today.

In turning to Islamic politics, they naturally rejected the official *ulemas* who represented complacency and cooptation. And, at the same time, they rejected the entire educational and institutional process that created and validated the *ulemas* as the only legitimate purveyors of Islamic thought. What began to emerge in the 1980s were thousands of new, religious autodidacts who fancied themselves Islamic intellectuals, a notion encouraged by Islam's tradition of anticlericalism. In their search for something that would validate their status as educated and disciplined members of the new religious cadres, they began to adopt a behavior of Islamic authenticity that included traditional dress, beards and codified language. As Roy notes, "The creation of a distinction, the marking of a difference with respect to the other, is based on the way one presents oneself, since neither the state nor the society furnishes institutional criteria for recognizing the category."[44]

Many have taken this process one step further and declared themselves to be members of a new category of mullahs and imams. Rather than expressing their frustration with the economic and social order through overtly political speech, they have set up impromptu mosques where they preach. They have set up loudspeakers in order to amplify their message beyond the narrow confines of their storefront mosques.[45] They denounce the official mullahs of the corrupted religious establishment and speak of returning to the authentic Islamic tradition, as they perceive it, of the self-educated religious scholar and preacher. They have adopted the dress and manners of the traditional mullah, including the white robe, skull cap, and beard (the popular Algerian term for them is *les barbes*, "the bearded ones," in French). They are similar to Christian evangelicals not only in their belief that all who are called may serve, but also in that they are strongly motivated to expand the areas of re-Islamization, which gives them a sense of personal and ideological fulfillment.

THE FUNDAMENTALIST MASSES

Les barbes have had a tremendous impact among residents of the poorest urban neighborhoods, many of whom trace their roots to the countryside and long for the personal connectedness to the mullahs and *marabouts* that they once had. As Esposito notes of the Middle East generally,

> Modernization as Westernization and secularization remained primarily the preserve of a small minority elite of society. Most important, the secularization of processes and institutions did not easily translate into the secularization of minds and cultures. While a minority accepted and implemented a Western secular worldview, the majority of most Muslim populations did not internalize a secular outlook and values.[46]

Indeed, while the new fundamentalists have had little impact in the countryside, where the peasantry remain faithful to the largely nonclerical Maraboutism of their ancestors, these new cadres of self-educated and self-authorized religious leaders have connected with the masses of frustrated and alienated urban Algerians, both of the generation removed from the countryside and the dissatisfied youth born and raised in the city. Not, says Roy in contradiction to Esposito, because these people have not internalized modern and secular values, but because they have been forced whether they chose to or not. "Modernity," he notes, "creeps into Muslim countries regardless of Islam."[47]

Burgat concurs. Critics of fundamentalism in Algeria and the West insist, he says, that the masses who are drawn to the movement are those suffering from the "sickness of modernity," those "who have tried to keep sheep in the bathtub to soften the absence of a genuine system of social protection; with those to whom a television was given before they were provided with a means of assessing at least a part of the lifestyle they were likely to see on it." But, he adds, an analysis of the FIS' election victories proves otherwise. "Rather than being recruited from pockets of archaism that had been excluded from the dynamic of modernization," he writes, "the vast majority . . . appear, in reality, to come from the modernist stratum of society," including "low-level civil servants and from the young."[48]

Thus, the modernized but dysfunctional social order of the Algerian metropoli represents a large and expanding field of activity for the new mullahs' endeavors. Algeria has rapidly urbanized in the post-independence era at a rate of 3.75 percent annually; approximately half of the population now lives in urban areas. The greater Algiers metropolitan area alone numbers approximately five million of Algeria's twenty-eight million people. The overcrowding of urban areas, the crumbling facilities, the lack of housing and occupational opportunities have created a context ideally suited for a mass movement based on Islamic principles, which proclaims that renewed morality rather than a more efficient economy will solve the country's problems. Unable to find housing and jobs, many young Algerians are forced to live at home long after they expect to be on their own. They cannot marry and raise a family, an extremely important goal in Arab societies. As "Kamel," a young resident of Algiers and FIS voter, told a reporter, "In this country, we always need a revolution just to get an apartment of our own."[49]

But as Barakat points out, this inability to establish their own households is only part of the source of the fundamentalists' appeal to the Algerian masses. Another is the Algerian (or Arab) family itself. It has been argued, he notes, that the intensely patriarchal Arab family creates a sense of dependency in the Arab personality. The ruler is equated with the father and both are expected to provide security and enforced guidance. When the ruler fails, the Arab is either unable to bring himself to condemn the ruler, leading to passivity in the face of authoritarianism and corruption, or else lashes out violently against all figures of authority who have failed him.

Arab families, he points out, are largely self-contained and isolated units that create both a powerful bond of identity and a mutual interdependence among their members. This, of course, is the source of the family's greatest strength, and its greatest weakness. When the larger society and political order begin to crumble, and the family naturally feels the effect of this, the Arab masses, oriented internally on the family rather than externally toward society, assume the problems have their sources within. This, of course, creates a sense of despair and desperation, as well as an openness to the blandishments of fundamentalists who offer the comforting argument that the failures of the larger society, due both to the government's incapacities and its intrusions into the *sharia*-defined sanctity of the private realm, are the causes of crises that are being felt in the family.

In the final analysis, scholars profoundly disagree over the depth and meaning of the fundamentalist appeal to the masses of urban Algerians. Some, like Esposito, say it is simply a reaction to the modernization and secularization of the post independence era and the social, political and economic morass that fundamentalists attribute to them. The Arab societies that have experienced the greatest explosion of fundamentalist politics, he says, include those societies that have undergone the most profound modernization, such as Egypt, Iran and of course Algeria.

Others agree with Esposito, but point to a more nuanced connection between modernism and fundamentalism. Roy, for example, points out that many Algerian fundamentalists display a kind of love-hate relationship with modernism and westernization. Consumerism, he says, has fully implanted itself in Algerian urban society, but the cultural models of consumption, cars, videos and other "ways of ostentatiously displaying one's place in the new social hierarchy based on money," symbolized in the liberalization period of the 1980s by the fancy European boutiques on Algier's better avenues, are out of reach of the vast majority of Algerian families.[50] To them, "modernization involves the juxtaposition of ostentatious consumption on the part of the new rich with the new needs of the poor," which, he says, explains the targets of the October 1988 riots and the current terrorist bombings: government buildings and such symbols of the *nouveau riche* lifestyle as upscale stores and cafes. And, he writes, this anger is intensified by sexual frustration.

> Impoverishment and overpopulation make it difficult for young people to have independent lives. Pleasure is only for the rich. The Islamists present a defense of chastity and virtue, a defense that is in fact widely divergent from a certain *art de vivre* inherent in Muslim civilization. They transform what was previously a reflection of one's degraded self-image into a source of dignity.[51]

A third school of thought holds that fundamentalism appeals to Algerians for positive reasons, and does not necessarily represent a reaction to modernism but a mode of thinking and living that offers a more appealing and relevant version of it. Like the arguments of Roy and Esposito, this analysis starts from the premise that for most Algerians the socialist and later liberalization policies of the FLN government have failed to deliver on the expectations of the revolution and, more important for the vast majority of Algerians who are too young to have experienced the struggle against the French, the promises of social and economic transformation that have been so much a part of the FLN's rationale for its single-party rule.

Because the Islamist discourse was not associated with this process, it has remained untainted by its failure. "Without being alien," Burgat says, "the vocabulary of Islam, returning from a long absence on the political front, has had the added attraction of novelty." But, he adds, and it is worth quoting him at length, it is more than a matter of newness, but one of authenticity. "The recourse to a political vocabulary nourished by categories produced by local societies restores to the references of the parent culture the universal qualities which had been lost to the political language from the North [i.e., Europe]."

> [It] permits the Arab political individual to renew his relationship with his own living and intuitive culture. In reconciling the individual with his or her ancestral culture, in which a symbolic affiliation becomes once again possible, the historical continuity that the imposition of western categories had interrupted is restored in the collective imagination. In doing this (and it is here that the secret of [Islamism's] formidable capacity for mobilization resides), the colonial parenthesis is closed at the symbolic level, at precisely the point where the more or less brutal recourse to representations fabricated by other social systems were able to have their most traumatic impact.

To Roy's argument "that the FIS's Algeria will do nothing more than place a chador over the FLN's Algeria,"[52] Burgat responds:

> If the addition of the word "Islamic" to the word bank thus allows the peasant . . . to enter into a relationship with financial institutions of national importance for the first time in his life, we may say that a mere ideological

production has reconnected the individual with his or her "public" environment and thus that a major step has been taken toward modernization.[53]

But Barakat adds a note of caution. The fundamentalist creation of an "alternative sense of coherence, unity, certainty, and inner strength," he argues, may allow the faithful to "insert themselves into a predictable and divine order and develop a sense of oneness," a sociological phenomenon that is hard to dispute when observing the hundreds of thousands of people attending FIS rallies in the late 1980s and early 1990s when the organization was still legal.[54] But the result, he says, may be increased alienation and anomie since the believers "lose control over their creations and activities, entering a relationship in which they deny rather than assert themselves," that is, "alienation in religion." They tend to see creativity and expression as God's purview and domain, seeing themselves as inferior, helpless and insignificant. They tend to see themselves as objects rather than subjects, downplaying their own capacities, efforts and achievements as external and estranged from themselves. Religious leaders, says Barakat, often utilize this alienation from self as "a mechanism of control, instigation, and reconciliation." But, he adds, when the human spirit rebels against such a self-destructive world-view, it cannot express itself in public because of the believer's fear of seeming anti-religious. Public taboos and prohibitions continue to be violated, but in private, thus increasing self-hatred, anger and anomie. "Taken together," Barakat concludes,

these phenomena alienate believers, who experience themselves as powerless objects rather than creative actors. Even when they enthusiastically support activist religious movements, the ultimate product of their engagement is impoverishment rather than enrichment, and repression rather than the transformation of reality.[55]

FUNDAMENTALIST ORGANIZATIONS

FIS

While Algerian political Islam traces its roots to al-Qadir in the early nineteenth century and the Association of Ulemas and Ibd al-Hamid Ben Badis in the early twentieth century, these early Islamic political leaders are not really part of the tradition of modern Algerian fundamentalism. For one thing, they are too distant and for another they have been largely appropriated by the government as heroes of Algerian nationalism and as precursors of the FLN itself. These personalities and their legacy, in other words, have been usurped by the enemy.

Instead, the origins of Algerian political Islam generally, and the FIS specifically, can be traced to the early post-independence-era activities of an Islamic organization known as al-Qiyam (The Values) and its review *Muslim Humanism*. The association advocated the establishment of a strict Islam-based moral code as the statutory foundation for a new legal code, and the eradication of all non-Islamic influences from Algeria. Some of its more headstrong members went as far as to try to destroy Roman ruins near Guelma in eastern Algeria. These extreme positions led Boumédienne to ban the group in 1966.

Under the Boumédienne regime, the government sought to head off Islamic organizing in two ways: outright bans, like the one against al-Qiyam, and the cooptation of Islamic symbols and rhetoric. Despite its largely socialist agenda, the 1976 Constitution represents the culmination of such efforts. It declared Algeria an officially Islamic state and formulated much of its socialist rhetoric in the strongly egalitarian language of Islam. A small group of religious opponents of the government formed around revolutionary leader Mohammed Kheiriddine in the mid-1970s, but it was largely formulated in the liberal religious tradition of Ben Badis and accepted the separation of church and state, making it very different from the Islamic politics that formed after Boumédienne's death. In short, the Boumédienne years were marked by a quiescence in Islamic politics. If the government faced any real ideological challenge during these years, it was from the Marxist and Maoist left in the universities. Doudi Mohamed Abdelhadi, an Egyptian-educated imam and early participant in Islamist politics, says that upon his return to Algeria in 1975, he found "a situation that was very fixed; there was immobility and passivity. No one bothered with religion."[56]

During the late 1970s, however, a series of "free mosques" were established outside the purview of the government and the official *ulema* establishment of Algeria. Abdelhadi speaks of one such mosque in the capital. "The Da'wa [preaching] was a free Da'wa where one could talk about everything that was happening in the country, all the truths. And since people always go to where the truth is being spoken, the mosque began to develop." By 1978, he says, the methods and aims of religious teaching in the free mosques were evolving.

> These were no longer lessons dealing with how to pray or perform a fast and all that. No, these were lessons at a high level in which we explained, or searched for a method by which we could live in an Islamic state . . . And we also touched on the problems which the Algerian nation was confronting. We spoke about everything. Of all the situations, the economy, of all the aspects of life.[57]

The precipitating event that led these religious leaders to take to the streets in opposition to the secular state was, of course, the Islamic Revolution in Iran and the coming to power of the Islamists there in 1979.

Clashes between the authorities and some of the early Islamist organizers, including future FIS leader Abbassi Madani, began shortly after that, especially after Islamic groups were formed in some of the nation's universities. Nevertheless, most of the verbal confrontations and even armed clashes were not with governmental authorities, but with the powerful Marxist organizations, like the Party of the Socialist Avant Garde (PAGS), already established there. While these leftist organizations will be discussed more thoroughly in Chapter 4, one important point needs to be made here. Islamists argue that PAGS and other groups were sponsored by the government. Opponents of the fundamentalists say that, in fact, the government was sponsoring the religious groups as a foil to the radical left, which it feared more in those early days of Islamic organizing.

The truth is that under the Boumédienne regime, the government had tried to coopt the student radicals by establishing its own student organizations. In 1979, when protests against the preferences for francophone students broke out among Arab-speaking students, the newly installed Benjedid regime changed tack and, with an eye on Iran, quickly sided with the latter in order to prevent the newly outspoken Islamic militants from gaining control of this movement.

Ruedy points out two important facets of this crisis. First, the more market-oriented Benjedid saw the Arabists as a natural ally, given their general conservatism, and largely gave in to their demands by initiating a far-reaching program of Arabization of university education and the nation's justice system. Second, the Arabization movement in Algeria has always been largely associated with religious politics while the French language has been associated with the FLN elite and their socialist and secularist agenda. Thus, the government's decision to give in to Arabophone student demands showed that it was allying itself with them in the hope of coopting the political Islamic movement. This new strategy was made clearer by the near total lack of concessions by the government to Berberist demands made during the uprising at the largely Berberist University Center of Tizi Ouzou in Kabyle.

But the new policy did not stop Islamic protests. Militants clashed with Berberist and Marxist groups on campuses throughout the country, intimidated female students who did not "abide by Muslim standards of dress or propriety," and in March 1981 went off campus for the first time to destroy a liquor store in the working-class Algiers neighborhood of Bab-el Oued.[58] But while the government gave in to Arabist demands on campus, it was determined to maintain control over the nation's religious institutions. When thirty militants seized an official mosque in the southern Algerian city of Laghouat to protest the arrest of one of their leaders, the authorities reacted strongly. The first death in the confrontation between Islamists and the government occurred when a policeman involved in storming the mosque was shot by the militants.

By 1982, the situation had escalated dramatically. Fundamentalists began distributing tracts calling for the abrogation of the socially liberal 1976 National Charter. When the new school year began that autumn, clashes between leftists and fundamentalists increased. When a leftist student was murdered in November, the government cracked down, arresting over 400 Islamic student activists. When 100,000 Muslim demonstrators marched on the downtown University of Algiers Mosque to protest the arrests, authorities were astounded. "It was," says Ruedy, "the greatest challenge to state authority since independence."[59] Two years later, when an elderly religious leader incarcerated by the authorities during the earlier crackdown (though never tried or convicted) died in prison, 400,000 attended his politicized funeral. Meanwhile that same year, Moustapha Bouyali, a regional commander of FLN forces during the revolution and a bureaucrat angered at the corruption and favoritism of the state corporation for which he worked, founded the militant Islamic Group for Defense Against the Illicit, an organization aimed at stirring up armed opposition to the government.

The government's response to these legal and illegal challenges included the predictable carrot and stick. The military and gendarmerie led a determined pursuit of Bouyali's group, leading to his death and the group's destruction in 1987. The civilian side of the government offered the socially conservative 1984 Family Code, which abrogated most of the liberal and pro-woman clauses contained in the 1976 Charter. In the face of the growing economic crisis of the 1980s, however, this dual approach would prove insufficient. Islamist student protests continued and increased in 1986, spreading to the labor sector in 1987.

But the October 1988 riots, brought on ultimately by long-term causes such as economic decline and government corruption, but sparked by a series of strikes in September, were largely spontaneous and popular. Beginning in Algiers and its environs, they quickly spread to urban centers around the country. There was no national leadership, though in certain localities leftist student groups, unions and, especially, fundamentalists began to lead attacks on government ministries and such symbols of the elite as shops, cafes and villas. The popular outrage at the government's heavy-handed and murderous response led the FLN to announce a future legalization of political associations and a plan for multiparty elections the following year.

Fundamentalists immediately took advantage of the government's concessions. FIS literature notes that the idea of forming an Islamic party came to two mullahs, Hachemi Sahnouni and Ali Belhadj, almost simultaneously in the months following the October 1988 riots and amidst the government's talk of legalizing opposition parties. The two then recruited an enthusiastic Islamic militant named Abbassi Madani. At a series of meetings in early 1989, a small circle of fundamentalist leaders formed the Majlis Shura, or Council of Advisers. On February 21, the group declared the establishment of the FIS. The group remained small and quasi-clandestine, however, until the government, violating its own election laws against religion-based parties, authorized the FIS in September. With its ready-built infrastructure of free mosques, independent religious schools and alternative social service agencies, most situated in the neighborhoods where opposition to the FLN leadership had already reached a critical mass, the FIS very quickly became the party of opposition for the vast majority of poor urban Algerians, whether they agreed with all of its Islamicizing agenda or not.

Despite the startling and rapid liberalization of the nation's press following the riots of 1988, the fundamentalist leaders felt that their political message was being ignored in the media. It was true that the government maintained a virtual monopoly over domestic TV and radio broadcasts (as it still does) and that there was a bias against political Islam on the part of much of the nation's press. But that was only part of the reason the FIS chose to campaign for public office in the streets. The audience and constituency they were after were largely those who didn't buy a daily newspaper or weekly newsmagazine. Whatever the case, their public showing was impressive. On December 29, in a response to a relatively small demonstration by liberal women protesting the nation's anti-feminist drift, the FIS mobilized tens of thousands of women in support of the Family Code. Despite the FLN's success in getting several fundamentalists to denounce a proposed rally in April 1990, the FIS drew hundreds of thousands of supporters. Its victories in the June elections, capturing the vast majority of municipal and provincial councils, were stunning, as was the electoral debacle of the FLN.

Yet despite these victories, many observers, including many in Algeria who were not supporters of the FLN, were left wondering what exactly this party represented. Indeed, when the High Council of State, the military junta that canceled the January 1992 election run-offs that the FIS was expected to win, outlawed the FIS immediately after taking power and imprisoned its leaders, it was able to cite the fact that the FIS, in violation of election law, had never presented a platform of ideas and programs.

What the FIS represents is a reasonable question. Along with its failure to put forth a platform, it never, the government claims, presented a list of its officers or its internal structure; its putative leaders, Belhadj and Madani, are simply listed as "spokesmen" for the organization. Moreover, the FIS has manifested itself in various guises—as a Leninist-type vanguard, a Western-style political party and a militant religious organization attempting to lead a revolution—each with its own methods and aims. Part of the reason for this is opportunism. As Roy points out, "The Algerian FIS has successively claimed to fit each of these molds, depending on whether it is denouncing or playing the political game."[60] But a larger part is the coalition that the FIS has tried to create.

As its name suggests and its two leaders' previous careers imply, the FIS is really more like a front than a political party, attempting to fuse two important constituencies with different aims, whose common bond is their opposition to the government. Madani represents one constituency. Born in 1931 and imprisoned by the French during the revolution, he went on to receive a Ph.D. in education at the University of London. Thus he stands with the older generation of university graduates, willing to compromise with modernism and who seek to maintain the Algerian state in its current form, albeit with a new Islamist orientation. They oppose the FLN both because they feel it has created a state based on nepotism, corruption and favoritism that is driving the country into social and economic ruin, and because they feel excluded from it. Often called "techno-Islamists" by scholars, they see themselves inserting themselves into the bureaucracy they attack, rather than bringing it down. Sympathizers say their motives are genuine. They want to fix and Islamicize the state in order to turn the country around; critics argue they're just frustrated, want to take power themselves and see fundamentalism as a means to that end.

Few, however, doubt the authentic anger and frustration of the other constituency, the impoverished, desperate and mostly younger voters of the FIS. Graduates of the nation's secondary schools, they remain crowded into the apartments of the poorer quarters of Algeria's cities, living with their parents, unable to find jobs, marry and get on with their lives. Their leader, Belhadj, is a Tunisian native born in 1956 who received a religious education and became a teacher of Arabic and a preacher before joining the FIS. He offers a scathing critique of westernization and speaks in nihilistic terms about the need for completely revamping Algerian society. As one journalist symbolized the difference between these two constituencies, the Madani group routinely watches, in great frustration, the many "seductive" foreign broadcasts available to those with access to the *paraboles* (satellite dishes), while Belhadj's constituency seeks to tear out the "forest of mushrooms that have sprouted over Algiers in recent years" and with them any connection to the modernism they see as so threatening.[61]

Finally, there is the matter of the FIS' financial support. The Algerian government claims that it is largely foreign in origin; the FIS claims it comes from constituent donations. They are both right. Undoubtedly, worshipers at the free mosques established by radical mullahs, parents whose children receive their religious education at the schools connected to the mosques and the general populace that takes advantage of the nongovernmental social services provided by the fundamentalists contribute funds to these institutions that end up paying for FIS campaigning.

But it is also clear that the FIS has received financing from the World Muslim League, based in Saudi Arabia. In its efforts to counteract the growing influence of Iranian Islamist radicals in the 1980s, the Saudi government established the league to support more conservative Islamic politicians and political organizations. The league publishes a vast array of pamphlets and literature that show up on the streets of Algeria. Most of these tracts, says Roy, are a mishmash of ideas, "half-preaching, half propaganda, destined for a very large and not very intellectual public."[62] Much of it, he notes, consists of "apologies" for Islam, listing the intellectual and scientific accomplishment of Islamic thinkers, designed to leave the impression that the West does not have a "monopoly on modernism." But the literature also has a clear political message: that the path to Islamicization is not through violent political revolution and the Iranian way, but through the creation of what students of fundamentalism call an "alternative public space," a complex of Islamic institutions that attempt to foster Islamic moral values and restrict Islamic political action to lobbying for Islamic social law. For the most part, these funds have dried up since the Gulf War, when Algerian fundamentalists broke with Saudi Arabia because of its permission to station non-Muslim troops there and ally itself with the West against a fellow Muslim regime.

OTHER RELIGIOUS OPPOSITION GROUPS

If Algerian religious parties could be placed on a Western political spectrum (a rather long stretch of the political imagination, but so be it), it might be said that the FIS is the centrist party, flanked on the right by the Movement of Islamic Resistance (Hamas) and other religious parties authorized by the government at the same time the FIS was, and on the left by the Armed Islamic Group (GIA) and other even more shadowy groups whose existence is largely known through the faxes received by the national and international press after some armed clash with authorities or act of terrorism occurs.

Hamas has never demonstrated anything close to the level of support received by the FIS. Lamamra claims this is because the desperate masses of Algerians who turned to the FIS wanted the most radical break with the existing order, something not offered by the more moderate leaders of Hamas, whom the conservative French newsmagazine L'Express described as men "who succeeded in creating the synthesis between Islam and democracy." The praise Hamas has received in the international press has led many fundamentalists to assert that Hamas is, in fact, a creation of the FLN, intended to split and confuse the FIS' constituency. Even its name, lifted from the radical Islamic organization in the Israeli-occupied territories (an organization much renowned and beloved among fundamentalists throughout the Arab world), is a consciously intended ruse, they say.

A far more significant group, the GIA, has emerged more recently and remains a far more serious competitor for power with the FIS. Originally, the GIA was part of the FIS, but broke with the latter organization because of its emphasis on electoral politics and its declared uneasiness with violent resistance to the government and attacks on supposed civilian collaborators of the FLN. The core of the GIA is a group of young Islamic militants known popularly as the "Afghanis," because many fought with the Mujahadeen in their struggle against the Soviets in Afghanistan in the 1980s. This participation, says Burgat, "conferred a prestige which was often disproportionate to their actual training."[63]

From the beginning, says Burgat, the Afghanis "constituted a needle in the foot of the Islamist Goliath."[64] They did not compete in the elections and some of their radical excesses embarrassed the FIS leadership as it tried to woo the vast majority of Algerians who abhorred political violence. The FIS leadership insisted from the beginning that the Afghanis represented a small minority within the party and that their actions did not represent the policies or methods of the FIS. But the media, largely hostile to the FIS, made no distinction, blaming on the FIS as a whole the Afghanis' threats against and attacks on shops that sell liquor, women who do not wear the veil and supporters of the government.

With the banning of political parties and the general crackdown on Islamic militants following the 1992 coup, the Afghanis split from the FIS to form the GIA, though many maintain that the two parties closely coordinate their activities. While the jailed FIS leadership has waffled on the question of violent resistance to the state, sometimes arguing for defensive action, sometimes offensive, but usually denouncing attacks on civilians, the GIA has waged an all-out war against both the government and that segment of the civilian population it sees as insufficiently Islamic, such as women who fail to wear the veil in public. It is also the GIA and groups like it that many say are responsible for the attacks on journalists, the recent terrorist attacks against French targets, the bombings of cafes and stores, and the September 1993 edict calling for the assassination of all foreigners in Algeria. These actions have led some Algerian opponents of the fundamentalists to label the GIA a collection of "psychopaths." As one Algerian academic opines,

> I have a feeling the GIA is just a diffused group of young people who don't really have a specific agenda, for whom violence has truly become a way of life, and they do it with great relish. If you look at the way in which they kill, like the passengers on Air France [during the hijacking in December 1994]. They just popped one of the passengers and the other passengers didn't even see how he did it. He was just so good. Obviously not anybody can do that. They must be trained to have complete contempt for life.[65]

The extent of the GIA's membership is not clear, but most observers suggest it is not very great, numbering anywhere between several hundred and a few thousand in the country as a whole, with a few small cadres in France and other European countries where they secure funding and weaponry. "Who knows how many?" says the Algerian academic. "They just keep issuing these ultimatums and threats." Reporters who have been able to penetrate GIA strongholds in the west of the country observed that they had typewriters, computers and weapons. "They were operating as if they were an autonomous group," the reporter noted.[66] Meanwhile in May 1995, *Le Monde* reported that a military garrison in a small town 30 miles from the capital was entirely surrounded by GIA militants who control the water supply and electricity to the base. And in early 1995, rumors began floating around Algeria that the GIA had issued an ultimatum to the FIS: fold your organization into the GIA and accept its leadership, or else become a target. The authenticity of this threat has not been acknowledged by the FIS or the government, and cannot be confirmed by outside observers.

NOTES

[1] Hourani, Albert, *A History of the Arab Peoples*, New York: Warner Books, 1991, p. 61.

[2] *Ibid.*

[3] Mansfield, Peter, *The Arabs*, New York: Penguin, 1992, p. 69.

[4] Gibb, H.A.R., *Modern Trends in Islam*, Chicago: University of Chicago Press, p. 11.

[5] Gibb offers a useful example. When coffee-drinking began to spread through the Middle East, Islamic jurists counseled leaders to ban it, and several coffee merchants and drinkers were executed. But it didn't stop the habit and eventually it was permitted. *Ibid.*

[6] Mansfield, *Arabs*, p. 70.

[7] As Mansfield notes, *itjihad* literally translated means "exerting oneself." *Ibid.*

[8] Kelsay, John, *Islam and War: A Study in Comparative Ethics*, Louisville, Ky.: Westminster/John Knox Press, 1993, p. 88.

[9] Roy, Olivier, *The Failure of Political Islam*, Cambridge, Mass.: Harvard University Press, 1994, p. 29.

[10] The Koran explicitly permits polygamy, but restricts it to four wives and requires a man to treat all four with perfect fairness. Some reformist scholars have insisted that requirement of perfect fairness is, in fact, a prohibition on polygamy since no man is capable of perfect justice. Mansfield, *Arabs*, p. 26.

[11] Barakat, Halim, *The Arab World: Society, Culture, and State*, Berkeley: University of California Press, 1993, p. 97.

[12] Mahfouz, Naguib, *Palace of Desire*, New York: Anchor Books, 1991.

[13] Lazreg, Marnia, *The Eloquence of Silence: Algerian Women in Question*, New York: Routledge, 1994, p. 153.

[14] Roy, *Failure of Islam*, pp. 10–11.

[15] *Ibid.*, p. 29.

[16] *Ibid.*

[17] *Ibid.*, pp. 9–10.

[18] *Ibid.*, p. 10.

[19] *Ibid.*, p. 132.

[20] Lazreg, Marnia, *The Emergence of Classes in Algeria*, Boulder, Colo.: Westview Press, 1976, p. 101.

[21] Cited in Roy, *Failure of Islam*, p. 137.

[22] Barakat, *Arab World*, p. 74.

[23] Hopkins, Nicholas, "Emergence of Class in a Tunisian Town" in Said, Ibrahim and Hopkins, Nicholas (eds.), *Arab Society in Transition: A Reader*, Cairo: American University in Cairo, 1977, p. 456.

[24] Duvignaud, Jean, *Change at Shebika: Report from a North African Village*, N.Y.: Vintage, 1970, p. 9.

[25] Burgat, François and Dowell, William, *The Islamic Movement in North Africa*, Austin, Tex.: Center for Middle Eastern Studies at the University of Texas, 1993, p. 3.

[26] This process was not, of course, confined to the Muslim world, as the examples of China and Japan during the same period illustrate.

[27] Barakat, *Arab World*, p. 314.

[28] *Ibid.*, p. 243.

[29] Cited in Khuri, Ra'if, *Modern Arab Thought: Channels of the French Revolution to the Arab East*, Princeton, N.J.: Kingston Press, 1983, p. 122.

[30] Roy, *Failure of Islam*, p. 33.

[31] We cannot examine here the differences between Shiism and Sunnism, even as these differences affect modern political Islam, since Algeria is almost entirely Sunni, although a few words seem appropriate here. Arising out of events of great antiquity and complexity, the profound Sunni-Shiite rift is about important questions of Muslim belief and ritual. Since Islamic political movements among both sects rely on the authenticity of their specific traditions, "true Sunni-Shiite ecumenism—that is, ecumenism based on mutual compromise" is, according to Islamicist Emmanuel Sivan, virtually impossible. Sivan, Emmanuel, "Islamic Radicalism: Sunni and Shi'ite" in Emmanuel Sivan and Menachem Friedman (eds.), *Religious Radicalism and Politics in the Middle East*, Albany, New York: State University of New York Press, 1990, p. 58.

[32] *Ibid.*, p. 41.

[33] Roy, *Failure of Islam*, p. 36.

[34] *Ibid.*, p. 75.

[35] *Ibid.*, p. 76.

[36] El-Kenz, Ali, *Algerian Reflections on Arab Crises*, Austin, Tex.: Center for Middle Eastern Studies, 1991, p. 95.

[37] Entelis, John, *Algeria: The Revolution Institutionalized*, Boulder, Colo.: Westview Press, 1986, p. 78.

[38] Perkins, Kenneth, "'The Masses Look Ardently to Istanbul': Tunisia, Islam, and the Ottoman Empire, 1837–1931" in Ruedy, John, *Islamism and Secularism in North Africa*, New York: St. Martin's Press, 1994, p. 29.

[39] Launay, Michel, *Paysans algériens*, Paris: Editions du Seuil, 1963, p. 371.

[40] Gellner, Ernest, *Muslim Society*, Cambridge: Cambridge University Press, 1981, p. 155.

[41] Knauss, Peter, *The Persistence of Patriarchy: Class, Gender, and Ideology in Twentieth Century Algeria*, New York: Praeger, 1987, p. 38.

[42] Ruedy, *Islamism and Secularism*, p. 79.

[43] Roy, *Failure of Islam*, p. 49.

[44] *Ibid.*, p. 94.

[45] *Bab el-Oued City*, a 1994 film by Algerian director Merzak Allouache, illustrates the intensity of these new mullahs. When a local baker, who has to sleep days and work nights, pulls down one of their loudspeakers that is keeping him awake, he is literally hounded out of the country by the defenders of the mosque.

[46] Esposito, John, *The Islamic Threat: Myth or Reality?*, New York: Oxford University Press, 1992, p. 9.

[47] Roy, *Failure of Islam*, p. 22.

[48] Burgat, *Islamic Movement*, p. 97.

[49] Mouffok, Ghania, "La cité de Diar el Kef" in Reporters sans frontières, *Le drame algérien: un peuple en otage*, Paris: Editions la découverte, 1994, p. 17.

[50] Roy, *Failure of Islam*, p. 55.

[51] *Ibid.*, pp. 55–6.

[52] *Ibid.*, p. 60.

[53] Burgat, *Islamic Movement*, p. 65.

[54] Barakat, *Arab World*, pp. 199–200.

[55] *Ibid.*, pp. 144–5.

[56] Cited in Burgat, *Islamic Movement*, p. 261.

[57] Cited in *Ibid.*

[58] Ruedy, John, *Modern Algeria: The Origins and Development of a Nation*, Bloomington: Indiana University Press, 1992, p. 241.

[59] *Ibid.*, p. 242.

[60] Roy, *Failure of Islam*, p. 46.

[61] Hakem, Tewfik, "La parabole de la démocratie" in RSF, *Drame algérien*, pp. 42–44.

[62] Roy, *Failure of Islam*, p. 112.

[63] Burgat, *Islamic Movement*, p. 290.

[64] *Ibid.*

[65] Anonymous, interview with author, June 3, 1995.

[66] *Ibid.*

···

4

SECULAR FORCES

Better a military dictatorship, than a fundamentalist one.
    —Anonymous Algerian man

*This time [FIS militants] are going to detention camps and they
are staying there forever.*
    —Anonymous military official

THE GOVERNMENT

In his magisterial *A History of the Arab Peoples*, historian Albert Hourani
points out perhaps the most striking contradiction of the post-independence era in Arab history. For all the profound and far-reaching social
and economic changes of the past fifty years, and despite the perception of
their volatility in the West, the regimes of the Arab world have by and large
been stable and long-lived.[1] Nowhere is this truer than in Algeria, which
has been led by the same party since independence in 1962. This continuity
of leadership, if not necessarily of policy, has several sources, including the
legacy of clans, the FLN's emphasis on collegial leadership, the peculiar
formation of post-independence class structure and the presence of a
powerful and, until the last decade or so, respected military establishment.
In Algeria, however, more than in most other Arab countries in the 1990s,
the clock appears to be running out on the ruling elite's stay in power.

CLANS

Two words, one a local idiom and the other from standard Arabic, help
provide the cultural context for the structure of rule that has emerged in
post-independence Algeria. *Mahgour* means a defenseless one. "In popular
culture," writes Algerian journalist Ghania Mouffok, "it is generally admitted that it is better to have sons, rather than daughters, to defend oneself
against one's enemies. As a Kabyle song goes, 'those who have no brothers
are *mahgours*.'" Women, by definition, are *mahgourantes* and "orphans are
the saddest of all."[2] Outside the family, *mahgour* takes on a slightly different
meaning. *Mahgours* are those without connection to a group that can
provide security and protection—in a society where the individual without
such connections is defenseless.

The Arabic word *assabiyya* describes the complex loyalties that form the basis of clan and tribal cohesion in the Middle East, a set of loyalties that have represented the great countervailing force in Arab history against which the pan-Islamic ideal of *umma* was formulated and has struggled for centuries, and which has only partially given way to the idea of nationalism in the twentieth century. "The medieval Arab historian Ibn Khaldun [of the fourteenth century]," write historians David and Marina Ottaway,

> singled out the pronounced clannishness of North Africa's predominantly Berber society as a primary cause of the instability of North African empires. His work contains some ideas that, *mutatis mutandis*, help to explain contemporary Algerian politics.[3]

The Ottoways' point is well-taken even today when we consider one thing. The stability of the state is clearly breaking down in contemporary Algeria, just thirty years after the French left, a relative blink of the eye in the millennium of North African history considered by the Ottoways. In fact, while the clannishness of the current government has provided remarkable stability in twentieth-century terms, it is clearly the key internal factor in the collapse of the current regime as well.

Of course, transepochal comparisons should not be stretched too far. The historical reason empires have been so hard to sustain in North Africa is that emperors and sultan's governors have been unable to transform the essentially feudal local political structure, based on tribute from tribal leaders, into a centralized kingdom of the early modern European kind. The FLN, on the other hand, has been able to create a unified, top-down bureaucratic state that goes beyond anything even the French colonial government was able to achieve. The technology and organizational structures available to twentieth-century governments have made this possible, as has, in the peculiar case of Algeria, the legacy of the revolution. The legitimacy attached to the party that led the revolution allowed those who controlled the party to make it the single ruling institution, first eliminating all potential outside challengers, then purging its ranks of virtually all dissidents.

Still, for the way the ruling elite has maintained its stability, power and, until recently, its unchallenged status, the transepochal comparison holds. Again, as the Ottoways note, the structures are much the same, except that the "clans" today are composed not of individuals related by blood, but of persons brought together by the struggle for independence, and their successors. These include men who formed the original FLN, struggled in the same *maquis* (resistance cadres), or spent time together in French prisons. "The system of alliances that brought Ben Bella to power," say the Ottoways, was very similar to that on which the sultans founded their empires. Around Ben Bella gathered a small group of well-known national figures, army officers, and guerrilla commanders, each man the leader of his own clan.[4]

Despite this connectedness, the FLN and the Algerian government—the two were inextricably bound together until the constitutional reforms and elections of the 1989–91 period—were really a front, as the FLN's name implies, rather than a political party in the European definition of the word. "The members of the alliance were held together by strictly personal ties and shared no community of ideals or common political program," the Ottoways note.[5]

This was true enough for the early years of the post-independence era, when the ruling alliance included the "romantic revolutionary" Ben Bella, the liberal democrat Ferhat Abbas and the statist-oriented but devoutly religious Boumédienne, who advocated returning the Algerian revolution to the "sources" of Islam. But as Ruedy notes, the decision to make the FLN the sole party, "catalyst and motor of the revolution," required a thinning of the ranks. During the revolution, he writes, the FLN "had to enlist the support of all segments of the population, even nonrevolutionary elements . . . [after independence], its task . . . was to purge itself of such elements in order that it could effectively serve as a guarantor of the revolution."[6]

Ironically, over the course of the Boumédienne regime from 1965 to 1978, the more ideologically consistent regime became less ideologically driven. For once the political program of the government was fixed upon, the various leadership cadres turned their attention and energies to the building of local and corporatist power bases, rather than to ideological struggle. The change in personnel at the secondary levels of the bureaucracy contributed to this transformation. The Boumédienne administration shifted its recruiting from political leaders to technocrats. "There emerged a new elite . . . who had spent the 1950s and 1960s in schools rather than in the maquis or in political infighting," Ruedy writes. "Their relatively apolitical outlook, added to the pragmatic approach of the military, served further to stabilize the system."[7] A group of FLN elites, often referred to as the Ouida clan, after the town in Morocco where Boumédienne oversaw the western wing of the Algerian Liberation Army (ALN), continued to rule, supported by a vast, officially neutral bureaucracy that claimed to serve nothing more than the cause of industrial modernization and nothing less than the Algerian nation as a whole.

Despite this effort to implant a neutral state apparatus, pursue the corporatist ideal and "put a halt to 'old rivalries,'" a decision reached rather early on in the revolutionary struggle against the French, "political groupings and clans succeeded in taking over the new institutions at independence." In short, backroom dealing among these "clubs of cronies and factions that surrounded and often hemmed in the president" became the norm in independent Algeria.[8] Under Ben Bella, the hidden power plays of this so-called *boulitique* were ideologically driven. After Boumédienne came to power, he spent the first two years of his administration eliminating these kinds of divisions and the fierce struggles they prompted. As economists Alan Richards and John Waterbury note, modern Arab ruling clans like the Ouida group around Boumédienne "are fragile, and power struggles within them can be brutal."[9]

Unlike the charismatic Ben Bella, who was overthrown because of the cult of personality he was attempting to create around himself, Boumédienne resurrected the collegial rule of the external cadres of the revolutionary FLN. But while decisions were reached collectively by consensus, each structural component of the regime, including the large state enterprises, the military, governmental agencies and the quasi-independent associations of workers and peasants made their voices heard and their impact felt based upon the relative power of the political and economic bases of their leaders.

In the mid-1970s, as rapid modernization and the influx of petrodollars put new strains on both Algerian society and government bureaucracy, a new purge took place at the top. When rifts over the new situation threatened the collegialism of the Boumédienne leadership, the president eliminated many of the remaining members of the Ouida clan from the ruling circle, replacing them with an even smaller circle of like-minded military leaders and technocrats as the sole source of advice. Overall, during the Boumédienne years, an ideological agenda was fused to the older clannish organization of rule. "The principle of collegiality advanced the mechanisms working in favour of the 'politics of chiefs,'" writes Tlemcani, "and thus obstructed the channels to leadership struggles to people who did not necessarily share the bureaucratic-military worldview."[10]

Despite the limited access to alternative opinion, elements within the Boumédienne administration were aware that the economic modernization of Algeria had reached an impasse by the mid-1970s. Vastly augmented foreign revenues (petrodollars) were not matched by anything near that rate of growth in industrial production and efficiency or elimination of unemployment. The Charter of 1976, introduced and shepherded into law by the military/bureaucratic inner circle, was quite explicit about the "disease of bureaucracy." But solutions to the problem had barely been conceptualized, much less implemented, when Boumédienne died suddenly at the end of 1978. The ruling circle decided that continuity of leadership at this critical historical moment was essential if a solution to the nation's problems—and the continuing rule of the FLN—were to be assured. The choice of Chadli Benjedid, a high-level functionary in both the FLN and military bureaucracies and "a perfect symbol of the army as guarantor and arbiter of the national interest," personified this policy. And indeed, during the first several years of his administration, Benjedid, preoccupied with consolidating his power and dealing with a series of ethnic and social crises, pursued "a cautious, middle-of-the-road policy consistent with his strong military identification and institutional loyalty."[11]

In the early 1980s, however, international economic and political forces combined with the changing internal dynamic of the Algerian bureaucracy to shift economic policy away from the old command structure to a heavier reliance on market forces and a program of liberalization. Despite these policy changes, the composition of ruling party leadership and pattern of bureaucratic formation stayed much the same. The inconsistencies between these two trends would eventually lead to the political crises of the late 1980s, the end of one-party rule and the elimination of the FLN as an institutional component of the ruling elite.

CLASS

As scholars Richards and Waterbury point out in their extended study of Middle Eastern economies, formation of distinct classes in the region is largely a recent phenomenon. "The only entrenched indigenous class in the region has been the landowners," they write, "and their roots are shallow, no deeper than the middle of the 19th century, when private title to land was extended to the rural notability by revenue-hungry governments."[12] This fact, especially pertinent in Algeria where European colonial rule was longer and more intrusive than anywhere else in the Middle East, means that social and economic class stratification in this region has been simultaneously with, and part of, the process of modern state-building.

In a pattern similar to that of many other postcolonial regimes, the inheritors of political power in Algeria were largely the *petit bourgeois* or lower-middle-class native administrators trained by the French. But because of the country's long and agonizing anti-imperialist struggle, Algeria presents several variations on the theme of the colonial inheritance in Third World postcolonial nation-building and economic modernization. First, the revolution partially radicalized those elements of the lower middle class who eventually took power under Ben Bella and Boumédienne, turning them toward a strongly anti-Western foreign policy, a statist model for economic development and a top-down revolutionary strategy for modernizing Algerian society. These choices led to the development of a state in which revolutionary symbols and rhetoric substituted for democracy and an economy that mixed some of the worst elements of statist and market-determined development.

During the early years of the revolution, both the workers and peasants of the *autogestion* movement and the leadership of the FLN spoke of democratizing the state and distributing economic power as widely as possible. But they were in fact speaking different languages. Workers and peasants envisioned self-management and a larger share of the national income based on their control of enterprises and farms. But the FLN, especially the Boumédienne faction, became enamored of the corporatist idea of establishing a neutral all-encompassing bureaucracy that would run the country, develop its economic base with an eye to import-substitution and large-scale enterprise, and mediate between interest groups through an all-pervasive party apparatus.

As the revolution became institutionalized during the Boumédienne regime, the emerging technocrats of the state bureaucracy and the military and administrative elites of the FLN and the ALN developed into a peculiar middle class, based not in the private sector but in state enterprises. While denying *autogestion* to the peasants and workers, they endorsed and created "a form of institutionalized self-management" at the highest levels. "By these means," says Tlemcani,

> . . . namely statization of autogestion, nationalization of foreign capital, industrialization and creation of new institutions, the bureaucracy succeeded in converting the colonial apparatus not only into a mere instrument for political power, but also into a source of economic power.[13]

In other words, the bureaucracy that was supposed to be technocratic and politically neutral was really neither. The efficient planning that was supposed to be the hallmark of a technocracy became instead a corrupt and wasteful economic process in which quasi-independent state firms and agencies tried, in characteristic bureaucratic fashion, to expand their budgets, take on personnel, funnel state funds to themselves and minimize the share of resources they contributed to economic development outside the walls of their factories. Thus, in Algerian sociologist Marnia Lazreg's formulation, "a form of socialism" coexisted in postcolonial Algeria within an economy and society that was "largely determined by capitalist relations."[14] At the same time, the Algerian bureaucracy perpetuated itself through nepotism (the opposite of *mahgourisme*) and the passing on of "cultural capital," that is to say, higher, French-language education largely inaccessible to the peasants and workers. Thus, through education and control of state firms, this class of high-level technocrats turned the bureaucracy into "the personification of capital in post-colonial [Algerian] society."[15]

As for the political neutrality of the one-party state, its largely rhetorical existence was the justification for this new middle-class bureaucracy's rule of Algeria in the name of the revolution and economic modernization. As Tlemcani asks,

> How can the state or the bureaucracy control the process of labour, organize the class distribution of the surplus value, "mediate" between competing class interests and reinforce at the same time its own privileges in the name of promoting national development?[16]

To outward appearances, then, Algeria under Boumédienne appeared quite radical. Algeria promoted the cause of Third World independence and beat the drum of anti-Westernism. This was done partly out of ideological conviction, but it also served to further the domestic illusion of an ongoing revolution. More important, the nationalization of foreign assets and the pursuit of "socialist" economic development was in fact a means for pursuing the economic consolidation of the technocratic and political elites as a privileged class within a radical and revolutionary, but largely symbolic, political context. By the late 1970s, however, even the pretense of revolution, social equality and one-party neutrality began to drop away. "On the eve of Boumédienne's death," concludes Tlemcani, "Algeria was marked, on one side, by shantytowns and food scarcity, on the other, by the flaunting of [the bureaucratic elite's] embourgeoisement."[17]

The first years of the Benjedid administration were marked by several very conspicuous reform efforts. One was an anti-corruption campaign initiated by the government; another was a dramatic restructuring of the command economy, including the breaking up of large state enterprises and privatization of some state property. The first component was, say many scholars and journalists, largely ineffective and perhaps even counterproductive. It was mainly, they say, a way for the new regime to consolidate its power base by targeting for prosecution those members of the previous regime it wanted to purge from its ranks.

But more important, even where a genuine attempt was made to root out mismanagement and malfeasance, it was based on the misguided notion that the problem of corruption was the behavior of a few bad individuals. The counterproductivity of the anti-corruption campaign, say its critics, lay in this: removing corrupt managers created the illusion that something was in fact being done about corruption and maintained the fiction that the problem was not inherent in the structural contradiction of a command economy operating under market forces. Thus the government made no effort to establish, for instance, effective independent watchdog agencies designed to monitor state enterprises and the bureaucracy in the future.

While the anti-corruption campaign led to no permanent changes in the way state enterprises and bureaucracies were run, the economic restructuring that accompanied it most certainly did. But that too was based on misguided assumptions, say critics, and inevitably perpetuated and worsened the economic crisis with a cure worse than the disease.

By the end of the 1970s, the incoming technocrats of the Algerian economy largely adhered to a school of thought once considered anathema to the revolution. Influenced by the free-market ideology that dominated the European and American management and graduate schools where they received their degrees, the new Algerian technocracy was determined to apply these new models back home. They were encouraged in this by the Benjedid administration, now fully purged of its Boumédienniste elements and composed largely of governmental, party and military functionaries who also favored the 1980s Anglo-American model of trickle-down economics, with privatization and export-driven development. In short, say observers, the Algerian bureaucratic state was being dismantled by the ruling quasi-capitalist class of technocrats that had been created and nurtured by it, but that now found it too restrictive to its own economic ambitions.

The early 1980s witnessed an explosive growth in imports, particularly of the luxury sort, and indulgence in blatant conspicuous consumption by a managerial class now free from the cultural restraints and austerity associated with the earlier, revolutionary period. As Tlemcani writes, "No longer [was] the Algerian bourgeoisie fearful and coy of showing off its material ostentation."[18] The increasingly conspicuous material gap between this class and the mass of the population was partially offset by the Algerian government's giving up its reluctance to borrow heavily on the international capital markets, expecting to be able to pay off the loans by ever-rising gas and oil prices. While much of the new debt went into luxury imports, some was used to maintain the payrolls of bloated state enterprises, no more efficient despite their breakup into small entities, and the subsidies on basic foodstuffs, education and health care.

When oil prices collapsed in the middle years of the decade, the new generation of technocrats, educated in many of the same institutions that IMF and World Bank officials had attended, readily adopted many of the prescriptions offered by these institutions, including a massive cut in subsidies, and would have gone further but for the growing public outrage expressed in rioting and elections. Nevertheless, governmental decision makers used the new crisis to further their economic reforms, now declaring the changes to be inevitable, necessary and in tune with the newest economic thinking. And while the bureaucracy made gestures toward public opinion, including taking cuts in salary, the better-situated were able to make up for these sacrifices through the perquisites of office. Property, including, for instance, houses, cars and country club memberships that belonged to the state were requisitioned for their exclusive personal use; state employees were assigned to garden their estates and clean their homes.

The political reforms of the late 1980s and the electoral crisis of the early 1990s only made the bureaucratic and managerial elite more determined to forward their reforms. In this effort, they were backed by the military, which demonstrated, in Black October, that it would brook no significant popular dissent. And while the military was forced to backpedal and accept the electoral reforms of 1989, it maintained its role as the final arbiter of power within the Algerian state and defender of last resort of the Algerian revolution, or what was left of it. Some observers have argued that the coup of January 1992 was carried out not so much to ward off a threat to Algeria's incipient democratic experiment but to prevent the discontinuation of Algeria's structural economic reforms.

In truth, the fundamentalists of the FIS never offered a systematic critique of the government's economic liberalization, and, if anything, seemed to embrace it. For the military junta to have believed that the economic reforms were endangered by the FIS would have required an almost total disregard or misreading on the military's part of the FIS' stated intentions. In fact, many critics believe the military leaders acted for more personal reasons, fearing that their dominance and that of the current class of technocrats to whom they were allied were being directly threatened. That is, the military and bureaucratic elite feared that the FIS would purge the existing leadership, much as the Benjedid regime had purged the Boumédiennists more than a decade earlier; except that the outsiders of the FIS could be expected to take this process further. After that, it would not be enough for the old elites simply to win the next elections, assuming there were any. They would need to build an entirely new political base in opposition to a newly entrenched bureaucracy of fundamentalists, their loyalists and their clients.

IDEOLOGY

Nationalism

From the early days of the revolution, the FLN leadership was guided by three principles: to build a "proud and independent" Algeria, free of foreign control and entanglements from West and East, though allied with other struggling and like-minded states in the Third World; to eschew the pluralism of Western-style bourgeois democracy and establish a single-party state guided by an all-inclusive revolutionary FLN; and to promote the essentially Islamic culture of Algeria while maintaining a firm separation of church and state. Of the three goals, only the first can be considered an unqualified success. Even the FIS rarely employs the kind of supranationalist Islamic political rhetoric familiar from Islamic movements elsewhere in the Middle East. Like the FLN, the FIS envisions a transformation of society within a strictly Algerian context.

The roots of secular nationalism in the Middle East, of which the FLN was among the most radical and determined variants, go back to the turn of the century. But Algeria and the Maghrib generally differed from the Arab east, where indigenous nationalist groups first formulated and pursued their goals within the context of the decaying Ottoman Empire. In the Arab west, the ruling empire was largely French (Libya was under Italian rule from 1911), and in Algeria included a European settler group that numbered about 10 percent of the population and owned the best lands and much of the industrial and commercial infrastructure. The existence of this population, and the fact that France had formally annexed Algeria, explains the ferocity with which France tried to hold onto its possessions there. It also explains much about subsequent FLN nationalism.

According to some scholars, the French presence in Algeria eliminated the tribal structures that persisted elsewhere, creating a more substantial foundation for Algerian nationalism, buttressed by the common experience of revolution, and obviating the need for the single powerful leader, or cult of personality, that emerged elsewhere in the postcolonial Arab world. Algeria had no need of a Nasser to provide a source of national unity and symbol of national identity. Instead, the FLN had the legacy of the revolution around which to build national identity and a small group of "historic [revolutionary] leaders" to develop national institutions.

Algerian economic modernization reflected the intense nationalism of the FLN and the Algerian people, and was made possible by the revenues earned from gas and oil. Direct foreign investment was limited to building "turnkey" facilities, which were turned over to Algerian ownership and management when they were completed and local personnel trained. In addition, during the first decade of independence, foreign-owned firms were gradually nationalized, culminating in the nationalization of the natural gas industry and 51 percent of the oil business, a move made in advance of most other Arab countries. The decision to nationalize the oil industry was aimed not only at gaining Algerian control, but also at creating a more competitive market for technology transfers and oil and gas sales. Instead of buying their equipment from and selling their oil and gas to France exclusively, the Algerians went into the international market. Finally, unlike Tunisia and Morocco, Algeria eschewed tourism. Algeria did not develop an infrastructure for mass European tourism, nor did it try to adjust currency rates to make it cheap for Europeans to go there.

Algeria's economic nationalism was matched by its anti-imperialist rhetoric, its studied neutrality during the Cold War, and its efforts to build a Third World coalition to redress economic and political imbalances between North and South. These policies were, of course, a predictable outcome of the Algerian revolution, but they also reflected the FLN's firm belief that Algeria represented a gateway between the Middle East and Europe, a Muslim-Arab nation with deep ties to France and Western Europe. Throughout the 1960s and 1970s, the Algerians also established close ties with revolutionary regimes such as Cuba and North Vietnam, as well as with other leaders of the Third World solidarity movement, such as Marshal Tito of Yugoslavia.

The only real blot on Algeria's foreign policy record has been repeated border disputes with Morocco, which led to several armed clashes in the 1960s, as well as the continuing dispute with Rabat over the status of the former Spanish colony of Western Sahara (annexed by Morocco in the late 1970s); Algeria's support of the Polisario independence movement), has partly prevented the achievement of an economic and political union of the

Maghribi states, a goal shared by all of them (Morocco, Algeria, Tunisia, Libya and Mauritania), at least rhetorically.

Algeria's neutrality in the Cold War also led it to avoid the kind of extreme anti-American rhetoric characteristic of other nationalist regimes of the Arab world. It was thus in a position to be instrumental in getting the Iranians to release the American Embassy hostages in Tehran in 1981. Its relations with the Soviet Union were lukewarm, resulting in part from the Soviets' coolness toward the Algerian revolution.[19]

Under the Benjedid liberalization, Algerian economic nationalism moderated. To cope with the shortfall in gas and oil revenues, the government has borrowed heavily in the international marketplace. Its foreign debt in 1994 was estimated at $26 billion. Meanwhile, Algiers has loosened restrictions on foreign ownership, allowing direct investment in certain sectors of the economy and repatriation of profits. As far as foreign policy is concerned, Algeria maintains its neutrality and has taken steps to resolve the crisis with Morocco in the Western Sahara, including cutting off much of its military and financial support for the Polisario guerrillas while pushing for elections to determine the territory's future sovereignty.

Corporatism

In 1959, Frantz Fanon, the internationally known theorist and ideologue of the Algerian revolution, wrote that what was happening in Algeria was a phenomenon rare in the postcolonial regions of the globe and unique in the Arab world. "While in many colonial countries it is the independence acquired by a party that progressively informs the diffused national consciousness of the people, in Algeria it is the national consciousness, the collective sufferings and terror [at the hands of the French] that make it inevitable that the people must take its destiny into its own hands."[20] But by winning the revolution against France and overcoming internal and external challenges during the Ben Bella years, the FLN became, in its own conception of things, the institutional manifestation of that destiny, "a willful construct," in Islamicist Rémy Leveau's words, "forcing destiny forward and imposing its will on it."[21]

The process by which the FLN took on this role began long before the Algerian revolution. Algerian national consciousness grew in stages during the final half-century of French rule, each stage moving the country further toward the ideal of a sovereign Algerian state. At each stage, new parties emerged, always proclaiming themselves the vanguard of Algerian nationalism and discounting the worth, credibility and even motives of the parties they were replacing. The FLN was the last, before independence, in this process of claiming national one-party leadership. The FLN's decisive role in the revolutionary struggle deepened and exaggerated these claims. The FLN had forced the French, who had tried and failed to find other legitimate and more moderate Muslim groups, to negotiate exclusively with it.

After the successful conclusion of the anticolonial struggle, the FLN went to war with itself. In order to establish itself as the sole party of the revolution, it had to purge its ranks of personnel and ideologies that threatened its unity, a process largely completed by the end of the second year of the Boumédienne regime. All political parties were then banned, including the Communists and those parties that had consolidated around former members of the FLN, such as Mohammed Boudiaf's Party of Socialist Revolution. The FLN, says historian Charles-Robert Ageron, had declared itself "the one and only party of progress" as early as 1963.[22]

At the same time, the FLN had eliminated virtually all of the competition for its role as mentor, leader and organizer of Algeria's transformation. It placed the self-management committees spontaneously organized by workers and peasants under its own bureaucratic control. In addition, by the early 1970s, the FLN had successfully incorporated or subordinated virtually all national organizations, including the national trade union confederation and peasant union, as well as the organizations representing women, youth and veterans. These organizations were then vertically integrated into the FLN party apparatus, with representatives from the groups both voicing their constituencies' interests at party congresses and funneling party mandates back to them. Even Algeria's intellectual establishment was subordinated to the party. "Lacking an [independent] intelligentsia," says Algerian sociologist Ali el-Kenz, "the state had intellectual servants . . . [and] bureaucrats."[23]

The FLN's vision of rule was based on the idea of corporatist representation. That is to say, the will of the people would be expressed through institutions that represented them in their primary social identities—as women, peasants, students and so on. Representatives of these institutions would be elected democratically by their constituents, but within limits established by the FLN. If the elected leaders challenged the FLN or its vision of Algeria's economic development, political participation or cultural identity, they would be eliminated by fiat from the party and replaced with others more amenable to party control. That is what happened when the trade union federation tried to establish more autonomy over strikes and other forms of labor activism in the 1960s. The party did likewise with the leaders of the youth federation in the early 1970s when they attempted to establish direct links to their counterparts among the peasant organizations—that is, when they attempted to create a horizontal political structure independent of the FLN.

The FLN leadership opted for this corporatist structure for several reasons. It believed that Algerian society had been severely handicapped economically by 130 years of French rule and needed to leap ahead in a short time. The FLN had been able to achieve national sovereignty through its united front during the war. Now it attempted to do the same thing for the political and economic structures of independent Algeria, an even more difficult task. Secondly, Algerians had not had the chance to develop independent political and cultural associations under French rule, and a sudden opening up of political and cultural life, according to the FLN, would lead to chaos, anarchy and extreme swings across the political spectrum. And finally, the unifying experience of the revolution had created the appropriate political *mentalité* and social context for one-party rule. Thus, the FLN leadership told itself, Algeria needed a vanguard party until economic development and political maturity had been achieved. According to Ramtane Lamamra, Algeria's ambassador to the UN, the FIS election victories of the early 1990s demonstrated that even after thirty years political maturity had not been achieved.

> A lot of people thought that change would not necessarily be for the better. But the lack of democratic culture and political sophistication led them to think that the most radical group would be the one most likely to get rid of the FLN and the system.[24]

Hence the belief, expressed by many members of the ruling circle, that the democratic process would have to be halted in favor of a more controlled experiment in political pluralism.

Critics of the government, both political and scholarly, cite less benign reasons for the establishment of the one-party state in Algeria. Tlemcani argues that the leaders of the FLN attached too much importance to the idea of national unity and viewed the struggle too much in terms of the noble Algerian versus the exploitative *colon*.

> This Manichean view of colonialism, very well articulated by Frantz Fanon, tended to obscure the very substantial socio-economic disparities among Algerians themselves . . . During the armed struggle (1954–1962), the FLN, in turn, ignored for political reasons, the existing social inequality that prevailed and greatly contributed to the legend that Algerian society was concretely classless.[25]

Lazreg cites another reason. Examining the FLN's approach to women, she argues that the party leadership saw in women a cause, rather than a force. It did "what western governments had done," she notes, "issuing liberal statements to declare universalistic principles that everybody has equal rights and that there shouldn't be any discrimination on the basis of sex, or creed, or race, or that sort of thing."[26] But what it failed to do, she says, was allow for the establishment of institutions that would have given women the opportunity to make their concerns felt in the corridors of power. Moreover, the government did not see in women a potential revolutionary cohort that could help it popularize and push forward their own specific agenda of gender equality, which FLN pronouncements claimed to support, as well as other revolutionary developments, such as democracy and economic modernization, that were of interest to the

Algerian nation as a whole. Other scholars have noted similar failings in regard to other sectors of the Algerian nation.

Ironically, whatever the reasons for the decision to establish a one-party state, the very institution that was supposed to be the heart of the system, the FLN, has gradually had its role and power circumscribed. "Though the party's ranks swelled during the Boumédienne years—to around 300,000 regular members by the late 1970s," writes Ruedy,

> it had become a bureaucratized symbol of revolution whose main function was to recruit and indoctrinate members. It was emphatically not an agitational party. It had lost its militancy and had been completely subordinated to the uses of the military, administrative, or technocratic elites.[27]

Under the Benjedid administration, the process of subordinating the FLN to the needs and demands of the elite cadres who really ran Algeria, and separating the party from national decision making, was largely completed. When popular pressure forced the government to accept multiparty democracy and elections in 1989, the pretense of the FLN as the vanguard of the revolution was dropped. The 1989 constitution failed to even mention the party by name.

In a sense the damage had already been done. The promotion of the FLN as the single institutional framework for popular participation in the revolution had led the government to eliminate rival political parties and to subject to its rule virtually every associative body in the country. But this revolutionary form of democracy was increasingly a sham. Real decision making was elsewhere and real democratic input into the decision-making process had been eliminated, long before the riots of 1988 made it obvious that Algerians no longer believed in the fiction of a revolutionary vanguard party. Unlike other Third World revolutions, like China or Cuba's, in which authoritarianism and elitism were at least somewhat ameliorated by a popular form of democracy at the local level (revolutionary committees whose function was to act as watchdogs over the local functionaries of the institutions of the state), Algeria had no such countervailing institutions. From the very beginning, with the takeover of the *autogestion* committees, the FLN/state bureaucracy had established centralized control over virtually all public institutions.

Thus, the sudden surge of oppositional associations made possible by the constitutional reforms of 1989 came as a shock to many of Algeria's intellectuals, who assumed that associative life had been destroyed by the FLN in its nearly thirty years of monopolistic control of public life. Equally, the leaders of the government were overwhelmed by the extent of opposition, believing that despite all that had happened, the FLN, in its new guise as a political party within a pluralistic democracy, still represented the will of the Algerian people. The election results proved them wrong. Instead, the vast majority of the electorate, if not of the population, turned to an institution and a political force that had long resisted FLN efforts to control it: Islam and fundamentalism.

Secularism

Journalists and other nonscholarly observers of the Arab world often oversimplify the relationship between religion and politics in Islamic societies. Indeed, the very structure of this book follows that pattern, that is, seeing the state as a secular force pitted against religious opponents. As noted above in Chapter 3, Islamism and fundamentalism are not purely archaic attempts at resurrecting a lost order. Similarly, the so-called secular governments of the Middle East have never attempted to extirpate Islamic principles in their pursuit of modernization. There are no purely secularist regimes, and Algeria's, though often cited as among the most radical and secular of Arab governments, is no exception.

In his work on contemporary Arab societies, Arabist Halim Barakat has listed three ways that governments in the Middle East have attempted to use religion: as a mechanism of social control, instigation and reconciliation. Of the three, Algeria's has most often employed the second. During the revolution, of course, the FLN strongly appealed to Algerian Muslims on the basis of a common cultural and religious heritage and way of life. At one level, this appeal made simple political sense given the heavy-handed way France and the *colons* tried to impose their European/Christian culture on Muslim Algerians. At another level, however, it represented a genuine commitment by much of the FLN leadership to find a way to harness Islamic ideals to their modernist and nationalist goals. This commitment was not universal. There were Marxists and radical nationalists, like Frantz Fanon, who believed that the revolution should and did propel Algerians toward a socialist ideal in which humanist values would prevail over Islamic ones. But there was also, says Algerian scholar Aïssa Khelladi, a "religious lobby which favoured the evolution of the movement and operated quietly within the FLN and the regime" from the beginning.[28]

The struggle between these two points of view lasted well into the post-independence era. "The problem of defining Algeria's identity within the framework of Islamism, Arabism, and Algerianism," says Ruedy, "was made all the more difficult by cultural disjuncture between the national political leadership and the rural or recently urbanized masses." In short, virtually all of the leadership and functionaries of the government were secularized by their French education and radicalized by the revolution. The former shaped their ideas on the separation of church and state; the latter led them to conceptualize and put forward programs and rhetoric based on class conflict; the two together "jarred Islamists, for whom the ideal community is one of brothers."[29] Ruedy may have exaggerated the degree to which the FLN promoted the idea of class conflict. Many scholars say that, if anything, its refusal to acknowledge class differences undid the potential radicalism inherent in *autogestion*.

In either case, the Boumédienne regime tried to find a middle ground, formulating a brand of socialism that it said was based on Islamic precepts while, at the same, trying to promote a version of official Islam that was compatible with the government's socialist ideals. In this balancing act, however, it is clear that when the government (and the personally devout Boumédienne) saw a conflict between promoting Islam and promoting their modernist agenda, they usually chose the latter. Rhetorically, however, the clash produced an ungainly and unsatisfactory compromise known as "Islamic socialism." According to Burgat, "an aseptic socialism—with all the mention of class struggle stripped away—receive[d] the guarantee of an Islam whose egalitarian vocation was emphasized."[30]

In seeking the happy compromise, however, the regime produced a decidedly unhappy vacuum. Sociologists since Emile Durkheim have written of the anomie at the core of modern and secular Western civilization, and the search for oneness that leads to a religious identity and faith so seemingly at odds with the rationalist values of twentieth-century civilization. As Barakat writes, modernization and secularization have been especially unsettling in some parts of the Arab world, where the process has occurred over decades rather than centuries, replacing a nearly universal, all-encompassing religio-cultural identity.

> The return of individuals and society at large to religion and authenticity seems to provide a compelling alternative sense of coherence, unity, certainty and inner strength. By choosing the sacred and universal, believers insert themselves into a predictable divine order and develop a sense of oneness.[31]

The FLN tried, in part, to create that "oneness" out of Algerians' collective experience of revolution and nation-building. It used a revolutionary rhetoric and built a network of institutions to reinforce this end. Whether a secular experience like revolution can ever match the power of religion is not really the issue here, since the rhetoric seemed increasingly hollow in the presence of gross social and economic disparities between the well-connected and the *mahgour*, and the state institutions had become obvious mockeries of democratic participation. When the various economic and social crises produced by rapid modernization and urbanization hit Algeria in the mid-1970s, people searched for faith and oneness in unsullied Islamic institutions (i.e., the free mosques) that spoke to them in a language pro-fundamentalists have called "authentic," opponents have labeled nostalgic, and all agree is effective.

There was nothing the FLN could do but Islamicize itself and Algeria. This does not mean that the religious stirrings of the late 1970s and early 1980s immediately threatened the party's hold on power. The FLN's choice was forced by its own sense of identity, the situation it had created and self-interest. First, the FLN viewed itself as the neutral vehicle of the people's will. If that will was demonstrably in favor of extending religion deeper into society, then the FLN felt it had a duty to do so. Second, if the party was to get on with the task of modernizing and developing Algeria's economy, and the revolution didn't provide the appropriate national will, it was willing to try Islam. And finally, the leaders of the FLN were genuinely worried about the growing power and popularity of the fundamentalist movement and hoped that by giving in on those issues dearest to the movement's heart, such as the Family Code, they could palliate it.

The policy proved insufficient, and not just because it was too little, too late. Rather, it ignored the history of the FLN's relationship with religious institutions, a history that had poisoned the well of goodwill. From the very beginning of the Algerian Republic's history, the government had tried to control the religious establishment and religious institutions. In doing so, it had compromised the official religion by forcing upon it an unseemly servility to the state. When the state failed to deliver the goods, so, it seemed, did official Islam. Radical Islamists took the equation one step further. They accused official Islam of compromising with modernism, socialism, secularism and all the other "isms" foisted onto Algeria by the West and its lackeys, the FLN.

At first, the government had seen in the rise of political Islam a potential ally in its struggle with Marxist students, a new political force that did not threaten the socioeconomic bases of the revolution or the elite's positions. But, as Tunisian sociologist Abdelbaki Hermassi notes, they were gravely mistaken in encouraging political Islam

> "as a counterweight to the leftist parties the establishments were trying to weaken, to get under control, or re-integrate into the political process. Islamist protest became dangerous at the point where its hostility ceased being directed against individuals and groups accused of deviating from Islamic norms and began targeting official Islam and the state itself. This was at a time (in the 1970s) when the state was becoming more vulnerable and was exhibiting signs of ideological fatigue and socio-economic bankruptcy.[32]

Some scholars argue that the surge of Islamic politics has had positive effects on the FLN. The pro-Islamist Burgat believes that it has forced the left "to deal with tradition so that the Islamists do not monopolize it completely."[33] Hermassi points out that it has led Maghribi governments in general and Algeria's in particular to confront systematically for the first time the issue of religion and state, and not attempt to deflect them with artificial compromises like "Islamic socialism." "It has in fact been the political advance of Islamism," he writes, "that has forced a public debate," though he wonders whether "the Maghribi intelligentsia today is sufficiently equipped to elaborate a theory of secularization appropriate to a Muslim milieu.[34]"

THE DEMOCRATIC OPPOSITION

Before the FLN embarked upon its economic modernization program for Algeria, it had to secure its political base. This entailed outlawing opposition parties of all political stripes and bureaucratizing into powerlessness the popular organizations of *autogestion*, a process that was largely completed by the mid-1960s. True, a number of liberal women and female veterans of the revolution, for example, organized to oppose the family codes of the early 1980s, but they were overwhelmed by government intransigence and a feeling that the vast majority of Algerians supported the more restrictive laws on women. On university campuses, left-wing students organized against the conservative direction taken by the government in the early 1980s, but they too were defeated by the government and Islamist groups, who soon seized control of the student movement. Several human rights organizations, sanctioned by, though independent of, the FLN, were denouncing government abuses as early as the mid-1980s. In addition, there were a number of revolution-era leaders like Ben Bella, Boudiaf and Ait Ahmed who led "minuscule opposition parties" from exile.

From the top, there were some slight openings, beginning with the new National Charter of 1976. For the first time since the early 1960s, the country experienced a serious and wide-ranging public debate about the direction of Algerian society. The government allowed people to discuss the charter and vote against it, but not campaign for its defeat; it overwhelmingly passed a national referendum largely as originally written. Then in the mid-1980s, Benjedid legalized political associations, though not parties, outside the purview of the FLN. But by and large, political life "had shrunk over the years," says Lazreg, "to the FLN . . . There was nothing else beyond the state, and that was the doing of the FLN." And that, she adds, is what made the "explosion of associations and associative life after 1988 so amazing."[35]

Indeed, no fewer than fifty-six parties were recognized by the government after legalization in 1989. But, as political scientist William Zartman notes, other than the Berber-based parties, "the largest number of third parties [i.e., non-Islamic, nongovernment] were salon parties, gathering together a living room full of the friends and family of the founder but unable to reach further." The reason for this is that most represented educated middle-class liberals with few interests in common with the masses of Algerian voters. "Many of the salon parties were made of *progressistes*," he adds, "and were more of a symbol of the regime's liberalism [before legalization] than of a leftist trend in the electorate."[36]

Nevertheless, other civic organizations, with constituencies among women, intellectuals and human rights activists, blossomed in the wake of political party legalization, hoping that they could use the new political parties to further their specific agendas. This proved an unsuccessful strategy. Like the FLN, the smaller democratic parties were swept aside in the FIS election victories at the municipal and national levels. None of these small parties won a single seat in the first round of the 1991 parliamentary elections, though three independent candidates succeeded. But clearly, the startling strength and victories of the FIS mobilized the democratic opposition. In the weeks leading up to the municipal elections in June 1989, democratic rallies in Algiers drew tens of thousands. Still, says Burgat, these groups were "failing to really open a 'second front' against the Islamists."[37]

The state of the democratic opposition can be judged by the fact that when the military launched its coup and canceled the elections in January 1992, many so-called democrats secretly and not so secretly expressed approval of this very undemocratic act. The relief, however, was mixed with worry. "While both the democratic opposition and the FLN power structure had reason to fear fundamentalist accession to power," notes Ruedy, "they were almost equally fearful of the military's new self-assertion."[38]

Part of the weakness of the democratic opposition is the lack of nationwide institutions and parties that was the consequence of the FLN's longtime policy of single-party politics. Independent national leaders could never emerge. The only potential democratic candidates were either sullied by their association with the FLN or had been rendered irrelevant by years in exile. Nor had political parties, other than the mosque-based FIS, been given a chance to build the institutional infrastructure necessary in such a geographically large country, in which the government continued to control the electronic media. Apart from the FIS and the FLN, there was only one political organization or movement on a national scale: that of the Berbers.

THE BERBERS

HISTORY

The vast majority of Algerians are descended from the original Berber tribes that had occupied the region from prehistoric times.[39] The present-day distinction between Arabs and Berbers is ethnic, that is, linguistic and cultural, and dates from the eighth century A.D. After the Arabs conquered Algeria at that time, the majority of flatland Berbers gradually adopted Islam, Arabic and much of Arab culture. Those in more isolated mountainous regions, particularly in the Grand and Petit Kabyle of central Algeria, converted to Islam, but retained their native tongue and culture. Today's Berbers number between 20 and 25 percent of the population.

Modern Berber history begins with the French occupation. Like other nineteenth-century Europeans of the upper and middle classes—that is, the "political" classes—French imperialists were taken with the power of racial theory and its offshoot, Social Darwinism, to provide a "scientific" and sociological justification for their own conquest and rule. In Algeria, these distinctions took two forms: the familiar elevation of European over non-European, and the superiority of the so-called Berber "race," which some

French sociologists even argued was descended from European (even Gallic) stock, over the Arab. This was the "Kabyle myth." Among the components of the myth were an ancient blood feud between the two peoples and the remnant of a potentially revivable pre-Islamic (i.e., Christian) culture. There was, of course, no physical evidence or historical basis for any of these notions or theories. As with so much nineteenth-century anthropology, biology and social theory, cultural assumptions and political interests, unacknowledged or unrecognized, influenced the course of scientific thought. And scientific thought in turn provided the basis for state political, cultural and economic policy.

While the French made a point of dismantling Islamic institutions throughout Algeria, they made a special effort in the Kabyle. French policy followed two tracks: the resurrection of ancient Berber laws and institutions; and the Gallicization of education. In 1898, the Berbers and Arabs were placed under separate administrations "so that the two peoples should not become used to contact with each other."[40] The aim was classic imperial strategy: to fashion a minority in the conqueror's image and use it as a tool for controlling the majority population. But as Ruedy points out, the policy was largely ineffective, and the French themselves were to blame.

> Attempts at evangelization were largely a failure . . . the number of berbero-phones was actually declining and . . . knowledge of Algerian Arabic was spreading rapidly. This phenomenon was the unexpected outcome of political and economic integration forced by colonialism. Wherever French railways and highways went, there also went dialectical Arabic as the principal language of commercial and intercommunal discourse.[41]

Only among a narrow minority at the top was French policy successful. Thus the legacy of the French Kabyle policy amounted to a high percentage of Berber trilingualists and a decided hostility among Berber elites toward their Arab counterparts. The full extent of their failure came home to the French only during the revolution. While there were substantial differences between Arab and Berber leaders of the insurrection, their common hatred of the French (and FLN discipline) kept those differences from dividing the nationalist movement. Indeed, says historian Alistair Horne, the internal disputes didn't even show up in the files of French intelligence agencies.

After the revolution, however, divisions between Berber and Arab leaders emerged into the open. Fearing Ben Bella's growing power, Hocine Ait Ahmed, a Berber FLN leader, began to organize a guerrilla movement to challenge the government from the mountains of Kabyle. Labeling Ben Bella's government "fascist," Ait Ahmed organized the Socialist Forces Front (FFS) as "a more authentic movement," but the differences between the FLN and the FFS eluded most Berbers and the movement fizzled.[42]

ECONOMIC GRIEVANCES

Nevertheless, economic and cultural grievances among the Berber population remained. The Kabyle people believe they have been shortchanged by
the government's economic modernization program, an assertion that,
superficially at least, seems at odds with reality. Rural Kabyle is no poorer
than other parts of the Algerian countryside and the regional capital, Tizi
Ouzou, is, by Algerian standards, a thriving place. But beneath these
superficial similarities, troubling differences remain. As Lazreg writes, part
of the problem resulted from the "unintended consequences of the modernization process, which either marginalizes minority groups or introduces
a new institution, the state, which each group seeks to control."[43] However,
she adds, the Berbers present a variation of this model, in which ethnic
nationalism results less from marginalization than from relative affluence,
itself a direct result of the colonial legacy.

Specifically, more Berbers continued to speak French and so more
Berbers immigrated to France for work. According to Lazreg, this raised
expectations among those Berbers who returned to the Kabyle and meas-
ured governmental economic efforts there against the vastly superior
facilities of France. When government spending fell as a result of the decline
in oil revenues, the Berbers read this in terms of ethnicity, that is, as a direct
affront to Kabyle people. In addition, she points out, Berbers have done
well politically, reaching high-level positions in many state enterprises and
bureaucratic agencies. There they have created fiefdoms where jobs are
made available to Berbers only. This increased the sense of tribal identity
among Berbers, who viewed typical internal politics within the bureaucracy
in cultural terms.

LANGUAGE AND CULTURE

Still, economic grievances among Berbers are secondary; the primary issues
around which the Kabyle people have organized, demonstrated and voted are
cultural, or more specifically, linguistic. From the time the early twentieth-century Algerian nationalists rallied to the cry "Islam is my religion; Arabic is my
language; Algeria is my fatherland," Arabization has been an integral part of
Algerian nation-building. Since independence, however, the Algerian government has been caught on the horns of several dilemmas. First, Arabization
implied de-Gallicization; but this goal contradicted the government's modernization effort. Technology and training required access to languages of the
West, and French was the obvious, most logical choice for Algerians. Second,
Arabization in the Algerian context (in contrast to the Arab east where the issue
is more neutral) has always been politically linked to Islamization, a goal the
government has been reluctant to pursue.

Nevertheless, the nationalist government was ideologically and economically bound to promote Arabic. French was associated with colonial

privilege, and no populist politician dared to admit the awful truth: that knowledge of French was one of the primary economic advantages of the elite, a barrier separating them from the masses in post-independence Algeria. In addition, if Algeria were to be a unified nation, it needed a single language. Thus the huge expansion of primary and secondary education that followed in the wake of the revolution was largely in Arabic. Needless to say, this infuriated and alienated the berberophones of Kabyle. "Kabyles saw the Arabization campaign as a threat to their culture," says Ruedy, "a negation of the rights they had earned by their wartime sacrifices, and an ill-disguised attempt by Arabs to impose themselves culturally and politically on their region."[44] As an Algiers-based Kabyle poet told travel writer Robert Fox, "I am not an Arab, but I am Algerian. Why should I have to submit to one form of cultural imperialism when we've only just got rid of another?"[45]

When arabophone students at the University of Algiers demonstrated during the 1979–80 academic year against the privileges afforded to francophone students, and then were joined by Islamist groups, the government moved quickly to defuse the dangerous situation. It pushed forward its Arabization campaign in the universities, Arabized the justice system overnight, and unintentionally set off a predictable protest among Kabyles. Not only did the Kabyles see Arabization as "suffocating" their culture, they also worried that the failure to promote French in schools would cut off one of their most lucrative forms of employment: temporary immigration to France. Berbers wanted Berber-language education in all Kabyle schools, and more media programming in Berber, since newscasts had always been in Arabic only and sportscasts were exclusively Arabic since the early 1970s.

The uprising in Tizi Ouzou in the spring of 1980 was sparked both by the government's cultural policies and by the economic squeeze being felt throughout Algeria. The government's response, a police crackdown and superficial concessions, did little to placate Kabyles who continued to commemorate the uprising annually through the 1980s in demonstrations that often turned violent when security forces were sent in. Thus, economic grievances became increasingly fused with cultural ones both in the Kabyle and among Berbers nationwide. The rise of fundamentalism in the 1980s further aggravated the situation.

BERBERS VERSUS FUNDAMENTALISTS

Like mountain and tribal peoples throughout the Middle East, such as the Kurds of the Arab east, the Berbers are generally not as religiously orthodox as their Arab neighbors. That is not to say they are less religious; rather, the inaccessibility of their homeland has made it difficult for Islamic institutions to operate. Where institutions are scarcer, religious ritual and practice often wane or take unorthodox forms. Fundamentalism, which aims at returning Islam to its "authentic" roots and which has displayed an intense hostility to the *maraboutist* practices that are especially popular in rural Kabyle, is thus anathema to most Berbers.

In more recent times, government efforts to Islamicize the state, thereby placating fundamentalists, have produced a reaction among Berbers who see the religious policy as yet a further indication of the state's desire to push Arabization, this time in an Islamic guise. Moreover, Berbers have generally been more leftist in their political affiliations and ideology. In the years leading up to the insurrection against the French, Berbers were more likely to vent their nationalist aspirations within the confines of the French and later the Algerian branch of the Communist Party. Since the revolution, their leaders have often voiced more radical economic positions than the mainstream of the FLN. Not surprisingly, many of the early university clashes between fundamentalists and leftists also represent the Arab-Berber split in the student body. Some Berber leaders even claim that the government has secretly tried to pit fundamentalists against Berberists. For their part, the fundamentalists see Berber resistance to their agenda as un-Islamic. In their quest for the unity of the Islamic *umma*, they see Berber assertions of cultural distinctiveness as an affront to God. Thus, they tend either to refuse to acknowledge the Berber issue as significant or to regard it as a threat.

The rise of fundamentalism and the opening up of the political system in the late 1980s produced a surge of Berber political activity. When popular protest was allowed to express itself in populist politics, it ironically took two forms that the secularist, modernizing FLN leaders had long considered atavistic and counterproductive: fundamentalism and Berber nationalism. But while fundamentalism demonstrated its remarkable capacity for organizing and activating the masses, Kabyle nationalism was largely an affair of Berber elites. According to Tlemcani, the masses of Berbers want radical economic change along with cultural autonomy, but leaders of the movement, largely middle-class businessmen or bureaucrats, want to divorce the two. Thus, in order to divert attention from pressing economic concerns, the Kabyle leadership has promoted a party of cultural nationalism, the Rally for Culture and Democracy (RCD), which one Algerian scholar called "a racist and fascist Kabyle-based group" with little appeal to Arab Algerians.[46]

This kind of Berber politics has produced a rather predictable outcome. Before the elections of 1990 and 1991, there was very little mass organizing or demonstrating by Berbers outside the context of democratic opposition politics. On the other hand, Berber nationalist parties, both the left-wing FFS and right-wing RCD, did moderately well in the parliamentary elections of December 1991.[47] Unlike nonfundamentalist Arab voters, Berbers who didn't want to vote for the ruling FLN had electoral options. The FFS received approximately 4 percent of the national vote and the RCD about 1.5. But because the Berber constituency was largely concentrated in the Kabyle districts, the FFS won 25, about 11 percent, of the seats decided in the first round.

OUTSIDE POWERS

FRANCE (AND THE EUROPEAN UNION)

To French men and women above fifty years of age, it might seem like the nightmare is back. War in Algeria has returned to the streets, metros and airways of France. The most spectacular incident involved the hijacking of an Air France jet in December 1994, allegedly by members of the GIA, who killed several passengers and planned to blow the jet up over Paris before being killed in an ambush by French paratroopers on the tarmac at the Marseilles airport. The next day the front page of Paris's *Le Monde* read "The Algerian War Has Crossed the Mediterranean."[48] The French government immediately cut off all direct flights to Algiers.

The paper's declaration proved accurate. Several bombings in the Paris metro, as well as an attempt on France's high-speed train, the TGV, claimed over ten lives in the first eight months of 1995. In response, the French police and the Interior Ministry stepped up arrests and random street searches in neighborhoods around the country where almost two million Algerians live and work. While another metro bomb went off in October and threats from the GIA continue, the security measures appear to be working as the terrorist attacks tailed off in 1996.

The crackdown naturally angers the emigrés. "The fundamentalist phenomenon in Algeria is a sociopolitical movement, so it has to have an echo among some Algerians here," said Djeloul Siddiki, a French-Algerian sociologist who works for Paris' largest mosque. "But I would say 95 percent of the Algerians living here want to live in peace and are very unlikely to be seduced by a militant fundamentalist call for any kind of action." At the same time, France has also closed all of its consulates in Algeria and is issuing visas to less than 1 percent of Algerians who apply, a policy that ironically hits the fundamentalists' opponents hardest. Algerian emigré critics argue that France has a special obligation to Algerian dissidents. "How can they talk about defending freedom and liberty if they fail to protect the most basic human right like staying alive?" asked an anonymous Algerian scientist.[49]

After the Algerian military coup of January 1992, the French government of François Mitterrand largely supported the government with intelligence, money, weaponry and international recognition. Fearful of antagonizing the anti-immigrant right, the French Socialists believed that the Algerian military was the only institution that stood between France and a massive influx of Algerian refugees fleeing a fundamentalist government in their country. But by early 1995, French authorities were beginning to hedge their bets. Some did so because they believed that the Algerian government was acting in an obstructionist manner, especially considering its out-of-hand rejection of the reconciliation platform offered to the military regime by a coalition of virtually all religious and secular opposition parties meeting in Rome. Others felt that the Algerian military had no solution to the crisis other than increased repression and violence. Increasingly, the Mitterrand government began to consider the possibility of an Islamist victory and its potential hostility to a French government that had supported the military up to the bitter end.

There was good reason for concern. FIS spokespersons continually reiterate a profound hostility toward Paris, which they believe still pulls the strings in Algiers. While FIS leaders profess what seems like a sincere effort to be conciliatory toward other Western powers, this approach is rarely extended to France. Thus, the more extreme elements of the Algerian religious opposition have made France a special target of their vengeance. Recognizing the dilemma and reaching the end of his 14 years in office, Mitterrand took a chance of offending Algiers by proposing a European Union–sponsored peace conference on Algeria. The reaction of the conservative-dominated cabinet of Premier Edouard Balladur was mixed. Interior Minister Charles Pasqua rejected the plan outright while Foreign Secretary Alain Juppé expressed cautious approval.

While Algiers' response was predictable and stern—it immediately recalled its ambassador from Paris—the European Union agreed to the proposal to base the conference on the Rome Platform outlined by the Algerian opposition in January (see Chapter 5, "Issues, Tactics and Negotiations"), though the conference has yet to be held. A basic division between France and Germany concerning European Union financial support may be holding it up. Germany wants a continuing emphasis on Eastern Europe, and France wants more money for North Africa. Other European countries, especially Spain and Italy, also have an interest in Algeria. Though their economic investment is significantly smaller than France's, both Italy and Spain are connected to Algeria by natural gas pipelines under the Mediterranean, and they, of course, have none of France's historical baggage there. On the other hand, foreigners of all nationalities are being killed under orders from Islamic militants in Algeria, including oil and gas workers from Italy and other European countries, and a gas pipeline was bombed in July 1995.

Meanwhile, other than the intensified crackdown on Algerians in France, it is unclear what the conservative government of President Jacques Chirac, which took power in August 1995, will do about the Algerian situation. But its response, says Algerian sociologist Marnia Lazreg, will be crucial.

The future resolution to the conflict depends in a way on whether Chirac's government will continue to support the Algerian government. It's important because the rest of the West is following France's lead, and the external debt has made the Algerian government bankrupt economically. If Chirac's government doesn't support the eradication policy [of Algiers against the fundamentalists] then the government might have to concede. But I doubt the Chirac government will do that. The Mitterrand government was racist and didn't want a wave of refugees, and Chirac's is even worse on this score.[50]

THE UNITED STATES

The United States is not the "great satan" of Algerian fundamentalists, as it was for the Islamists of Iran in the 1970s and 1980s. France is the opponent upon whom the fundamentalists focus their concerns about Western control and support for the existing government. The United States is not seen as a major supporter of the Algerian junta and, in fact, the Clinton administration has tried to occupy a middle ground between the fundamentalists and the government. While authorizing agricultural credits and supporting loan restructuring plans between the IMF and the military regime, the Clinton administration has also made its concerns about human rights abuses known to Algiers.

While Algiers has been muted in its response to Washington, for fear of jeopardizing its relations with the IMF and American banks, France has been an outspoken critic of United States policy in Algeria. Paris has not forgotten American policy of the 1950s and 1960s, when it openly broke with France's military approach to the Algerian rebellion. Now, it sees the United States doing the same again. Moreover, France believes the United States is being extremely naive about the effectiveness of working with so-called Islamist moderates. "Hindsight suggests that the French think the United States is naive about 'moderate' Islam, just as the Reaganites thought the French were naive about 'moderate' leftists in Central America," writes journalist Charles Lane.

> The French may have realism on their side in both cases—in the ironic sense that the threat of communism essentially died out when the Soviet Union collapsed, whereas Islamic rebellion belongs to every historical epoch, pre- and post-cold war.[51]

Despite the Iranian debacle and the influential though widely disputed argument of the American political scientist Samuel P. Huntington that future world conflicts will involve clashes of civilizations (e.g., Christian versus Muslim) rather than ideologies, the Clinton administration has avoided an anti-Islamist approach generally, with Algeria being the test case. "The American quarrel with Iran should not be misconstrued as a clash of civilizations," national security advisor Anthony Lake wrote in March 1994.

Washington does not take issue with the Islamic dimension of the Islamic Republic of Iran . . . America has a deep respect for the religion and culture of Islam. It is extremism, whether religious or secular, that we oppose.[52]

In fact, the policy is not new. Like the conservative Saudi regime, the United States viewed the surge of Iranian-style Islamist politics as a direct threat to its interests in the 1980s. Thus, not only did the United States try to support so-called Iranian moderates, it also worked with the Saudis in establishing the World Muslim League, which aimed at propagandizing and organizing conservative fundamentalism throughout the Sunni Muslim world, as a kind of preventive vaccine against the more revolutionary and anti-Western Iranian variety of Islamic politics. While it would be overstating the case to say that the FIS is entirely the result of this policy, especially since it broke away from its Saudi benefactors over the 1991 Gulf War and the events preceding it, the fundamentalists of Algeria are, at least in part, America's stepchildren in the Islamic world.

Thus far the United States has been saved from the GIA's assaults on foreigners. While this may have something to do with the Clinton administration's studied neutrality, it may also be a legacy of American Cold War policy. In Algeria, GIA militants are known as "Afghanis" because they are veterans of the Mujahadeen struggle against the former Soviet Union there in the 1980s, a struggle largely funded by the United States. The GIA's hesitancy to go after American targets in Algeria may reflect an unspoken agreement on the part of its leaders to abstain from biting the hand that once fed them.

NOTES

[1] Hourani, Albert, *A History of the Arab Peoples*, New York: Warner Books, 1991, pp. 447–8.

[2] Mouffouk, Ghania, "La *hogra*" in Reporters sans frontières, *Le drame algérien: Un peuple en otage*, Paris: Éditions la Découverte, 1994, pp. 30–1.

[3] Ottaway, David and Marina, *Algeria: The Politics of a Socialist Revolution*, Berkeley: University of California Press, 1970, p. 5.

[4] *Ibid.*, pp. 6–7.

[5] *Ibid.*, p. 7.

[6] Ruedy, John, *Modern Algeria: The Origins and Development of a Nation*, Bloomington: Indiana University Press, p. 204.

[7] *Ibid.*, p. 208.

[8] Zartman, I. William, "The Challenge of Democratic Alternatives in the Magrib" in Ruedy, John (ed), *Islamism and Secularism in North Africa*, New York: St. Martin's Press, 1994, p. 209.

[9] Richards, Alan, and Waterbury, John, *A Political Economy of the Middle East: State, Class, and Economic Development*, Boulder, Colo.: Westview Press, 1990, p. 332.

[10] Tlemcani, Rachid, *State and Revolution in Algeria*, Boulder, Colo.: Westview Press, 1986, p. 64.

[11] Entelis, John, *Algeria: The Revolution Institutionalized*, Boulder, Colo.: Westview Press, 1986, p. 208.

[12] Richards and Waterbury, *Political Economy of the Middle East*, p. 401.

[13] Tlemcani, *State and Revolution*, p. 6.

[14] Lazreg, Marnia, "Bureaucracy and Class: The Algerian Case Dialectic" in *Dialectic Anthropology*, vol. 4, 1976, p. 295.

[15] Tlemcani, *State and Revolution*, p. 10.

[16] *Ibid.*, p. 10.

[17] *Ibid.*, p. 158.

[18] *Ibid.*

[19] The Soviets generally supported France, hoping that by bolstering Paris, they might pull the anti-NATO de Gaulle closer to Moscow.

[20] Fanon, Frantz, *A Dying Colonialism*, New York: Grove Press, 1965, p. 28.

[21] Leveau, Rémy, *Le sabre et le turban: L'avenir du Maghrib*, Paris: François Bourin, 1993, pp. 128–9.

[22] Ageron, Charles-Robert, *Modern Algeria: A History from 1830 to the Present*, Trenton, N.J.: Africa World Press, 1991, p. 132.

[23] El-Kenz, Ali, Algerian *Reflections on Arab Crises*, Austin, Tex.: Center for Middle Eastern Studies, 1991, p. 25.

[24] Lamamra, Ramtane, interview with author, June 23, 1995.

[25] Tlemcani, *State and Revolution*, p. 45.

[26] Lazreg, Marnia, interview with author, June 1, 1995.

[27] Ruedy, *Modern Algeria*, p. 208.

[28] Khelladi, Aïssa, "Les islamistes algérien à l'assaut du pouvoir" in *Les Temps Modernes*, January/February 1995, p. 139.

[29] Ruedy, *Modern Algeria*, p. 224.

[30] Burgat, François and Dowell, William, *The Islamic Movement in North Africa*, Austin, Tex.: Center for Middle Eastern Studies at the University of Texas, 1993, p. 250.

[31] Barakat, Halim, *The Arab World: Society, Culture, and State*, Berkeley: University of California Press, 1993, p. 144.

[32] Ruedy, *Islamism and Secularism*, p. 94.

[33] Burgat, *Islamic Movement*, p. 83.

[34] Ruedy, *Islamism and Secularism*, p. 98.

[35] Lazreg, interview.

[36] Zartman, *Islamism and Secularism*, pp. 212–3.

[37] Burgat, *Islamic Movement*, p. 277.

[38] Ruedy, *Modern Algeria*, p. 256.

[39] The word *Berber* is of Greek origin and means barbarian; the Berbers lived outside the limits of Greek coastal civilization. The word was adopted by the Romans, Arabs and Europeans in turn. The Berbers call themselves the *Imazighen*, or "free and noble men."

[40]   Cited in Ageron, *Modern Algeria: A History*, p. 73.

[41]   Ruedy, *Modern Algeria*, p. 92.

[42]   Ruedy, *Modern Algeria*, pp. 201–02.

[43]   Lazreg, Marnia, "The Kabyle-Berber Cultural Movement in Algeria" in Schwab, Peter and Pollis, Adamantia (eds.), *Toward A Human Rights Framework*, New York: Praeger, 1982, p. 233.

[44]   Ruedy, *Modern Algeria*, p. 225.

[45]   Fox, Robert, *The Inner Sea: The Mediterranean and Its People*, New York: Alfred A. Knopf, 1993, p. 330.

[46]   Anonymous, interview with author, June 3, 1995.

[47]   The FFS boycotted the municipal elections of 1990, believing that the FLN had gerrymandered districts in its favor; only 24 percent of the electorate in the Kabyle went to the polls and voted largely for the RCD.

[48]   Le Monde, December 24, 1994, p. 1.

[49]   New York Times, September 7, 1995, p. A3.

[50]   Lazreg, interview.

[51]   New Republic, February 27, 1995, p. 12.

[52]   Foreign Affairs, March 1994, p. 9.

5

ISSUES, TACTICS AND NEGOTIATIONS

*The suspension of these [1991] elections . . . was to
ensure a genuine and irreversible democratic process.*
— Noureddine Yazid Zerhouni, Algerian
Ambassador to the United States

*The FIS [Islamic Salvation Front], which has at least
shown some honesty and frankness in this area, said it is
not democratic, that it is against democracy, that it does
not want democracy.*
— Ali Haroun, Algerian Interior Minister

ISSUES

POLITICAL ISSUES

Fundamentalism and Democracy

Algeria is a nation deep in the throes of civil war. The indiscriminate violence
of the state and its religious opponents has nurtured a host of grievances
and recriminations that continue to fuel the conflict. Both the government
and the leaders of the religious opposition, as well as human rights organizations, cite the violence and the abuse of human of rights as the major
obstacle to a negotiated settlement of the war. But before Algeria's fall into
civil strife, there was the original political sin: the abrogation of the
parliamentary election results and the coup d'etat by the military in January
1992. In plain language, the military's unilateral action to prevent the FIS
from coming to power started the war. This basic cause and effect reflects
the fundamental issues at stake in Algeria. The military, as well as large
sectors of the Algerian public, believes that fundamentalist rule is incompatible with democracy; hence the coup. The religious opposition counters
that the coup was an illegitimate, undemocratic seizure of power; hence
their armed resistance. Let us begin with the first issue: is political Islam in
Algeria compatible with democracy?

"The FIS was unequivocal in following the rules of the game," insists
Mohammed Seghir, a longtime American-based spokesman for the Algerian political Islam movement (though he is not directly affiliated with the

FIS). And indeed, despite charges of fraud and the relatively low election turnouts, the FIS generally played by the constitutional rules and garnered a solid plurality of the popular vote, winning control of a majority of municipal councils and apparently poised to do the same in the National Popular Assembly (APN). "The Islamic Front for Salvation [FIS], a political party that has emerged from the people of Algeria as an expression of their identity and their aspirations, and whose mission is political, economic, social, cultural and civilizational," writes Anwar Haddam, president of the FIS parliamentary delegation to Europe and the USA, "is however being unfairly denied its victory at the polls, based on the false assumption that Political Islam is a threat to the West."[1]

In fact, FIS delegates and their allies from other parties in the APN consider themselves a government in exile. To charges that the FIS represents a threat to democracy, the party's leaders point to the obvious: they have followed the rules; the military has not. The FIS threat to democracy is a "chimera", they argue, the military's actions are facts. "We cannot speak of the government," Haddam explained in 1995, "because according to the Constitution, there is no government now."[2] Contrary to the military's assertion that Islamic politics means "one man, one vote, one time," adds Mohammed Seghir, FIS leaders have consistently demonstrated their willingness to surrender power. "A government must have strong opposition," he notes.

> One day the government is for you and one day it is against you. The FLN ruled and now its day has gone. And the FIS' day will one day pass and someone else will rule. This was declared even before the 1991 elections.[3]

The fundamentalists' clear democratic victory in the parliamentary elections is the basis for the FIS' claim to power. That they played by the rules of the electoral game underlines their professed commitment to democracy. But what kind of democracy do they envision for Algeria? Algeria's political Islamists admit, indeed explicitly profess, that their vision of democracy is not that of the West, nor, they say, does it resemble the socialist regimes' "people's democracies." But while the political structures and terminology differ, Islamic democracy adheres to the same universal values of political pluralism, individual liberties and minority rights as liberal Western democracy. "Political pluralism as a way for people to govern themselves is being recognized by most nations of the world as a way to achieve prosperity, civilization development, stability and technological advancement," writes Haddam. "It is indeed an efficient and self-safeguarding path against tyranny, despotism, and dictatorship."[4] In fact, there is a constant theme of resentment in FIS literature and speeches that the West has claimed the universalist ideals of democracy as its own.

Theoretically, of course, the relationship between Islam and democracy in Muslim civilization is tenuous. The ideal prince of Islam's classical era was supposed to rule in conformity to God's will, not the people's, though God intended that the prince rule in the best interests of the people. The relationship between ruled and ruler was based on the *baya*, literally a covenant between ruler and ruled that left little room for popular expression. This lack of democracy in classical Islam is admitted by modern Islamists, but its significance for today is downplayed, at least by the movement's more liberal elements. There is a tendency in the West, they say, for "overestimating the impact of the past, to deprive the Muslim community of precisely the ability that, in its time, provided its force in other civilizations: the capacity to evolve and to adapt its normative universe."[5]

Indeed, the idea of an evolving Islamic theory of democracy is a major theme of the FIS and in the literature of scholars sympathetic to the movement. The anti-democratic pronouncements of FIS leaders, especially the radical Ali Belhadj, says Islamicist François Burgat, reflect the lack of political sophistication of the movement. The FLN's monopoly of political expression and organization, he says, stifled the maturation of political thought of the FIS.

> Undoubtedly, that is one of the reasons the Algerian movement remained longer than others in the primary phase of affirmation that is part of the growth of all opposition movements, and showed little embarrassment at using in its rare doctrinal expressions a strongly idealized language of rejection [of democracy].[6]

Yet, he goes on to say, "It remains the case that most of the Islamist leaders have one by one surmounted this reactionary phase and one after another have adhered in an explicit manner to the principles of democratic pluralism."[7]

Political Islamists, however, insist that their commitment to democracy is not only equal to that of the West but also more authentic, that is to say, more rooted in the experience, beliefs and history of Muslim peoples. This argument rests on a critique of Western democracy as corrupt, especially in its watered-down versions in the Middle East, and their belief that political Islam represents a more genuine and appropriate expression of democracy for the Muslim world. "Once certain of the failure of the West," notes Maghribi Islamic scholar Salah Eddine Jourchi,

> we discover the comedy in which we have lived and in which we continue to live. We believe that we are developing and civilizing ourselves by marching toward the same failure as the West. It is time that we open our eyes and realize that we are running after an illusion whose name is the "powerful West" when in reality it is weak and sick . . . A little courage, patience, faith, of conscience, of action, and fears and complexes will disappear. Then we will regain control.[8]

The emphasis on authenticity is the most important key to understanding both the appeal of Islamic politics and its ability to express the Algerian masses' deep-felt desire for political expression. "One cannot express the rejection of the West, using its language and its terminology," writes Burgat.

> How better to mark the distance, how better to satisfy the demand for an identity, than to employ the language that is different from its own, along with a system of codes and symbols that seem foreign to it? . . . At a time when the first manifestations of this quest for identity expressed itself through concepts forged by the West (nationalism, socialism, or liberalism) and therefore were marked with a deficiency, the specificity of the Islamist discourse and a large part of its effectiveness stemmed from its privileged recourse to a stock of references perceived as untouched by foreign influences.[9]

Appeals to authenticity and legitimacy, of course, beg the question: authentic and legitimate to what? What precisely is a genuinely Islamic path to democracy? In Algeria, the FIS and Islamic political theorists emphasize a democratic politics imbued with morality and ethics. Much of the political literature of fundamentalism elides questions of how power is to be attained and exercised; it focuses on the virtue of those who wield it. "The plans for the creation of [democratic] institutions," notes Islamicist Olivier Roy, "are terminated while still on the drawing board in favor of a discussion of the qualities and virtues of their leaders."[10]

This emphasis has its sources in both ancient Islamic precedents and post-independence Algerian history. First, as noted, the righteous Islamic prince ruled in God's name, according to Islamic law and custom. While guided and advised by religious scholars, the prince based his decisions upon his own virtue. Islamic history and scholarship is replete with stories and anecdotes of the righteous prince. It also specifies what constitutes virtue: close observation of the *sharia*, devotion to faith and concern for the *ijma*, or will of the people—not as the responsibility of a democratic representative but as the duty of an upholder of the customs, expectations and right living of the faithful. Ultimately, however, the political success of a regime, and the happiness, stability and prosperity of the society it rules, depends on the ruler. "Who designates the amir?" Roy asks.

> The ideal solution, which runs throughout the [Islamic] debate, would be for the amir to be *index sui*, his own indicator; that is, by merely appearing he would be instantly recognizable. Hence, no doubt, the incessant quest for a charismatic chief, which is transformed in political life into a quest for a leader. The only criterion for designating an amir would therefore be the man himself, his virtue, his personality.[11]

The quest for the moral and virtuous leader seems especially relevant in the current Algerian context. Algerians speak of *hogra* when referring to

FLN rule. "*Hogra,* an untranslatable word, means at once the abuse of power, arbitrariness, and humiliation," writes Algerian journalist Ghania Mouffok. "By extension, the *hogra* means all cases of power abuse or social injustice by political leaders."[12] Given the corruption and venality of FLN rule, especially in its last decade, Algeria's recent rulers have failed to live up to expected standards of virtue and morality. The FIS, having been kept out of power, has been tainted neither by association with an immoral regime nor through its own exercise of power. It has the positive virtue of being, in the current American term, a party of political outsiders.

Oddly, though, for all the emphasis on the righteousness and morality of the Islamic ruler, the FIS and the Algerian fundamentalist movement generally have not cast up a leader of the stature of Ayatollah Khomeini in Iran. This can also be explained in terms of both Islamic precedent and Algerian history. The FLN, of course, has made it a point to discourage charismatic leaders like Ben Bella and the cults of personality so common in recent nationalist and socialist regimes of the Arab world (and elsewhere). In addition, Sunni Islam eschews the kind of charismatic leadership typical of Shiite Islam. For specific historical and scriptural reasons, Shiism seeks to embody the precepts and ideals of Islamic society in a powerful cleric and leader. Sunni Islam does not. In a sense, then, there is a hole at the center of the FIS' political thinking: the emphasis on the virtuous leader without the theory or means for discovering, evaluating and empowering him. Hence, the FIS has never established a hierarchy of party leaders. Officially, the two most prominent members of the Front, Belhadj and Abbassi Madani, are known as "spokesmen."

That inconsistency, say critics of the FIS, is only one of many in the fabric of Algerian political Islam. More important, they say, are the major contradictions between the idea of the Islamic polity and democracy, and the way the FIS elides this problem by avoiding any formulation of a political platform. Specifically, many FIS observers ask, how can the idea of a God-directed society be reconciled with democratic expression? The simple answer, they say, is that it can't. [12A] "The rejection of even a chimerical notion of democracy is actually inherent in Islamic religious doctrine, which in its present-day militant reaffirmation, is fervently monist," writes Islamicist Gilles Kepel.

> There is only one organizing principle in the world—God—and human freedom is reduced virtually to zero. In Islamist thinking there could be no room for autonomous political activity outside the control of the shar'ia, the Law codified by Islamic scholars from revealed scripture. To introduce democracy is to destroy the case put forward by the re-Islamization movements.[13]

Islamist scholar A. Maududi concurs. "Whatever human agency is constituted to enforce the political system of Islam in a state will not possess real

sovereignty in the legal and political sense of the term," he writes, "because
... its powers are limited and circumscribed by a supreme law which it can
neither alter nor interfere with."[14]

Of course, since the time of the Prophet, God has not revealed His
intentions for how human society should be run. A leader desirous of being
God's "vice-regent" on Earth has to look to scripture and official interpretations of scripture by Islamic scholars past and, if he is committed to the
idea of *itjihad*, or free interpretation, present. This fact reveals another
contradiction between political Islam and democracy. Virtually any definition of the latter includes the notion of checks and balances, both between
the various branches of the government and concerning the government's
power over the people. But, says Roy, there is a fundamental flaw in the
Islamic conception of these checks on power. Since sovereignty emanates
from God alone, by way of His vice-regent on Earth, no elected assembly
has the power to legislate—only to counsel.

Moreover, the process of selection of that assembly and the way it
goes about its work ignores the problem of political power. One can
arguably maintain a commitment to democracy while believing that a chief
executive can be simultaneously God's vice-regent on Earth and the
representative of the collective will of the people to have a virtuous ruler,
but the commitment becomes problematic if one also supports an Islamic
parliament. Democratic representation implies accommodation of compet-
ing interests, but political Islam fails to recognize this idea, insisting instead
that parliamentarians be chosen on the basis of virtue alone. While democracy does not require that representatives be of the same social background
and class as their constituency—few Western democracies would meet such
a criterion—it does require that they speak on their behalf. This basic
principle of democracy, however, implies social divisions and conflicts—the
much-condemned *fitna* of the scriptures.

Here we see a straightforward contradiction between political Islam
and the concept of political pluralism. How can those who believe that they
represent the will of God tolerate those who oppose them? Even if fundamentalists do not believe that they alone represent God's will, how can they
accept the victory of political forces that openly oppose the idea of the
sharia? According to Barakat, they cannot. "By claiming to implement
God's will," he writes,

> they create an order that cannot tolerate dissent or even different interpreta-
> tions of religious texts. New ideas are dismissed as *wafida, nabt ghareeb,
> mustajlaba* (borrowed, "alien plant," inauthentic). The concept of authen-
> ticity (*asala*) is meant not only to assert national identity and a genuine search
> for roots, but also to restrict free discussion.[15]

Although echoing the sentiments of the Algerian junta, these Islamic
scholars are no apologists for the current government in Algiers. The

democracy to which the rulers of Algeria "paid lip-service" was, says Kepel, a "meaningless catchword . . . and the people knew it. Thus it is easy nowadays to cast 'democracy' as the ugly sister, because it has remained largely unknown in the Muslim world as an operative political system."[16] Many FIS leaders do not express it in those terms, however, insisting instead that the FIS is committed to democracy and assuring a skeptical world that, if rejected at the polls in the future, they would accept the will of the people and leave office, even if their successors did not adhere to their program for the Islamicization of Algerian society.

Is the FIS committed to democracy or does its commitment to the Islamicization of the political order preclude pluralism, checks and balances and the sovereignty of the people? Part of the difficulty in answering this question comes from the difficulty in assessing the relative weight of the people speaking in the FIS' name. Because of its ephemeral structure and its lack of an established hierarchy, problems exacerbated by the party's having had to go underground since January 1992, it is hard to tell whether the liberal wing of the party, best represented by Madani, or the radicals under Belhadj are currently in control and would be dominant in the government should the FIS come to power. The current willingness of the FIS to cooperate with other opposition parties, including the FLN (see Chapter 6), in forcing the military junta to relinquish power speaks for the rise of the liberal wing. But, as Barakat points out, the history of political Islam suggests otherwise. "Once in power," he writes, "past experience has shown us, the moderates among the religious absolutists are most likely to become sacrificial lambs."[17]

But it is precisely this conflict between liberal and conservative traditions, say some Algerian fundamentalists, that proves political Islam's compatibility with political pluralism. "Since the dawn of Islam," says Seghir,

> there has always been a literalist and objectivist approach [to the application of Islamic political rule]. The objectivist approach is also part of the pluralistic heritage of Islam. A state of equilibrium between these competing views of bettering Islamic society is the goal of political Islam. It aims at reestablishing Islam as the basis of life through the institutionalization of government as a stable system which ought to be representative of Algerian society in its plurality . . . The FIS is nothing but an expression of this ancient tradition.[18]

Islam in its political manifestation, he adds, makes the law supreme and thus returns Algeria to the rule of law and not men. Others, like Mokhtar Maghraoui, concur. "The intent of the [Islamic] lawgiver is to provide for and protect the well-being of the human beings," he begins. "This is . . . not a theocratic, suprarational assertion, it is a legal assertion, in the rational world, through legislation, through the interpretative power of human reason. It's the only way in the post-prophetic era."[19]

Both Seghir and Maghraoui cite a traditional commitment to democratic principles in Algerian political Islamic thought. Among the thirteen principles outlined in 1956 by Mohammed Nouadiz, an Islamist opponent of the French and an important precursor of the current fundamentalists, was that no one has the right to lead the *umma*, or Islamic community, without the consent of that community and that the *umma* had the right to place checks on that leader as he carried out his duties. "There have always been five principles of [modern] political Islam," notes Maghraoui, "human rights, a social contract between ruler and ruled, elections, pluralism, and the supremacy of the law. All schools [in Algeria] agree on these principles, even if the details vary."[20]

Yet other pronouncements by FIS leaders call into question the assertions of more liberal Islamists that there is an inherent compatibility between democracy and Islam. "Among the reasons for which we [the FIS] refuse the democratic dogma," says Belhadj,

> there is the fact that democracy relies on the opinion of the majority . . .
> Starting from this principle, one sees the heads of the democratic parties trying to win over the greatest possible number of people, even if it is to the detriment of their faith, of their dignity, religion and honor . . . As for us, the people of the Sunna, we believe that justice (*haq*) only comes from the decisive proofs of the Sharia and not from a multitude of demagogic actors and voices.[21]

Then, to underline Islamic precedent for this assertion, he adds, "Those who followed the Prophet were a very small number, while those who followed idols were a multitude."[22]

Regardless of which view predominates in an FIS-dominated Algerian government (given the fluid situation in the country, it is by no means certain which will prevail), the simple fact remains: the future of democracy and the future of Islamic politics are inextricable. "No political system can claim to be legitimate if it lacks political sovereignty," notes political scientist John Entelis,

> and no political sovereignty can be achieved without a congruent mass political culture. In the Arab world that political culture is rooted in Islam . . . Any notion of democracy in the Arab world that does not incorporate Islam into its analysis is simply a nonstarter.[23]

In short, the search for an appropriate form of democracy is confounded by a paradox: Islamic politics and democracy may not be compatible, but the exclusion of Islamist politics makes a mockery of democracy. "This paradox of democratization in Algeria," writes Maghraoui, "is difficult to resolve. But no theorist or advocate of democracy could argue against popular sovereignty without creating yet another paradox: violating the basic democratic principle of universal political participation."[24]

Fundamentalism and the State

In theory at least, Islamic politics can make no room for the national state, for two reasons. First, the only communities recognized as legitimate by Islam are the community of believers and the community of the family; one a supranational entity and the other an organic, self-contained micro-community outside the state's purview. But Algeria's Islamic politicians dismiss as impractical the idea of a pan-Islamic super-state of all Muslims. When asked about the priority the FIS placed on a pan-Islamic state, a spokesman responded, "We can dream, can't we?"[25] Unlike the revolutionary Shiite regime in Iran, Algeria's FIS has never claimed universal applicability for its message or movement, insisting that it is dedicated to the Islamicization of Algerian society only.

The second theoretical obstacle to the harmonization of the national state and Islamic politics, however, is more pressing and immediate. According to Roy, Algerian fundamentalism challenges the very functions for which the national state exists. "Neither the people nor the parliament nor the sovereign can be sources of law," he writes.

> The state has no positive power in and of itself. What is the point of precisely defining political institutions, when in any case the executive, legislative, and judicial powers have very little room to maneuver? Sovereignty lies with God alone, and the law has already been given.[26]

In effect, political Islam pulls the rug out from under the state, since it is impossible to imagine a nation-state or even a reason to have one in the absence of supreme sovereignty—regardless of whether that sovereignty is bestowed directly by God through scriptural revelation or by the people. Since any government that hopes to rule effectively has to possess sovereignty, the argument that Islam negates the idea of the state would seem to be nothing more than casuistry.

But the theoretical incompatibility of Islamic politics and the modern idea of the nation-state has a rather important consequence for the functioning of such an Islamic nation-state. An effective state requires institutions to regulate the affairs of its citizens and implement the programs of the government. But, say many scholars, the fundamentalists of Algeria are averse to the idea of such institutions, even Islamicized ones. Just as they focus on the morality and virtue of political leaders, rather than the dynamics and functions of political power, so they see institutions as moralizing agencies rather than functional entities. "Institutions [of an Islamic state]," notes Roy,

> exist to oblige the individual to be a good Muslim (it is the duty of "ordering the good and chasing the bad"); once the members of the community are truly virtuous, there will be no need for institutions. Islamist authors evade any definition of institutions, which they essentially mistrust, in favor of reflections on virtue (taqwa).[27]

Thus, in theory, political Islam delegitimates the state by denying it both sovereignty and the institutional means to exercise it.

Part of the reason for this rejection of the state comes from the fundamentalists' interpretation of the ideal Islamic community, the community of the prophetic era before the assassination of the fourth caliph. Why this ideal has become so compelling to contemporary Algerians can be explained only by examining the modern history of the Algerian state. The FLN conceptualized the state, state institutions and the party as the vehicles for fulfilling the goals of the Algerian revolution: economic modernization, political consensus and national sovereignty. In pursuit of these goals it arrogated vast powers unto itself and used them to attempt to control all aspects of society. As Barakat summarizes, the state no longer served the people, the people served the state; the state began to be "perceived as needing citizens to govern, rather than as needed by citizens to regulate their affairs"; the state no longer protected the citizens but required the citizens to protect it; "objects of governing became subjects." In other words, a form of totalitarianism crept into the FLN's concept and management of the Algerian polity.

> Bureaucracy . . . dominates [citizens'] lives, exercises power over them, and interferes in their private affairs, while proclaiming its own independent existence.[28]

Practical day-to-day fundamentalist politics, however, are more informed by attacks on the specific uses of state power. Aside from its extensive documentation of human rights violations by the state, FIS literature generally focuses on the government's treatment of religion and its cozying up to Western powers. While these seem to be disconnected topics, they are in fact related. According to the FIS, the government never effectively decolonized society and continued the French tradition of secularization, separation of church and state, and assaults on Islamic institutions. "The French thought they were smart and they put at the head of Algeria . . . some of their puppets," notes Haddam. "And it's still the same thing, but now the people have made it too costly to maintain the charade of [independence from Western contamination]."[29]

While this position seems almost counterfactual given the FLN's hostility to the French as evinced in its nationalization of French oil interests, its removal of French bases before the date laid out in the peace treaty and the government's long-standing commitment to Third World solidarity, the message rings true on a deeper level. Many Algerian fundamentalists and, indeed, many Algerian Muslims believe, and not entirely mistakenly, that the West, and France in particular, fears Islamic politics and will do anything to prevent it from coming to power. Thus, the government's history of control, manipulation and restraint of Islamic institutions and resistance to Islamicization of society is seen in terms of a foreign plot.

"These values provide the extremists with a set of criteria for judging the present state of affairs . . . [as] irreligious, apostate," writes Islamicist Emmanuel Sivan. "This is their most crucial function, for the primordial impulse of all these extremist movements is one of religiosity in a state of siege; that is, a defensive initiative designed to thwart the demise of . . . Islam, undermined from within by 'nominal (hypocritical) believers,' who are in fact . . . Westoxicated."[30] In short, as far as the FIS is concerned, the French have never left.

Over thirty years of FLN and military rule, then, has taught Algerians an important lesson in state power. Its sovereignty comes from the barrel of a gun. And the institutions it has created simply impose themselves on the people, without democratic input and, since the coup, without even the basic consensus of the governed. It is no wonder then that Islamic politicians and their constituency conceptualize the state and its institutions in purely negative terms, though they don't see it that way. They believe they are pursuing a millennialist vision, based on the idea of re-creating, through the institutions and power of the state, a virtuous community from the idealized past. In an ironic twist of history, the Algerian fundamentalists borrow from the millenarian vision of their erstwhile Marxist enemies: once the state and the institution have created this idealized community, they will wither away. In the final analysis, Algerian society is trapped between a government that has corrupted the idea of the state through its actions and an opposition that bases its political program on the delegitimation of the state. The results have been anarchy, political anomie, nihilism and savage violence. As Roy notes,

> The rejection of institutional validation accentuates the process of the dele-
> gitimation of the state, which is always latent in Muslim countries, and again
> raises the problem of authority: who is the master? . . . One's differentiation
> from the "other," those who don't know . . . can be established only through
> a decisive, even violent act, for want of a set of procedures recognized by the
> [fundamentalists]. This is the violence of the [fundamentalist] faced with the
> violence of the state.[31]

SOCIAL ISSUES

The Crisis in Contemporary Algerian Society

All sides to the conflict agree that Algerian society is experiencing a crisis of grave proportions. For the vast majority of the nation's urban citizens, the quality of life has deteriorated significantly from a standard that was never high to begin with. Good jobs are scarce, money is short, medicines are lacking, water supplies are dwindling, costs are going up. For the poor, the basic necessities of life are becoming luxuries, while much of the middle class has grown accustomed to a standard of living not much above that of the poor during the flush years of the 1970s. "Running water is practically a luxury in Algiers," writes journalist José Garçon, "unless one can install huge cisterns that collect the water when it flows and distribute it when people want it. But this can cost $500 per person, and goes up whenever shortages get worse."[32]

Housing is probably the most frustrating problem facing urban Algeria today. Journalist Ghania Mouffok describes a typical apartment in a planned complex in the Constantine suburb of Diar el Kef, a "town that looks like a Lego toy, covered by dust and rocking with constant explosions from nearby quarries." It was built by the French in 1956 when they feared a social explosion in the nearby *bidonvilles* and "was not built to last." A typical family, she notes, lives in "a two room apartment, parents sleeping in the only bedroom and eight brothers and sisters sleeping in the living room, which at night becomes a veritable dormitory of foam mattresses. Bodies up against each other limit the decency about which Algerians are so persnickety."[33]

The future does not bode well. The housing shortage, say experts, will affect six million by the year 2000 when the country's population may reach 50 million. Meanwhile, Mouffok continues,

> people try to cope with a crisis that they feel less and less like they are going to get out of. They demolish walls, kitchens are whittled away, balconies are enclosed and become bedrooms, children's clothes are kept in valises . . . When they run out of room children are sent to live in the building's public lavatories on the ground floor.[34]

Such living conditions, however, are only a part of the problem. There is a sense that Algerian society is coming apart, that it was coming apart even before the current wave of violence began in the early 1990s. To many Algerians, it seems as if their leaders have abdicated their responsibility and retreated to their well-protected villas and enclaves in the suburbs, "completely cut off from the torn apart Algeria which they are supposed to be managing."[35] The government appears to have no ideas while the democratic opposition flounders, unable to find its voice or build consensus. Only the fundamentalists maintain a coherent vision for the future, and that vision deeply frightens many Algerians of all classes and backgrounds.

The social pathologies of contemporary Algeria, most agree, are especially endemic among the young, the three-quarters of the population under twenty. On the streets of Algiers and other cities, tens of thousands of young men hang out. Most have been educated through high school, but few will find jobs. The Algerians even have a word for them: *hittistes*, literally those who keep the walls standing (by leaning against them). "Lacking an apartment, a job, or a place to entertain themselves, they hang out in the street," writes Algerian journalist Thé Hash. "They're young, but they don't move, they are just there, always in the same place. Backs to the wall, watching life go by, they see time itself passing them by."[36] A bitter joke circulating around Algiers after the fall of the Berlin Wall was that the German government should have shipped the remains to Algeria rather than tear it down. Meanwhile, drug abuse has become an increasing problem. Older Algerians turn to hashish smuggled in from the countryside and Europe, while the young go in for pills smuggled out of hospitals and clinics by underpaid doctors, or sniffing industrial solvents and glue.

In the broadest sense, a spiritual crisis has descended on Algerian society. "The abandoned generation, as it defines itself," says Mouffok, "doesn't really know what it wants, it only knows that the crisis has killed all hope, and that they will not have decent housing or jobs for a long time." There is also a strong feeling of entrapment. "Petroleum shock? Economic crisis? What the Algerians remember most clearly from that horrible time [1985] was the laconic communiqué that told them there will be no more 'allocs,' tourist allotments," writes journalist Tewfik Hakem. "The terrible message was clear and terse: an end to the conversion of 1500 dinars to 1600 francs that the state banks offered to Algerians 18 years old and above who wanted to go abroad." It was, he declares, "the end of a dream!"[37]

The only form of escape for many is emigration. Packet boats leave daily from Algiers and Oran, with their loads of Algerians looking for work in Europe. But the main destination of the emigrés, France, is experiencing a revival of anti-immigrant politics and is seeking to curtail the flood, thus adding to the sense of entrapment. French journalist Thierry Leclère writes of the new Algerian myth:

> The boat for Australia. It will embark with candidates for exile and will carry them to the antipodes to find work and a welcome there. Relayed by this rumor, the myth . . . comes up from time to time in conversations. It was born from a successful theater piece which evoked the imminent arrival of this mysterious boat.

Foreign embassies, he adds, are surrounded by long lines every working day as "obtaining a visa has become the national sport." But for most, the "dream of exile remains a fantasy . . . When the city and its curfews and raids becomes too oppressive, many leave for uncles or cousins in Kabyle, or in the douars [villages] of the interior, another form of the 'Australian boat.'"[38]

And amidst the crisis, the world continues to come into Algeria in the form of Western consumption patterns and broadcasts from abroad. During the short-lived boom period of the early 1980s, when consumer imports poured in, Algerians were introduced to a new world of goods and a new form of social identity: Citizens became consumers. But with the collapse of the economy, consumption dried up, producing frustrations in all strata of society, especially among the young. Increasingly conditioned to identify themselves through possessions, fashions and diversion, the country's youth felt the collapse not just as hard times but as a threat to their identity and their way of life.

Since the late 1980s arrival of satellite dishes, Algerians have had access to a world of images and information from Europe, especially France, among the most broad-minded and risqué of national broadcasters. While only the middle and upper classes can afford the "paraboles," working-class and unemployed Algerians have access to the broadcasts at cafes and friends' homes. Watching TV has become one of the last affordable pleasures in contemporary, war-torn Algeria. Hakem explains the social and political impact of the dishes. They open "windows on mass consumption" that make the viewers' own poverty-stricken lives seem that much more intolerable.

> Algerians find themselves caught between Europe and the Islamic umma, between pleasure and guilt . . . The satellite dish is a metaphor for the democratization of society, so many choices makes people a little crazy. Thus, they choose the FIS which intends to end their choices.[39]

The Promise and Threat of Fundamentalism

Fundamentalists argue that they offer an alternative to the escapism of exile and televised diversion. This alternative, the implementation of a social order based on the *sharia*, is based on a different reading of Algeria's social ills. While the government and the secular opposition see the crisis largely in economic terms, the fundamentalists conceptualize the problem as a moral and ethical one. The inability or failure to modernize Algeria is not the problem, they say. The problem is modernity itself, or at least the failure to adopt only those aspects of it appropriate to a Muslim society.

Most fundamentalists, for instance, decry the *paraboles* and what they represent, a destructive force capable of undermining the moral values of Muslims, especially the young, by bombarding them with the values and imagery of the modern West. At the core of the Islamic critique of Algerian society is the idea of "westoxification," a term invented by Iranian Islamic scholars to describe Muslim societies forced to absorb Western (popular) culture. Weakened by the secular values of the state, which encourages Muslims to think in terms of Western materialist ideas of development, progress and modernization, citizens have no defense against this "discourse of seduction." This, they say, explains the despair and hopelessness that have saturated Algerian society since the economic collapse "made the western dream a nightmare." "What is strange," writes Islamic scholar Salah Eddine Jourchi,

> is that the nation which has been invaded, accepts and blesses this occupation and puts all its energy into deepening it and giving it roots. With our goods and machines, we have imported ideas . . . but we have won nothing and lost our religion. We have rid ourselves of the past with a fever that we suffer from still.[40]

The fundamentalists' message has obvious appeal, says Mouffok.

"Caught in the contradiction [of a semi-modernized society] these searchers [Algeria's young] look about where they find themselves: Doesn't faith move mountains after all? The mosques give them something neither the state bureaucracy nor the western model can: landmarks, daily ritual, five pillars [rituals of Islam], a discovery of self, a collective identity, that these other identities do not.[41]

The diagnosis is simple: failure to implement the *sharia* and establish a social order based on its precepts is the source of all of the country's social ailments, from unemployment to psychological stress to political authoritarianism; its implementation is the cure. "Political Islam ideologizes reality by inverting cause and effect and presenting non-application of the *sharia* as the cause of national failure," notes Algerian sociologist Ali el-Kenz, "whereas it is this failure that made it possible to ask such a question."[42] El-Kenz is not necessarily praising the political authorities for allowing this critique of their policies to be aired in public. He is saying that the failure of their attempt to build a modern society has created the context for such a critique. Or, in Roy's words, "It is not that the Middle Ages are invading our modern world, but rather that modernity itself produces its own form of protest."[43]

Thus, the key to understanding Algeria's fundamentalists is the way they conceptualize modern society and social dysfunction. The question is: are the fundamentalists engaged in a genuine intellectual critique of modernity, or are they responding to it in frustration and religious reaction? Are they, to use Islamicist John Esposito's construct,[44] "more specific about what they are against than what they are for?" Or is Burgat's descriptive phrase for their approach, "selective appropriation rather than rejection" of modern ideas, more accurate?[45]

To begin answering these questions about fundamentalism and modernity let us examine the statements of the FIS itself. "The intention of Algerian Political Islam," says Anwar Haddam, president of the FIS parliamentary delegation to Europe and the United States,

is not to replace the present by a mythical past, but to restructure the modern social order so that it conforms to Islamic principles and values. This does not mean, however, that under Islamic reforms everything Western is to be discarded. A selective interactive approach to western political, economic and social expression is undertaken so long as there is no violation of Islamic moral principles.[46]

The effort to reform society is premised on a return to the *sharia*; fundamentalist literature insists that the effort to resurrect the ancient tradition is not medievalist. Instead it will allow the fusion of traditions, so that Algerians may thoughtfully select and incorporate those aspects of Western modernity that are appropriate to a Muslim society.

From an outright rejection of Western and modern values, described in the 1970s as "weak and sick," fundamentalism has evolved, says Burgat, a more nuanced approach. The vocabulary of present-day political Islam rings true for the average Algerian, enabling him to understand and resist all-encompassing modernity. Critics are less sanguine about political Islam's ability to reconceptualize modernity in an Islamic framework. The problem, they say, is twofold. First, and most obviously, modernism "creeps into Muslim countries regardless of Islam." "Protest against the West," says Roy, "is on the same order as Western [anti-industrial deep] ecology or anti-immigrant movements: They are arguments one propounds when it is too late. Just as France will never return to a preindustrial society, and its immigrants are there to stay, so Muslim cities will never return to the harmony of the bazaar and of the guilds.

In fact, says Roy, the fundamentalists themselves accelerate the process. By insisting on rejecting what he calls "the real tradition of Islam," including *maraboutism*, popular practice, indigenous but non-Islamic customs and the sensuality that is an integral part of the Muslim social tradition, "they themselves deny and undermine what is and was Muslim civilization and ensure the triumph of fast food (*halal*, of course—religiously correct), of jeans, Coke, and English." In its place, they project what he calls an "imaginary tradition" that does not and will not resonate with the semiwesternized and modernized society of contemporary Algeria. Unless the "neo-fundamentalists" plan on tearing down all the *paraboles*, a task even the Islamists of Tehran have shied away from, they will render Algerian Muslim society more vulnerable than ever.

Unable to confront the modernization within the Algerian soul, say critics, the fundamentalists go after its outward symbols: cafes, nightclubs, alcohol, casual dating, the cinema, video clubs, among other things. There is nothing new in the puritanical streak in Islamic fundamentalism, but unlike the Western variety, it is a strong, still-living tradition, not an attenuated survival within Christian fundamentalist conservatism. "'[Islamic] Puritanism' is characterized by the rejection of all distraction, of music, theater, and all diversion . . . and the desire to eradicate places of pleasure and leisure," writes Roy.

> Preaching focuses on a return to the essentials: religious practice and fear of God. There is a kind of a millenarian pessimism, which is actually rather far from traditional Islam, in which pleasure is legitimate as long as it does not transgress either the *sharia* or the superior goals of man.[47]

The coming to power of the fundamentalists will, in fact, bring the inherent contradictions of their program and philosophy into the open. As even the most radical of Islamist theorists have pointed out, the full imposition of the *sharia* can take place only in a society that has already been Islamicized and where people are already virtuous. In the absence of that condition, hypocrisy and duplicity will result. Transgressions will continue to take place, but underground, as is the case in Saudi Arabia. In the Islamicized environment, most will be afraid to express their more joyous selves in public or risk criticizing the fundamentalist agenda for fear of being labeled anti-religious. At the same time, the wealthy will continue to watch forbidden videos on home VCRs and indulge themselves at private country clubs or on holidays abroad. Thus the realization of the fundamentalist social agenda will only exacerbate the basic problems in contemporary Algerian society: boredom and alienation among the young, a heightened sense of social injustice, and pleasure as the exclusive preserve of the well-off and the well-connected.

Nor, say opponents, does the fundamentalist social agenda realistically cope with another problem in recent Algerian history: the lack of associative institutions and space. As Roy points out,

> "The only model for sociability in Islamism is personal devotion within the framework of the mosque. Why create associations, leisure activities, opportunities, for individuals to blossom, when the only model of behavior is devotional? Between the sacred family space (the *haram*), the mosque, and the institution of the state, viewed as a simple instrument of Islamicization, there is no structure for the social space, except through traditional or business solidarities, which are obviously not open to the young unemployed generation.[48]

In a sense, the fundamentalists may do for society what the FLN government did for the economy in its first several decades of power. In the name of nationalism and the revolution, the FLN under Boumédienne tried to suppress all consumer expression and indulgence, except for the elites who could get around the state restrictions. This policy produced a frustrated, angry citizenry. The restriction of social life to mosque and family may be no more satisfactory—especially when a major problem for the young is the economic near-impossibility of supporting a family to begin with.

Women

During the War of Independence, the French and the FLN presented their arguments in terms of women, says Algerian sociologist Marnia Lazreg, and made of them a symbol of Algeria's future: the Islamic Muslim woman versus the Europeanized Muslim woman. The use of women to symbolize Algeria's identity continues in the current civil war. "If you want to establish a government according to what you perceive is the word of God," Lazreg notes, "it makes logical sense to begin with women because this is the area where it's very clear that men are empowered over women." Women, she concludes, have become not just symbols of alternative visions of Algerian society, but the battlefield, "the main contested ground" of the conflict.[49]

Algerian society, like other Arab societies, has traditionally assigned women a subordinate status in several ways: segregation and seclusion; limited roles in society; and discriminatory codes concerning personal status and behavior. All of these have been supported by a general religious perception, shared with Christianity and Judaism, that women are a source of evil, social disorder and deception. The Book of Genesis story of the fall from paradise as a result of woman's curiosity and trickery is part of the Islamic heritage as well. Thus scripture and traditional patriarchy have created a social climate that reinforces second-class citizenship for women.

Religious scholars say that Islam originally offered liberation for women from the stifling and hostile environment of the Arab tribe. But given that female children in pre-Islamic Arabia were routinely killed, and women often bought and sold as slaves, this is small comfort. In more recent times, however, Islamic scholars have presented an argument that conceptualizes women as different but equal within certain limitations. Islam, says one scholar, decreed equality between the sexes "where equality was possible . . . [but] preference was admissible where equality was impossible." Essentially, Islamic scholars consider gender equality within two separate and distinct contexts. On the one hand, in the spiritual realm, Islam insists that all believers be submissive to God. Thus, say more liberal interpreters of the Islamic tradition, a woman is liberated by her faith from submission to the men in her life. But in the secular realm, God has clearly said that

> "men are superior to women"; [and] made it the duty of man to struggle and to provide for dependents, and relieved woman from such burdens on account of her physical potential, personal circumstances, and financial responsibilities.[50]

While Algerian fundamentalists insist that the current disorders in Algerian society are due to a failure to implement the *sharia*, including rules on the role of women, el-Kenz offers an alternative explanation. The patriarchal order in Algerian society, he says, has never gone away; thus the fundamentalists are guilty of "an inversion of reality[,] presenting the preservation of patriarchal relationships as a product of religion, whereas in reality it is the relative continuity of the patriarchal structure that provides the basis for a religious interpretation."[51] Other scholars concur. According to sociologist Peter Knauss, "The movement away from traditional patriarchal practices and law has been much slower [in Algeria] owing to the fear of nationalists of being considered disloyal to their long-suppressed Islamic culture or of being thought turncoats, or *M'Tourni*, of Algerian nationalism," as evidenced in the Family Code of 1984.[52] An Algerian academic puts the argument in stronger terms. "The government has been disgraceful on the issue of women," she says.

> While the various documents, the Constitution and charters have identified women as a noteworthy group, the government has not engaged in any policy that was directed at women, for the social, political and economic program of women.[53]

It is in this context that the FIS presents its ideas about and programs for women. As in the case of social issues generally, Algerian fundamentalists insist that they intend to liberate Algerians, in this case female Algerians, from a false freedom concocted in the West and foisted onto Algerian society. At the heart of their agenda is the revival of the veil, or *hijab*. "The Hijab is certainly a symbol of the rejection of an imported and imposed modernity," writes Islamic journalist Fariba Adelkhah, who also points to "the inanity of the Western discourse when it sees in the imposition of the Hijjab, a simple sign of the repressive character of the Islamic regime."[54] Theoretically, the *hijab*, these scholars say, allows women to assert their submission to God above all secular authority, including men.

In addition, say fundamentalists, the wearing of the *hijab* is not really a rejection of modernity, but an adjustment to it. "When a girl takes the Hijjab and renounces 'mixing,'" writes Islamic scholar Mohamed Tozy,

> she certainly appropriates a cultural identity. But this identity is effective to the extent to which it is in response to a concrete obstacle. In a university restaurant with endless lines, or on an overcrowded bus where promiscuity often threatens physical integrity, the Hijjab becomes a vital requirement.[55]

That many Algerian women embrace the *hijab* is beyond doubt. Fundamentalist women insist that veil-wearing allows them to break out of their assigned role in Algerian society and pursue an education and a career. As one female student explained.

> I have six brothers and I am the only girl and the youngest. Before, everyone used to say: "Where were you? Where are you going?" Now I am free, I go to the mosque, even at night during Ramadan. They allow me everything.[56]

Women also take advantage of the social space created by the revivalist mosques. There, in a segregated space, they meet and discuss issues with other women. Older venues like the baths, or *hamman*, have declined in Algeria since the water shortages began a decade ago.

On the other hand, women are virtually excluded from the cadres of the FIS. There are no major female party leaders or spokespersons. Moreover, say many critics of the fundamentalists, women adhere to FIS practices out of fear rather than conviction. As a woman manager of a factory in western Algeria admitted,

> None of us wants to wear the veil, but fear is stronger than our convictions or our will to be free. Fear is all around us. Our parents, our brothers, are unanimous: "Wear the veil and stay alive. This will pass."[57]

The main problem with the veil issue, and the larger program of *sharia* implementation of which it is the most visible part, says Lazreg, is not whether a woman wears the veil or not, but what happens if she chooses not to. Algerian history, she adds, is filled with devout Muslim women who chose to flout the rule of the veil. (In fact, the veil is not mentioned in the Koran, but is part of the religious tradition of later centuries.) But in contemporary Algeria, the veiled woman has become the prime symbol of society's Islamicization. The FIS, say critics, has linked the veil with faith and faith with the survival of the polity. Disregarding the veil is thus understood as a direct attack on the nation. Likewise, the veil and the implementation of the *sharia* has "been presented simplistically as the word of God," says Lazreg, "instead of man's attempt to create a legal system he deemed close to God's word."[58]

In the violent atmosphere of contemporary Algeria, flouting the fundamentalist Islamic rules on women can be fatal. According to Algerian journalist Amal Boumédienne, 400 women have been murdered "because they were women and because they were in public." (FIS spokesmen point out that the party has never advocated attacks on any citizens, and, in fact, has consistently called for a neutral commission to look into cases of civilian murders, as it has in the cases of government torture.)

Fundamentalists also argue that nothing in their program says women cannot play a full role in society. The future of women in society is subject to debate within a democratic Islamic context, and they point to the tradition of free religious interpretation (*itjihad*) as offering a defense of women's rights. For example, says Maghraoui, different Islamic legal theorists have reached entirely different conclusions about whether a woman needs a guardian's permission to marry. Critics maintain that this is all casuistics and distraction; in no polity where Islamic politicians rule has *itjihad* ever taken hold. But in the most important such case, Iran, the record is mixed. The government in Tehran did make an effort to impose the *chador*, or head covering, and it gender-segregated public life, but it never denied women's right to pursue an education, drive a car, have a career or travel without an escort. True, says Roy, but the Algerian "neo-fundamentalists" are more reactionary than their Iranian Islamist counterparts.

> Islamist [Iranian] politicization allowed women access to the public sphere, where the [Algerian] neo-fundamentalists are now taking it away. Whereas there were female Islamist militants, there are no neo-fundamentalist militant women . . . The neo-fundamentalists are exerting pressure to limit women's right to vote . . . The question of personal status (wives, family, divorce) is becoming the principal area of neo-fundamentalist assertions, which brutally reestablish the letter of the *sharia* without the social and educational measures that the Iranian or Egyptian Islamists favored.[59]

Finally, over the issue of women in the workforce, the fundamentalists have formulated a position that melds their economic and social programs and reveals their differences with the Islamists of the Arab East and Iran. According to Roy, the FIS denies women's right to work outside the home, "a right that Khomeini considered self-evident."[60] Indeed, FIS spokesmen have on occasion offered a radically simple solution to Algeria's direst social and economic problem: fire women and hire unemployed men in their place. Unmentioned is the reality that 9 percent of the workforce is female and is dwarfed by the unemployed, who constitute as much as a third of all adult Algerian males.

ECONOMIC ISSUES

The Crisis in the Contemporary Algerian Economy

Like many others in the Middle East, Algeria's economy is one of speculation. Because the state plans and directs macroeconomic development, businessmen realize profits through their contacts with the state bureaucracy. Rather than making independent decisions based on the marketability of products and the costs of production, they expend their energy and time maintaining those connections and speculating based on inside information they receive from bureaucrats. Moreover, the bureaucrats at the helm of state enterprises act as both state functionaries and businessmen, with disastrous results. That is to say, they engage in speculative investment with state funds, knowing full well that they are ultimately not responsible for any losses that might come from such investments. Rational planning, the presumed benefit of a command economy, is defeated even as the mitigating factor of risk inherent in speculative capital investment is eliminated.

To find a way out of this dilemma, the Benjedid administration embarked on a program of economic reform that included making managers more independent, but more responsible for the profitability of their firms. Given the clannish nature of the Algerian government, however, independent decision making was also accompanied by built-in protections for managers who either made gross business errors or lined their own pockets with profits from state property. "There were appeals to the private sector to produce more, but the result was speculation," says Algerian UN ambassador Ramtane Lamamra,

> it was speculation. No risks, no guarantees that the government's agenda would be carried out, no entrepreneurial spirit, just bazaari [petit-bourgeois] mentality. "I will invest so much, and I will get back so much more." So money was invested in restaurants, hotels, videocassettes, [satellite] dishes, nice cars. In other words, nothing productive.[61]

The other element of the reforms, the breaking-up of large state firms into smaller and more efficient units, was ruined by its contradictory agenda.

Its goals were more efficiency *and* a way to create more jobs for the technocratic graduates of the nation's universities, especially the restless Arab-speaking cohort. The result of this downsizing, therefore, was even more bloated bureaucracy. "The program was not conducted in terms of efficiency, that is, keeping administrative overhead down, but [as] a way to make jobs," says Lamamra. Today, the government admits that industrial production is running at just 50 percent of capacity and that 70 percent of Algeria's food is imported, a rate that consumes approximately one-third of Algeria's gas and oil revenues.

With its vast population of un- or underemployed people and an official economy constricted by IMF-induced austerity programs, Algeria has produced a flourishing underground economy. Despite the fundamentalists' hostility to Western goods and values, Algerians remain absorbed in the consumer culture they joined during the debt-driven boom years of the early 1980s or while working in France. Moreover, with the war and fundamentalist edicts closing off public space, Algerians with disposable income are turning to private consumption, the only form of leisure activity they can participate in without risking their personal safety or reputations. And because state firms are unable to supply the demand, smuggling has grown. "According to official statistics, Omar [a pseudonym] is young (really in his 40s) and unemployed and excluded from the schools," writes Mouffok of one such *trabendist*, or smuggler.

> Twice a week, he returns from Barcelona and Marseilles with valises of jeans, clothes that must say Lacoste, soaps and tights. All of these are prohibited from importation. His role is to get them through Algerian customs, as if he had simply been on a vacation. His enemy is the customs officer. The officer knows what is going on but for a bribe he closes his eyes . . . the buyer waits. He is much younger, very rich, but of course he has relations. He's the one who finances Omar's trip, who is in charge of the valises . . . In exchange for the risk [Omar] receives about $100, a fortune on the black market where $1 brings 75 dinars.[62]

According to Mouffok, the buyer "manages a small battalion of soldiers" and the product ends up on sale in a variety of locales around Algiers. "You see," says the buyer, "I am not allowed to import these products, but I can sell them and I pay taxes on them at the end of the year." The state economy is not immune. The black market, says Mouffok, has become so powerful that it influences legitimate retail business. At major state-run emporia, smuggled goods are plentiful and their prices reflect black-market rates. Nor are the fundamentalist rank-and-file immune from the lure of the underground economy. "A bearded one will sell you some tempting underwear and bras at 1000 dinars [about $12], and then afterward he goes to pray," writes Mouffok.

Like the rest of them [fundamentalists], he has voted for the FIS in the last elections to bring down this impious state which controls commerce. They have voted for the FIS to end the corruption. In the meantime, they live and are nourished by the wages of sin. "The Prophet, may blessings be upon Him," the bearded entrepreneur intones, "wasn't he a businessman?"363

Meanwhile, people are forced to scramble for the basic necessities of life. Patients are required to bring their own medications with them when they go to hospital, but pharmacy shelves are bare. The cars whose presence was made possible by subsidized oil prices, an extensive road-building program and debt, go unserviced for lack of parts. Public transportation is in a sorry state, the planned metro for Algiers is popularly known as the "phantom" and finding a taxi in Algiers "requires patience and strategy."64 And while the most basic foods can still be purchased at subsidized prices in state-run markets, Algerians looking for variety in their diet are forced onto the black market where prices can be exorbitant.

Government and FIS Economic Programs

As bleak as the current economic picture of Algeria appears, the future may be even worse. Neither the government nor the FIS, say many critics, seems to have a realistic program for fixing what ails the Algerian economy. The government offers what it has offered for the past decade or so: liberalization and economic austerity. "Things are different now," insists Lamamra, "because we have to present a program to the IMF and so we have parameters of an almost scientific nature for prices, currency values, and without subsidies. This was not done in the Benjedid era and so did not produce the benefits of liberalization."65

In fact, the government's macroeconomic program has changed. It is now almost entirely based on attracting foreign investment, something not fully realized in the Benjedid era. The "radical but pragmatic economic reforms" include new commerce and investment codes that "define an attractive legal environment which offers maximum guarantees to foreign investors," "formalization of a free currency market . . . [with] free convertibility [of the dinar]," free-enterprise zones and "unrestricted participation" by foreign investors in public enterprises "without any [of the] present limits." This would even include access to the previously sacrosanct oil and gas sector in which, until recently, foreign investment was limited to pipelines and other transport infrastructure.66

In addition, the government plans to accelerate a recently announced domestic privatization program and "more efficient support in favor [of] private enterprises which manage about 50 percent of the country's GDP."67 As one government spokesman announced, "there is no more discrimination between the public and private sectors," although, he insists, the government intends to act "pragmatically to avoid the chaotic situation in other countries which probably acted in a hasty manner." In fact, government economists appear extremely mindful of the problems that befell the Soviet bloc economies during rapid liberalization, and insist that Algeria has learned from these errors.[68]

Nevertheless, strict austerity measures have been in place for a decade. To take one example, medical care is no longer provided free, though the government insists that the indigent will be taken care of. "It didn't make sense that everyone was given hospital care, whether they could afford it or not," says Lamamra. "Since the doctors weren't being paid enough, everyone suffered from poor medical attention under the old system." But equitability of Algerian medicine seems to be threatened. Those who can afford private care will get it; those who go to public hospitals will now have to pay for service that may deteriorate even further, as the best doctors leave the public system and shortages become more intense as scarce foreign reserves are spent on medicines and equipment for private clinics. As one critic pointed out, the solution is worse than the cure because it exacerbates the feeling among Algerians that the privileged are not sharing in the pain of austerity.[69]

Meanwhile, the government insists that the Algerian people be patient and understand that the new economic measures will take time to take effect and have an impact. Agriculture is one instance. It will take years, say government agronomists, for land privatization to have an effect on food prices. The housing crisis, among the most significant socioeconomic problems facing the country, is another. It was never a priority for the government, and it will take some time for the bureaucracy to get moving. "It takes many years, buying raw material, giving more permission [to private contractors]," says one government official. "Lots of people have the means to build, but can't find the land and so the government is easing way for the municipalities to distribute land, opening up to imports of basic [construction materials], and encouraging banks to lend money more easily for the construction of low-cost housing." The same applies, another official says, to the employment problem. "We must have a crusading spirit," he adds.

> Algerians have always dreamed of turning our Sahara into a California. We are floating an idea to send young people to the South. We will tell them: "all your needs are taken care of, but your salary will be given to you in five years. After five years work in the South, you will have the capital to build a home or open a business."[70]

Whether these plans become a reality will be decided in the future, but given the explosive economic and political situation, will that future ever be reached? The FIS, citing past failures of the planned economy and the pain of current austerity measures, insists that the government's economic programs are as bankrupt as its political credibility.

Fundamentalists and their opponents acknowledge that the socioeconomic crisis engulfing Algeria has been a boon to religious politics, though they disagree about why. Critics say it has created a desperate populace in search of simple answers that zealous and/or opportunistic religious leaders have used to their own advantage. The fundamentalists claim that the economic crisis was the result of a spiritual crisis, not the other way round, and that the current woes have awakened Muslims to the truth: the pursuit of secular, godless material goals leads to spiritual and economic catastrophe.

The specific solutions offered by the FIS do not sound all that different from the current government's programs. Foreign investment will be encouraged, though for slightly different reasons than those offered by the government. While both believe that an influx of capital and expertise is necessary, FIS spokesmen emphasize the continuing chokehold France has on the Algerian economy and the need to break it by inviting in other investors. The preoccupation with French capital surprises many outside observers who argue that the FLN effectively yanked Algeria out of France's economic orbit in the 1970s with its nationalization of the oil and gas industry and its establishment of direct pipeline and tanker links with Italy, Spain, the United States and Japan. The FIS also emphasizes increased Algerian participation in the global market, and so does the government. "One will have to favor certain sectors of the economy (export-oriented sectors as [an] example) at the expense of others," reads one FIS statement. "Obviously to implement such a policy one needs to have political stability, which cannot be recovered without political democratization."[71]

On perhaps the most critical economic issue facing Algeria in the near future, privatization, the two sides seem to be heading toward common ground as well. The government is pushing for accelerated privatization, despite some left-wing opposition in its ranks and among secular opponents in other parties. The FIS, once hostile to all government interference in the economy, increasingly includes in official communiqués the need for some central planning, though, admits Haddam, this represents just one school of thought within the party. "It [privatization] has to go gradually," he says. "I'm from that part of the party, because we know the free market economy cannot be introduced at once. We see what happened to eastern Europe and the Soviet Union."[72]

Despite such disclaimers, the basic intent of the FIS' economic program appears to be a rapid and thorough privatization of the economy. This ideological position, of course, is not new for religious leaders. As Burgat points out,

> The nationalization of the 'Agrarian Revolution' launched by the regime in November, 1971, offered a . . . terrain for [religious] recruitment. The language of religion was used . . . to discredit the egalitarianism in the land distribution of Boumédienne. Rumors circulated that a prayer made on nationalized land was not valid.[73]

And indeed, religious spokesmen argued that the expropriation and nationalization of resources was un-Islamic. "We said in fact," a hard-line Islamist explained later in the 1980s, that this was only a revolution for agriculture, and that it could not in any way bring happiness to the Algerian people by itself. For that we have a religion which takes care of everything and which shows everything. It leaves nothing to chance, neither that which is small nor that which is grand.[74]

Echoes of that sentiment can be heard in the utterances of fundamentalists today. "The government damaged our agriculture in 1971 by the revolution," says Haddam.

They nationalized the agricultural network. It was a very devastating thing. We have to give this back to the people. The state should not be considered as a manager. The state farms, the state factories should never have happened.[75]

The Algerian fundamentalists do not hide their hostility to socialism and socialist ideas. As Roy points out, "It is Marxism that is the mirror and foil of the Islamist effort."[76] And, in fact, the fundamentalists say there is nothing in Islam to prevent someone from becoming rich. "We had a long debate about this in the universities [in the early 1980s] with the communists who base their [philosophy] on differences in classes, on struggle. We don't have that," says Haddam. "You have the right to become rich, but not at the expense of others. We will have institutions to prevent this, but after all God is watching."[77]

Statements like these that try to balance the need for human laws and institutions with a reliance on God as the determiner of a just economic order, are what critics have in mind when they say the fundamentalists ultimately do not have a realistic economic program. And, as noted in Chapter 3, Islamic tradition generally eschews class struggle as a form of *fitna*, division, the pitting of Muslim against Muslim, even if it takes the form of non-violent, state institutions established to redistribute wealth, such as the progressive income tax. Even the *zakat*, and *sharia*-mandated tax in support of the poor, say some fundamentalists, does not justify state intervention. "There can be no intervention of the state," insists Haddam, "you can't intervene. As long as they [the wealthy] are obeying the rules [and] paying their duty to the community, you cannot interfere."[78]

Thus, it is not a "massive lacuna in the programmatic outlook of Algerian Islamism," as political scientist Hugh Roberts argues, but rather an inherent contradiction at the heart of fundamentalist thought that makes it seem as if "Algerian Islamism [has] virtually nothing to say about economic policy."[79] But that contradiction is dismissed by fundamentalists as a product of Western thinking, either of the classical capitalist or socialist varieties. Islam, they say, offers a simple solution. If a devout Muslim conforms his economic activities to the *sharia*, the inherent problems of capitalism will be solved without the need for redistributive institutions or social revolution.

Critics, however, say that this is casuistry. "The Islamization of the economy is largely rhetorical," says Roy. Besides conforming to the *sharia*, an Islamic businessman who wants to apply Islamic principles to his economic activities is reduced to laundering his money, that is, achieving "the purification of profits" through institutions like Islamic banks. "But as far as the economy goes, these institutions function between two models," writes Roy, "neither of which is specifically Islamic: the declining model of the centralized, socialist-leaning state, or the triumphant model of liberalism and capitalism."[80] The problem, say scholars, is that the Algerian fundamentalists do not engage themselves with economic theory, nor do they offer analyses of specific economic problems, such as the causes of inflation, surplus value and the like. As in the case of political institutions, economic programs are based on individual virtue and a moral order deriving from the revealed word of God. "The idea of building a modern economy that would function only through the virtue of the economic actors is an illusion," says Roy,

> a sweet one to be sure in terms of collectivist utopias, but for this reason totally nonfunctional, as various attempts [Iran, Pakistan] have shown. And, in economics as in politics, when virtue doesn't function, its opposite emerges: the abuse of power, speculation, and corruption, the banes of "Islamicized" economic systems.[81]

TACTICS

THE GOVERNMENT

The Algerian government's current struggle with the fundamentalists is not entirely a case of "those who sow the wind, reap the whirlwind," but the adage is clearly relevant. Tradition, faith and declining oil prices are obvious factors in the rise of fundamentalism that lie beyond the government's purview. Nevertheless, as pointed out in Chapter 4, FLN policy may very well have encouraged fundamentalist politics in the 1970s and early 1980s as a foil to what then seemed a more threatening radical left. Despite the example of Iran and the explosive growth of fundamentalism in the early 1980s, as evidenced by the ever more massive crowds at the religious opposition's political rallies, the government continued to hope that it could either use the fundamentalists for its own ends, or at least absorb them into the FLN party apparatus. Thus in 1989 the government, in contravention of its own constitution, legalized the FIS.

The landslide victory of the FIS in the municipal elections of 1990 provided a wake-up call. As FIS spokesmen and independent observers note, the government immediately embarked upon a several-pronged offensive after the 1990 elections. It tried to undermine the effectiveness of the municipal councils with new national regulations limiting the juridical powers of the municipalities and scaled back national revenues. When the fundamentalists turned militant in the spring of 1991, organizing street demonstrations against gerrymandering in the upcoming national parliamentary elections, the government responded with a show of military force and postponement of the elections, but also with the appointment of an FLN critic as prime minister, a new, more equitable electoral law and rescheduled elections at the end of the year.

The government's increasing use of religious rhetoric and its acceptance of a fundamentalist-inspired Family Code also played into the hands of the growing religious opposition. "The result of all these processes . . . is what might be called the ideologization of Islam," writes Maghribi sociologist Abdelbaki Hermassi,

> the shift of contemporary Muslim thought from the traditional theological field to an ideological field whose tendency is to formulate the content of Islam in terms of socio-economic and political rather than spiritual norms and values.[81A]

The intent, he adds, was to add a religious luster to a nationalist regime, "to sanctify principles of national cohesion centered on the political leaders," but the strategy proved counterproductive. Not only did it politicize Islamism, but it also served to highlight the discrepancies between the moral pronouncements of FLN leaders and their obvious corrupt practices. The government both failed to achieve its primary objective, religious sanctification of the state, and it ideologized the most important nongovernmental institution in the country, that is, the network of mosques. In so doing, it created a locus around which religious opponents of the regime could rally the faithful masses.

During this entire process, government leaders remained deeply divided about the policy of trying to encourage and coopt Islam and fundamentalists. Reformers around Benjedid correctly believed that the fundamentalists shared their commitment to economic liberalization and hoped to forward their agenda by "capturing" them, offering social concessions as bait. Hard-liners, particularly in the military, disagreed. Iran was always on their minds, especially the systematic and, in their view, disastrous purging of the Iranian military after the 1979 revolution. Military leaders and their allies at the top of the FLN and state enterprise bureaucracy believed they recognized the fundamentalist threat for what it was: a revolutionary movement bent on the political extermination of the *ancien regime*. Whether the military acted out of ideological conviction—a commitment to the ongoing democratization process, as supporters argue—or self-interest will probably never be determined definitively unless the fundamentalists come to power and, following the lead of the Iranian Islamists, publicize the inner doings of the government they've replaced.

Whatever the reasons, the military coup dramatically altered the government's approach to fundamentalist politics. One of the first acts of the new military junta, the High Council of State, was to ban the FIS. On February 9, 1992, a twelve-month state of emergency was declared, and has not been lifted since. The government also moved on the previously sacrosanct space of the free, or non-government-funded, mosques and arrested a number of FIS imams for "inciting and insulting" sermons.[82] In addition, in a dramatic reversal of previous policy, the government has cracked down on what many considered to be the freest press in the Arab world. Since the imposition of the state of emergency, opposition journalists of all political stripes have been imprisoned without trial and over a dozen newspapers shut down.

While the specifics of the government's crackdown since the coup will be explored in Chapter 6, the approach can generally be described as harsh, violent, thorough and in violation of basic due process of law and human rights. Human Rights Watch, as well as a number of independent Algerian human rights organizations, asserts that thousands of prisoners are being held in camps in the Sahara (many built by the French decades earlier to imprison the same people now running the government) and that torture is widespread. Where suspected militants have received trials, says Human Rights Watch, those proceedings have been conducted in special military courts established by Legislative Decree 92–03 "Relative to the Struggle [against] Subversion and Terrorism" of September 1992. Basic defendants' rights such as access to attorneys, appeal and knowledge of an accuser's identity have been ignored.

The government has also banned the FIS from the upcoming elections, though it is allowing individual members to run as independents and is encouraging other religious parties to forward candidates. "The government," says journalist Alfred Hermida, "is trying to include Islamic efforts to put in place the illusion . . . of democracy."[83] Of course, as political scientist Mary-Jane Deeb points out, the more moderate groups have been ideologically, if not institutionally, swallowed up by the FIS, "due to their inability to organize and mobilize people around their leaders and the fact that their agendas were not radically different from that of the FIS."[84] Thus, rather than bringing stability to Algeria, the crackdown has aggravated the violence. Many of the more moderate FIS leaders have been imprisoned, leaving the field to the more radical and violent Armed Islamic Group (GIA). But as journalist Alfred Hermida points out, the "crackdown may be too late, as extremist measures by both sides have helped to radicalize the fundamentalist movement."[85]

FUNDAMENTALISTS

The lack of a defined social and political program and a broad amorphous structure, which make the FIS so popular and successful, also make it problematic as an effective voice of opposition. The party is capable of speaking in many ideological voices and, until its banning, could act as a revolutionary front organization, a religious movement or a Western-style political party as mood and circumstances dictated. The party's initial congress, held in March 1989, clearly reflected this ideological ambivalence and tactical mutability. According to Islamicist Severine Labat, the delegates' failure to reach an agreed-upon platform led them to choose the "least common denominator" instead. "It is noteworthy," she says,

> that the debates that troubled the FIS were almost always over questions of strategy and not on the plan for society that the party intended to set out . . . Ideological quarrels were put off until power had been secured, and were never permitted to interfere with the quest for that power.[86]

If this sounds like the FLN of the 1954–62 period, it is because the two organizations approached the attainment and use of power from similar perspectives. Convinced of the rightness of their project and hoping acts of militancy alone would win over the masses, neither really concerned itself with presenting a plan of governance to the people. Whether the FLN's success at defeating a powerful and entrenched enemy will be repeated by the FIS is hard to say. But the incessant government propaganda that sanctified Algerian militancy over the past thirty years has, say many observers, played an important role both in the approach taken by the Islamic militants and their initial popularity among the masses.

Others disagree with this assessment. Burgat, for one, says it is not fair to criticize the FIS for its lack of programmatic precision since it is charting new political territory and has yet to take power. Moreover, he adds, the party's popularity comes from its ability to speak in an authentic language that anchors Algerians to their heritage and their values at a time when that alone seems like a solution to the nation's crisis regardless of what specific programs it undertakes once in power.

> The 'Allah Akbar [God is great]' that emanates from the mosques, therefore, usually has a double message of rejecting both the West and the secular government accused of being its servant. On the economic level, Islamic discourse gives coherence to the expression of all types (from the student looking for a job to the consumer with nothing to buy), and it facilitates their articulation in political demands . . . This is the essential Islamist theme (simplistic, perhaps, but as such very effective), and the basis of its formidable capacity for mobilization.[87]

Vague or compelling, the real strength of political Islamic discourse, observers agree, is its ubiquity. The omnipresence of Islamist discourse is partly due to traditional factors: the deep faith of the vast majority of Algerian people and the nation's vast religious infrastructure. But it is also a result of the political program of the fundamentalists, and the government's reaction to it. Since the idea of the *jahaliyya*, or break with apostate rulers and corrupted Muslim societies, was first forwarded by the Muslim Brotherhoods of the early twentieth century, and brought to its culmination in the writings of Sayyid Qutb, political Islamists have formulated two approaches to organizing, evangelizing and taking power. One might be called the Iranian model: massive popular agitation and a revolutionary seizure of the government. This approach, especially appropriate to Shiism with its ready-made hierarchy and structure, has never effectively taken hold in Sunni Muslim countries like Algeria.

Instead, fundamentalists outside Iran, especially in recent years when many Islamic politicians wrote off Islamic Iran as an ideological failure, have pursued power by means of another strategy. Since at least the early 1970s, Algeria's religiopolitical leaders have embarked on the gradual systematic Islamicization of society from the bottom up. These "Islamicized spaces," as many call them, allow both political activists and those simply frustrated with contemporary society to create a kind of model society in miniature. The method is quite effective, because it allows supporters to live their political convictions on a daily basis and invests everyday actions with political meaning. Building a life around these Islamicized spaces is at once both a method of separation from the corrupt and apostate society and a political statement that literally demonstrates that actions speak louder than words. Moreover, it jibes with the two most powerful forms of religious practice in Islam (and in Christianity as well): evangelization and ascetic withdrawal.

"Re-Islamization 'from below' is first and foremost a way of rebuilding an identity in a world that has lost its meaning and become amorphous and alienating," writes Islamicist Gilles Kepel. At first, he says, disciples largely came from the lower strata of society rather than Islamic militants: "unemployed labourers or young people with no prospects, fathers upset by children over whom they had lost traditional authority, often turning, in their distress, to drink, drugs or crime, until brought back to the path of true religion by the itinerant preachers of these movements."[88]

These pietist movements were largely tolerated by the government, which saw them as conservators of the social order, providing necessary services like schooling, health care and welfare in the poorest communities where governmental institutions were scarce. But by the end of the 1980s the movements had grown and evolved. "The movements of re-Islamization 'from below' were [now] at the head of powerful networks, which sometimes controlled whole districts and had become the indispensable intermediaries between the public authorities and marginalized social groups," notes Kepel. "At that point a change occurred in relations with the government: these movements began to take part in political life, a field into which they had seldom ventured before."[89]

Specifically religious space in Muslim societies has an ancient tradition. The purpose of the Islamic state has always been the creation of an environment in which the faith can thrive. As Roy notes, "The state is an instrument and not an end in itself."[90] This implies that the Islamic prince should not interfere in those spaces, specifically the mosque and the family, where a higher law, the *sharia*, applies. But the idea that these spaces, either literal spaces such as neighborhoods or institutional spaces such as banks, should serve both as models for the larger society and state and as bases for an assault on that society and state is something new to fundamentalism. "One can prepare for the Islamic society through local militancy, associations, cooperatives, and other institutions," says Roy, "in this sense neofundamentalism is to Islamism what social democracy was to Marxism."[91]

The Islamicization of social space is a step on the path to the perfection of man, man's institutions and human society. This millenarianism is the source of the vagueness of the Islamists' political program. As Roy points out, to fundamentalists "it is the ethical disposition of one's soul that gives unity to one's knowledge and practices . . . Knowledge is not the result of analytic reasoning, but a mystical object, which is refracted and fragmented into the many facets of the world."[92] Therefore, he says, the fundamentalists are predisposed to a rejection of *itjihad*, or free interpretation of scripture, an embrace of a priori argumentation, and a reliance on charismatic leaders, all hallmarks of the Algerian fundamentalist movement, say critics. The result is an inherent contradiction between belief and rhetoric. It is in the spirit of *taqlid*, imitation," says Roy, "that one demands *itjihad*, critical innovation."[93]

Another contradiction, say critics, arises when fundamentalists move from the traditional sphere of theological discussion to overt political discourse. In its desire to influence social policy and gain access to political power through electoral means, the FIS has compromised itself on the one principle that underlies its entire agenda. That is to say, the FIS has abandoned godly rhetoric for populist demands, thus violating the basic Islamist principle that all sovereignty comes from God. In fact, says Roberts,

> its impatience to exert influence has left it wide open to being manipulated. Only if it had . . . left lobbying and populism to the other tendencies in Algerian politics, could the Islamists have made themselves intellectually and morally independent of the FLN state . . .[94]

By adopting an electoral strategy, says Roy, "the autonomous functioning of the political and social arenas wins out, but only after the religious sphere has been emptied of its value as a place of transcendence, refuge, and protest, since it is now identified with the new power."[95]

The results have been predictable. Those elements within the FIS who disagreed with the electoral strategy from the beginning have broken from the movement, to form the more militant GIA, though the government asserts that there are still connections between the two. While the FIS publicly maintains a commitment to the electoral process, and has formed an alliance against the military junta with a number of opposition parties, including the FLN, the GIA has decided to confront the government directly with acts of violence and terror. While the GIA's campaign will be outlined in Chapter 6, it should be noted here that the GIA's tactics have worked, to a degree. If the social crisis of the 1980s is what gave the FIS its political momentum, then the heightened tension of an Algeria at war with itself creates an ideal atmosphere for the GIA's brand of militant politics. Its members can idealize themselves as defenders of the people, and its militancy is appealing to precisely those elements of Algerian society who are most frustrated with the existing order, the alienated young supporters of the FIS.

Still, it is not clear who is responsible for some of the more violent acts in Algeria and in France. The GIA often does not take responsibility for terrorist actions, like the wave of bombings and attempted bombings that struck France in 1994 and 1995. Meanwhile the FIS has vacillated publicly on its use of violence. Some FIS spokespersons have asserted that the organization does not condone violence in any form; others say it is used defensively, with targets restricted to military and police personnel. But the huge number of civilian deaths, especially of critics of the FIS and those who flout Islamic rules of propriety, suggests fundamentalist death squads. Moreover, the FIS has not clearly and publicly outlined its relationship to the GIA. When asked if the FIS was in fact in control of the GIA, Haddam would say only that given the government's violence against the FIS, the organization needed a means of self-defense. Many observers inside and outside the government, however, wonder whether events have spun out of the FIS leaders' control. "Maybe the leadership that we [the government] know are no longer accepted by their militants," said Lamamra

> but those leaders have yet to agree to the constitutional due process and denounce violence. That would help to clarify the whole picture. Violence can be done anywhere of course, but at least it wouldn't be done in the name of the FIS.[96]

To which the FIS' representative to the United States and Europe responds:

> There might be these terrorists operating in our name. We can't control everybody and anybody can sign whatever. The policy we have tried [is to] let our people understand what the movement stands for. The struggle is against the military who took over the institutions of the state. We are not struggling against the people. According to international law, unfortunately, we have no right to have an armed wing. Therefore we have decided to keep the FIS as a political party.[97]

The official position of the party remains:

[We] have never viewed force or violence as the *only* means for solving the problem . . . Following the coup . . . and the crackdown on our people (more than 30,000 arrests within the first 3 days), we tried our utmost to contain any views calling for escalation toward the use of force. We gave firm instructions to our constituency to avoid any provocation and confrontation. We declared, following the cancellation of the elections, that we would resort to legal means. [emphasis added][98]

Secular opponents of the FIS claim that the organization is definitely involved in the murder, kidnapping and torture of civilians, including the shooting of women who do not wear the veil and journalists who criticize the party. After detailing horrific tortures of journalist friends, including beheadings and disembowelments, at a symposium on Algerian women held in New York in June 1995, one female Algerian reporter told an American-based Islamist spokesman, who was unaffiliated with the FIS, that if he did in fact represent the party, "I would have spit on you and left this forum." In response, the spokesman reiterated the FIS' official line on civilian murder: the party does not know who is responsible and that outside observers do not know who is responsible, hence the need for an independent and neutral commission to look into the allegations and punish those who have perpetrated them whether they work for the government, are Islamists or are part of secular death squads like the Young Algerians for Freedom who have been accused of murdering women for wearing the veil in public.

NEGOTIATIONS

It is never easy to determine the status of negotiations, especially in civil conflicts, and particularly in Algeria, where the government usually reaches important decisions in secret and where the opposition speaks with many voices. Nevertheless, objective conditions, including street violence, official human rights abuses and harsh rhetoric from both sides, would seem to indicate the sides are perhaps further apart than they were when the military seized power in January 1992. The essential points of contention have not changed since that time: the military junta does not believe that the fundamentalists can be trusted with power and the FIS says that they represent the real government of Algeria, "the only legitimate representatives of the Algerian people," and that the current regime is founded on an illegal and unconstitutional seizure of power.[99]

Despite these differences, there has been a series of unofficial but high-level negotiations between FIS leaders Madani and Belhadj and the military-appointed Algerian president Liamine Zeroual. In December 1993, then minister of defense Zeroual moved to have Madani and Belhadj removed from prison and placed under house arrest at a government-owned villa near Algiers. "[Zeroual] was under the impression that something was possible to do if [the FIS leaders'] conditions were improved and if they were given access to communications facilities," says Lamamra. "The hope was that they would appeal to the armed groups not to use violence anymore. And when Zeroual became president in early 1994, they were given access to telephones, faxes, visitors and they had a lot from the government."[100] In June 1995, the two FIS spokesmen were put back in prison after one last series of direct negotiations between the FIS and Zeroual failed to reach an agreement.

According to the government, Madani and Belhadj failed to live up to their end of the bargain. Government spokesmen claim that about one year after the two were moved to Algiers a message from Belhadj was found in the pocket of an Islamic militant killed by the security forces. The note, says Lamamra, paraphrasing it, was that the FIS leader

> supported war and jihad, just the opposite of what he promised the government he would do. It said if sometimes you hear that we have to be flexible in our public statements. Don't believe what we say in public. You have to proceed with your strategy. It's some kind of division of labor, and this is [the radical] Belhadj talking, not [the more moderate] Madane.[101]

This, say official government communiqués, indicated that the FIS leaders were unwilling to accept the basic prerequisite, renunciation of violence, for participation in the transitional government. The decision to try a new round of elections, rather than to seek a negotiated transfer of power or sharing of power with the FIS, was reached by the end of 1994 and, say government spokesmen, was made when it was clear that the FIS was committed to a continuing campaign of violence and an unwillingness to abide by the country's constitution. "Remember," says Lamamra, "that even when the FIS was a legal party, its spokesmen made public statements on TV and in rallies [that] they were against the constitution, only [for] what God and the Prophet say is the law of the land."[102] Meanwhile, the government insists that the FIS will not be able to run in the upcoming elections, though individuals associated with the organization may, if they renounce violence. "It may very well be an election of the FIS, without the name," adds Lamamra. In fact, the FIS boycotted the November 1995 presidential elections.

While negotiations between the government and the fundamentalists have come to almost nothing, talks among the various opposition parties have proved more fruitful. In January 1995, virtually all the major opposition parties, including the Berberist Socialist Forces Front (FFS), the FIS, Ben Bella's Movement for Democratic Action (MDA), the FLN (officially removed from power by the junta) and the main Algerian human rights organization, the Algerian League for the Defense of Human Rights (LADDH), met under the auspices of the Sant'Egidio religious brotherhood in Rome, and signed "a platform for a political and peaceful solution of the Algerian crisis."[103] The government turned down an offer from the brotherhood to attend.

The so-called Rome platform was a general statement of purpose rather than a specific set of procedures for the restoration of democracy. As had the government, the signatories called for a renunciation of violence, respect for human rights and equality of gender, as well as the end of the dictatorship and a "respect for popular legitimacy." In a direct slap at the junta, the declaration stated that "institutions freely elected cannot be questioned except through the people's will." It also set a list of conditions that would have to precede negotiations, including "full freedom for the FIS leaders and all other political detainees," "abrogation of the decision to ban the FIS," cancellation of all emergency rule measures including those on the press, an end to capital punishment, extrajudicial killings and "reprisals against the civilian population," and the establishment of an "independent commission of inquiry to investigate these acts of violence and serious violations of human rights."[104] Both the GIA and another shadowy militant group known as the Armed Islamic Movement (MIA) rejected the platform and said they would keep up the armed struggle.

The Algerian regime, meanwhile, has publicly dismissed the Rome platform as an unacceptable ultimatum. "They didn't want to negotiate with the government," says Lamamra,

> they wanted to impose their platform as the basis of the solution. [The signatories] are saying ridiculous things. That is, as soon as the government releases Belhadj and Madani, the FIS will stop killing civilians and taking hostages. Then if the FIS is established as a formal political party, then something else will take place . . . Completely forgotten is the Constitution [which] says that the government is the only institution that has a legitimate right to the use of violence according to international law. It puts the armed groups on an equal footing.[105]

In the meantime, the government established a set of procedures for the revival of the democratic process. It began with a presidential election in November 1995. This was a nonpartisan poll. Individual candidates, without party affiliation, could run. As a government spokesman pointed out, winning this first election would be critical because the president will implement the electoral laws for the parliamentary elections. After winning the election handily (receiving 61 percent of a 75 percent turnout), Zeroual announced a constitutional referendum for 1996 and legislative elections in 1997, though the terms of the latter were not announced.

The reaction of the Rome signatories was mixed. A spokesman disputed the government's high turnout claims, saying it was less than half, and cited numerous cases of fraud and voter intimidation. Still, there were signs that both sides saw the elections as a watershed event and that negotiations between the government and the Rome signatories should be revived. With their boycott largely ignored, the FIS was put on the defensive. "We are ready to dialogue with that regime in order to contribute to a return of peace in Algeria," said Rabeh Kebir, the FIS' chief overseas representative. Zeroual, bolstered by his victory, was conciliatory as well. As an editorial in *El Watan*, Algeria's largest daily, noted, Zeroual had "won the legitimacy that would allow him some political freedom" to negotiate.[106]

The talk of rapprochement, however, was brief, and negotiations never got off the ground. The FIS, caught up in a growing confrontation with the GIA and with most of its members in jail or exile, was not in a position to initiate them, while the government, bolstered by its decisive win in the elections, was not in the mood. As for the secular Rome signatory parties, many of their leaders believe they had erred in joining the FIS' boycott.

NOTES

[1] Haddam, Anwar, "The Algerian Crisis: FIS Viewpoint," unpublished manuscript, 1995, p. 9.

[2] Haddam, Anwar, interview with author, August 30, 1995.

[3] Seghir, Mohammed, "Political Islam and Government: Agenda and Method," talk given at Symposium on Political Islam and Women in Algeria, New York: Hunter College, June 23, 1995.

[4] Haddam, "Algerian Crisis," p. 9.

[5] Burgat, François and Dowell, William, *The Islamic Movement in North Africa*, Austin, Tex.: Center for Middle Eastern Studies at the University of Texas, 1993, p. 124.

[6] *Ibid.*, p. 247.

[7] *Ibid.*, p. 127.

[8] Cited in *ibid.*, pp. 73–4.

[9] *Ibid.*, p. 64.

[10] Roy, Olivier, *The Failure of Political Islam*, Cambridge, Mass.: Harvard University Press, 1994, p. 61.

[11] *Ibid.*, p. 43.

[12] Mouffok, Ghania, "La *hogra*" in Reporters sans frontières, *Le drame algérien: un peuple en otage*, Paris: Éditions la découverte, 1994, pp. 30–1.

[12A] Islamic fundamentalism is not unique on this score. Both Christian and Jewish fundamentalism place scriptural authority above secular authority. But current Christian doctrine draws a distinct line between the two that allows most believers to retain a faith in the literal correctness of the gospels while allowing them to accept the democratic will of the people. Jewish fundamentalism offers a closer parallel in that many ultra-Orthodox either don't accept the legitimacy of secular Zionism or believe that Mosaic law should be adopted by the state of Israel.

[13] Kepel, Gilles, *The Revenge of God: The Resurgence of Islam, Christianity and Judaism in the Modern World*, University Park, Pa.: The Pennsylvania State University Press, 1994, p. 194.

[14] Maududi, A., *The Islamic Law and Constitution*, Lahore, Pakistan: Islamic Publication, 1980, p. 218.

[15] Barakat, Halim, *The Arab World: Society, Culture, and State*, Berkeley: University of California Press, 1993, p. 281.

[16] Kepel, *Revenge of God*, pp. 193–4.

[17] Barakat, *Arab World*, p. 281.

[18] Seghir, Mohammed, "Political Islam and Government."

[19] Maghraoui, Makhtar, "Political Islam and Civil Society: Human Rights, Women's Rights and Individual Freedom," talk given at Symposium on Political Islam and Women in Algeria, New York: Hunter College, June 23, 1995.

[20] *Ibid.*

[21] Cited in Burgat, *Islamic Movement*, p. 125.

[22] *Ibid.*

[23] Entelis, John, "Islam, Democracy, and the State: The Reemergence of Authoritarian Politics in Algeria," in Ruedy, John (ed.), *Islamism and Secularism in North Africa*, New York: St. Martin's Press, 1994, pp. 219–52.

[24] Maghraoui, Abdeslam, "Problems of Transition to Democracy: Algeria's Short-Lived Experiment with Electoral Politics" in *Middle East Insight*, July–October 1992, p. 25.

[25] Haddam, interview.

[26] Roy, *Failure of Islam*, pp. 61–2.

[27] *Ibid.*, p. 62.

[28] Barakat, *Arab World*, p. 151.

[29] Haddam, interview.

[30] Sivan, Emmanuel, and Friedman, Menachem (ed.), *Religious Radicalism and Politics in the Middle East*, Albany, N.Y.: State University of New York Press, 1990, p. 5.

[31] Roy, *Failure of Islam*, pp. 99–100.

[32] Garçon José, "La vie sans l'eau" in Reporters sans frontières, *Le drame algérien: un peuple en otage*, Paris: Éditions la découverte, 1994, pp. 18–20.

[33] Mouffok, Ghania, "La Cité de Diar el Kef" in Reporters sans frontières, *Le drame algérien*.

[34] *Ibid.*

[35] Mouffok, Ghania, "Le Club des pins" in *ibid.*, pp. 18–20.

[36] Hash, Thé, "Hittistes: les murs ont des dos" in *ibid.*, pp. 27–8.

[37] Hakem, Tewfik, "'Kech devises?'" in *ibid.*, pp. 25–6.

[38] Leclère, Thierry, "Un Bateau pour l'Australie" in *ibid.*, p. 31.

[39] Hakem, "La Parabole," pp. 42–7.

[40] Cited in Burgat, *Islamic Movement*, p. 72.

[41] Mouffok, Ghania, "Une société déchirée" in RSF, *Le drame algérien*, pp. 13–5.

[42] El-Kenz, Ali, *Algerian Reflections on Arab Crises*, Austin, Tex.: Center for Middle Eastern Studies, 1991, p. 112.

[43] Roy, *Failure of Islam*, p. 1.

[44] Esposito, John, *The Islamic Threat: Myth or Reality?*, New York: Oxford University Press, 1992, pp. 163–4.

[45] Burgat, *Islamic Movement*, p. 81.

[46] Haddam, "Algerian Crisis," p. 11.

[47] Roy, *Failure of Islam*, p. 80.

[48] *Ibid.*, p. 197.

[49] Lazreg, Marnia, interview with author, June 1, 1995.

[50] Cited in Barakat, *Arab World*, p 103.

[51] el-Kenz, *Algerian Reflections*, p. 112.

[52] Knauss, Peter, *The Persistence of Patriarchy: Class, Gender, and Ideology in Twentieth Century Algeria*, New York: Praeger, 1987, p. 142.

[53] Anonymous, interview with author, June 3, 1995.

[54] Cited in Chafiq, Chahla, *La femme et le retour de l'Islam*, Paris: Editions du Félin, 1991, p. 146.

[55] Cited in Burgat, *Islamic Movement*, p. 103.

[56] Cited in Slyomovics, Susan, "'Hassiba Ben Bouali, If You Could See Our Algeria': Woman and Public Space in Algeria" in *Middle East Report*, January–February 1995. p. 10.

[57] *Ibid.*

[58] Lazreg, Marnia, *The Eloquence of Silence: Algerian Women in Question*, New York: Routledge, 1994, p. 219.

[59] Roy, *Failure of Islam*, p. 83.

[60] *Ibid.*

[61] Lamamra, Ramtane, interview with author, June 21, 1995.

[62] Mouffok, Ghania, "Trabendo" in RSF, *Le drame algérien*, pp. 22–4.

[63] *Ibid.*

[64] Mouffok, "La pénurie de médicants" in RSF, *Le drame algérien*, p. 21.

[65] Lamamra, interview.

[66] Zerhouni, Nourredine Yazid, "Algeria: The Struggle for Democracy," unpublished manuscript, 1992, p. 11.

[67] *Ibid.*

[68] Lamamra, interview.

[69] *Ibid.*

[70] *Ibid.*

[71] Haddam, "Algerian Crisis," p. 13.

[72] Haddam, interview.

[73] Burgat, *Islamic Movement*, p. 255.

[74] Cited in *ibid.*, pp. 255–6.

[75] Haddam, interview.

[76] Roy, *Failure of Islam*, p. 133.

[77] Haddam, interview.

[78] *Ibid.*

[79] Roberts, Hugh, "Doctrinaire Economics and Political Opportunism in the Strategy of Algerian Islamism" in Ruedy, *Islamism and Secularism*, p. 124.

[80] Roy, *Failure of Islam*, pp. 144–5.

[81] *Ibid.*, p. 145.

[81A] Hermassi, Abdelbaki, "The Political and the Religious in the Modern History of the Maghrib" in Ruedy, *Islamism and Secularism*, p. 96.

[82] Human Rights Watch, "Human Rights in Algeria since the Halt of the Electoral Process," New York: Human Rights Watch/Middle East, February 1992, p. 7.

[83] Hermida, Alfred, "The Battle of Algiers" in *Africa Report*, January–February 1994, p. 42.

[84] Deeb, Mary-Jane, "Islam and the State in Algeria and Morocco: A Dialectical Model" in Ruedy, *Islamism and Secularism*, p. 285.

[85] Hermida, "Battle of Algiers," p. 42.

[86] Labat, Severine, "Islamism and Islamists: The Emergence of New Types of Politico-Religious Militants" in Ruedy, *Islamism and Secularism*, p. 105.

[87] Burgat, *Islamic Movement*, p. 77.

[88] Kepel, *Revenge of God*, p. 35.

[89] *Ibid.*, p. 36.

[90] Roy, *Failure of Islam*, p. 14.

[91] *Ibid.*, p. 79.

[92] *Ibid.*, pp. 100–1.

[93] *Ibid.*, p. 104.

[94] Roberts, "Doctrinaire Economics" in Ruedy, *Islamism and Secularism*, p. 144.

[95] Roy, *Failure of Islam*, p. 199.

[96] *Ibid.*

[97] Haddam, interview.

[98] Haddam, "Algerian Crisis," p. 7.

[99] Islamic Salvation Front, "Call to the Participants of the U.N. Human Rights Commission," unpublished manuscript, March 1995, p. 1.

[100] Lamamra, interview.

[101] *Ibid.*

[102] *Ibid.*

[103] Haddam, "Algerian Crisis," after p. 14.

[104] *Ibid.*

[105] Lamamra, interview.

[106] Reuters On-Line Information Service, November 18, 1995.

6

··

UPDATE AND CONCLUSION

No one can take power by force or remain in power by force.
—Anwar Haddam,
Islamic Salvation Front spokesperson

I am a democrat, but I strongly support the army's takeover. Between that and an FIF government, I have no choice as a citizen and a woman.
—Amina Zerrouk, publisher

THE COUP AND ITS AFTERMATH (JANUARY–JUNE 1992)

January 11, 1992, 8:30 in the evening: first came the strains of Algeria's national anthem and then the familiar white-maned and mustachioed face of the nation's president. In what the *New York Times* called a "dramatic television appearance," a tired-looking Chadli Benjedid announced his resignation from office and from "a heavy responsibility that I cannot accept." His stated reasons were vague: "to safeguard the interests of the country and the nation." His appeal seemed strained: "Please consider this resignation a sacrifice on my part in the interest of the stability of the nation." Indeed, as Algerian commentators immediately concluded, the whole telecast seemed forced. While the military remained silent that night, few in Algeria had any doubts about who was behind the startling announcement.[1]

The following day, all speculation was laid to rest, when a junta of military officers and hard-line cabinet members canceled the second round of parliamentary elections—elections that the fundamentalist FIS was likely to win—and announced the formation of a joint executive body known as the High Council of State (HCE). While the body was evenly divided between civilians and military men, it was self-evident to most Algerians and international observers who was calling the shots.[2] "Mr. Chadli's resignation," noted *The Economist*, "was, in effect, a takeover by the army. Improvising with bits and pieces of constitutional camouflage, the generals have set up a series of councils; the strong man on these bodies remains the minister of defense, [General] Khaled Nezzar. Algeria is no more than a step from martial law." Five days later, in a further effort to legitimize the coup, the HCE recalled Mohammed Boudiaf, one of the so-called *chefs*

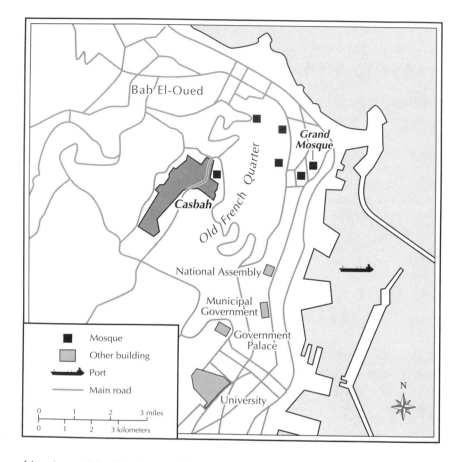

historiques of the Algerian revolution, from twenty-seven years of exile in France to serve as acting president. In a TV speech on January 15, the government's human rights minister explained why he supported the military's actions.

> What threatened us after January 15 was an Islamic state . . . The FIS, which has at least shown some honesty and frankness in this area, said that it is not democratic, that it is against democracy, that it does not want democracy . . . As a minister of human rights, my question is: Who is there to defend the notion of human rights? Am I going to allow a situation, where, in a month or two, people will no longer have any rights? I cannot do that.[3]

To which the FIS' highest nonimprisoned official, Abdelkader Hachani, responded:

> If an Islamic state were to be established in Algeria, all freedoms would be guaranteed. Ulterior motives have been unjustly ascribed to the FIS. It has been condemned even before it has come to power . . . Within the framework of our own values and our own civilization, [other] parties will be allowed to exist. Politics will be enriched by this.[4]

Hachani also cited the municipalities governed by the FIS since the elections of 1990 as examples of the way the party intends to run Algeria. "The fact that there has been no repression in those places . . . is disregarded," he noted. "Other parties' officials retain their posts. They include even women who do not wear the veil."[5]

Nevertheless, the FIS was clearly caught off-guard by the army's move. It took over forty-eight hours for its unjailed leaders to issue a communiqué. When it came, the statement was stern and revealed the FIS' belief that somehow the ruling junta was a puppet of foreign powers, most likely France.

> We call upon veteran fighters, intellectuals, religious leaders, senior army officers and soldiers, sons of martyrs, social organizations and all those who love Algeria to take a stand against this oppressive clique of *foreign* agents that has usurped power. [emphasis added][6]

Other parties that won seats in the first round of parliamentary elections, including the once-ruling National Liberation Front (FLN) and the Berber-based Socialist Forces Front (FFS), condemned the coup. The FLN even called on all Algerian parties, including the fundamentalists, to form a political alliance in opposition to the junta.

Popular opinion was mixed. Virtually all Algerians expressed disapproval of the military's actions, but many were clearly relieved that the FIS had not come to power. "When I saw the tanks rolling through the city streets, I began crying," a twenty-year-old told a reporter. "Not because I was fearful of the army nor afraid of the Islamic Salvation Front, but because I suddenly saw disappear in a matter of moments the liberty that we had struggled so hard to achieve these past three years."[7] Despite tanks in the streets of Algeria's major cities, a strange calm prevailed in the first few days, as people waited for Friday, the Islamic sabbath, the day for religious services and sermons. Nothing happened then but by the end of January, violent skirmishes were reported at mosques in Algeria's major cities, despite a government ban on political sermons, while running battles with police in Algiers' impoverished fundamentalist stronghold were described as "Beirut-like." In the southeastern city of Batna, police clashed with protesting fundamentalists, killing eight and wounding fifty.

The junta also began to beef up police garrisons and made preemptive raids on headquarters of the "Afghanis," Islamist Algerian veterans of the war in Afghanistan, widely considered the most militant of fundamentalists. At the same time, homemade bombs were lobbed at the Justice Ministry and the French consulate. Yet moves by both sides indicated an effort to win hearts and minds by less violent means. The government announced an imminent public works bill to help eliminate unemployment, and the FIS called for a "great peaceful confrontation" in Algiers after prayers on February 4.[8] The general calm and FIS' apparent shock at the coup, said one journalist, had led the army to "dare to hope that it had got away with it."[9] But the increasing violence forced itsr hand. On February 9, the government imposed a state of emergency. A few hours later, ambushers in the Casbah of Algiers, hotbed of the original Algerian revolution, raked two police cars with gunfire, killing six.

THE ASSASSINATION OF BOUDIAF (SUMMER 1992)

Despite the rise in violence, calm continued to prevail through the first few months, due in large part to FIS leaders who, despite fiery speeches about the illegal junta, appealed for civil peace. Hachani told worshipers in his first post-coup sermon, "[The junta] want[s] us to bring the people out into streets so that they can shoot them, but we will not give them a pretext." It seemed, in those first few weeks, as if Algerians were praying for peace, but reluctantly preparing for war. "Even if we are killed or go to prison," Hachani noted in another sermon, "we will one day have an Islamic republic."[10] When Hachani's words proved prophetic and he was jailed, an FIS foreign affairs spokesman again appealed for calm. "I ask you for vigilance and to avoid all provocation . . . pray in calm, go out again in calm, and . . . give no one the opportunity to rejoice in the misfortune of a Muslim."[11]

The regime also appeared to be divided. While the military contingent pushed for a harsher crackdown, Boudiaf and the other civilian members were urging a two-pronged approach in the FLN tradition: a police crackdown ameliorated by an anti-corruption campaign and a massive public works project to alleviate the unemployment and housing crises. Boudiaf also spoke of a sixty-seat interim national assembly from which both the old-line FLN and FIS leaders would be excluded and advocated the release of several hundred militants being held without trial. On June 29, 1992, the internal divisions within the junta burst into the public's conscience in a hail of bullets. While delivering an address in the eastern city of Annaba, Boudiaf was assassinated. In a videotape shown on Algerian TV, Boudiaf uttered these words just before being shot: "We must know that the life of a human being is very short. We are all going to die. Why should we cling so much to power?"

Initially, fingers pointed to the FIS, whose leaders, Belhadj and Madani, were about to go on trial. "It is the FIS," a senior government official announced hours after the attack. "This time they are going to detention camps and they are staying there forever." Boudiaf's family disagreed, and it soon became clear that hard-liners in the military were responsible, indeed, that the gunman had come from one of the elite units of the army. The assassination did not help the military's cause. Among its other consequences, concluded the *New York Times*, it "seems certain to set back the halting progress made by the Government to attract foreign investors." Desperately in need of a capital infusion, the government had offered to sell gas and oil fields valued at some $6 billion.[12]

While most observers expected the junta to get rid of its civilian members and dispense with any constitutional pretext for holding power, it appointed another veteran of the revolution, Ali Kafi, as head of state. The appointment was seen as a largely futile gesture. Kafi was even more a figurehead than Boudiaf, who accomplished little in his anti-corruption campaign. By the time of the assassination, only one senior general had been tried for embezzlement. While some members of the HCE were hinting at a return to elections by the end of the year, most considered the possibility unlikely, a view confirmed at the end of 1992 by the new prime minister Belaid Abdesselam who said he favored a "pause of three to five years, to enable Algeria to tackle its mounting economic woes."[13]

In July, the long-awaited trial of Madani, Belhadj and five other FIS leaders resumed. The military's ban on the FIS had already been approved by the Supreme Court in March. Neither Belhadj nor Madani appeared in court, however, believing that they had been condemned in advance. On July 15, a military tribunal, given power to try civilians under the Emergency Law of February 9, sentenced Madani and Belhadj to fourteen years and gave four-to-six-year sentences to lesser defendants. This was widely considered a conciliatory gesture by the court, since the prosecution was asking for the death penalty and said it would appeal both the convictions and the legality of the military tribunal to the Algerian Supreme Court. The judges, however, quietly admitted that "extenuating circumstances" had been taken into account.[14] Given the mood of FIS and the country generally, "extenuating circumstances" struck many as an understatement. According to journalist Alfred Hermida, "The conviction of the FIS leaders provoked a wave of fundamentalist demonstrations across the country."[15]

THE JUNTA CRACKS DOWN (1992–93)

Street violence, endemic since the 1980s, took a new turn following the coup. Along with continuing illegal demonstrations that turned into violent confrontations with police, there were clandestine attacks on security forces, undertaken by militants as an escalation in their confrontation with the junta. From March to October 1992, over one hundred police officers were killed by assassins, and a large number of weapons was stolen. "The raids follow a familiar pattern," noted Hermida.

> The extremists generally attack police officers late at night as they are returning home. Officers are either fired upon or knifed in the back. In one of the most fatal attacks in July, five police officers were killed when their cars

were sprayed with bullets as they were driving down a country lane on the outskirts of Algiers.[16]

By the end of the year, the toll stood at over 200 soldiers, police and gendarmes (national police) dead. Meanwhile, a number of bystanders were killed as demonstrations were set upon by security forces. In one such incident, a man was shot to death as he gathered his children when protesters set fire to market stalls in a suburb of Algiers. Witnesses said he was shot by security forces because he was bearded like many of the fundamentalist militants.

As society spun out of control, many ordinary Algerians remained hopeful that some form of reconciliation between the junta and the fundamentalists was possible. This hope was destroyed in February 1993 by the attempted assassination of Khaled Nezzar, defense minister and "strong man" on the ruling HCE, during a "weekend of more-than-routine violence." While denying involvement in the attack, the FIS was obviously pleased. "This can be considered a clear warning from the mujahideen [Islamic warriors] to the tyrants who openly fought God and his prophet," said Rabah Kebir, the party's information chief, from his exile "somewhere in Europe."[17]

Most outside observers agree, however, that the junta's crackdown against the fundamentalists preceded the violence directed against security forces. In the days following the coup, police moved on the nation's mosques, banning the use of streets for overflow crowds and removing loudspeakers used for that purpose. More provocatively, some fifty clerics were arrested and held incommunicado. And throughout the spring and summer of 1992, massive raids were conducted against suspected Islamic militants. The junta's main targets were cadres of extremist Afghanis. In February, six members of the Expiation and Sin group, including a woman, were arrested with documents that the government said included plans to set fire to food warehouses to produce a shortage during the holy month of Ramadan (March–April), when Muslims fast from dawn to dusk.

By the end of the year, some 10,000 had been incarcerated in camps in the Sahara where daytime temperatures soar to 120 degrees. Most, according to Amnesty International, were incarcerated without being formally arrested or indicted, in clear violation of the 1989 constitutional provision limiting *garde à vue* (police custody or observation without being charged) to forty-eight hours. Authorities did permit visits by Algerian and international human rights organizations shortly after the camps were set up in March 1992, but these were stopped in June. Amnesty International reported that many detainees were being denied medical attention, contrary to Algerian law, and that the isolation of the camps prevented visits by family members. The government claims it is providing adequate shelter, food and medical attention, and that the camps were set up because Algeria's prisons were not designed to handle such large numbers of detainees.

Trials were held for about 1,000 prisoners during the first year, including many for capital crimes. Between March 1992 and January 1993, almost fifty people were sentenced to death and two were executed. Under laws passed in October 1992, which applied retroactively to all cases since the beginning of the year, the government could double sentences for criminal violations that involved "subversive and terrorist acts," thereby transforming acts punishable by life imprisonment to capital crimes. Moreover, the term "subversive and terrorist" now applied to any act that "threatens state security, territorial integrity and the normal functioning of institutions by acts such as endangering life, property, hindering freedom of movement, impeding public authorities, offending against republican symbols, impeding the functioning of public institutions and hindering free worship and public liberties." To handle the flood of cases under this broad interpretation of the law, three Special Courts were set up under military jurisdiction.[18]

In virtually all of the capital and noncapital trials before the military tribunals, procedures have "lacked some of the safeguards which are maintained under civil justice," according to Amnesty International. Many of the cases were held in closed court. In January 1993, twenty people were sentenced to death, including sixteen *in absentia*, for "plotting to cause massacres and devastation." When defense lawyers protested and walked out, they were replaced with military-appointed attorneys. Meanwhile, of the more than twenty-five cases of death or wounding of bystanders by security forces, none was the subject of an official inquiry.[19] Along with violations of due process in the first year of the junta, including lengthy detentions, anonymous judges, limited public courtroom access, retroactive legislation, limited rights of appeal and arbitrary trial deadlines, came reports of human rights abuses. In March 1993, Amnesty International said it had received testimony from dozens of "victims of torture and ill-treatment" in police stations and prisons throughout the country. "Torture, which was virtually eradicated in Algeria, has now become widespread, and perhaps systematic, in detention centres," the organization explained. "It is used to obtain information, to extract confessions, or simply to punish detainees suspected of having killed or wounded members of the security services."[20]

While the emphasis was on rounding up militants, security forces were also attempting to win the propaganda battle as well. On January 22, 1992, the crackdown on the press, widely considered to be one of the freest in the Arab world following the political opening of the late 1980s, began. Twelve journalists were arrested and several mostly Arabic-language papers closed down including *al-Khabar* (*The News*) for publishing an FIS communiqué calling for soldiers "to disobey the regime" and a "malicious report" about the elite Republican Guard having resigned. A secretary in the newsroom told French reporters, "When the police came, they did not choose, they took with them everyone who happened to be in the editorial office at that moment." Another targeted paper was the pro-Islamist *al-Balagh* (*The*

Message) whose editor and director were arrested for publishing articles critical of the military and a cartoon captioned "The army has betrayed Muslims and taken the side of communists."[21] At the same time, the government tried to prevent foreign reporters from covering demonstrations and police activities. In February 1992, four Spanish journalists were ordered out of the country after filming clashes between police and fundamentalists at an Algiers mosque.

In addition, the regime took to televising the confessions of murder suspects. Between July and September 1992, Algerian TV aired the confessions of Hocine Abderrahim, suspected of planting a bomb at Algiers airport, and members of a group alleged to have carried out several murders in Constantine. As Amnesty International noted, Abderrahim later said his confession was exacted after he had been tortured. "Such televising of confessions," the organization pronounced, "undermines the presumption of innocence guaranteed by the Algerian Constitution."[22]

FUNDAMENTALIST VIOLENCE (1992–94)

The year 1993 marked a dramatic and troubling escalation in the Algerian conflict. During the previous year, killings were mostly confined to security personnel, fundamentalist militants and the odd civilian caught in the crossfire.[23] Though the killings and detentions of fundamentalists were often based on little more than the fact that the suspect wore a beard (beards are a mark of commitment to the teachings of the Prophet, though many fundamentalist militants and supporters began shaving their beards to avoid suspicion), a sense of boundaries to the conflict was maintained. Not so in 1993. From January 1993 to January 1994, casualties doubled over the previous year, while hundreds of civilians were targeted for assassination, often after abduction from the streets by armed militants or security personnel. Agence France-Press, the French wire service, put the toll of casualties in the two years since the coup at 1,017 Islamists, 427 security force personnel and 327 civilians. "Increasingly," Human Rights Watch (HRW) reported in January 1994,

> the violence involved abduction-killings and ambushes of civilians. The victims came from all walks of life, and included prominent writers, professors, public figures and foreigners working or living in Algeria. Both civilians and security forces members have been found dead after having been abducted and murdered in custody.[24]

While the human rights organization blamed the majority of the killings on security forces, it also pointed out that

> there is little doubt that Islamist groups were responsible for some of the killings, despite the absence of claims of responsibility for virtually all acts of violence not committed by uniformed or identifiable security forces. Middle East Watch deplores the fact that, to our knowledge, FIS leaders speaking on behalf of the party have made no statements condemning in clear terms the killing of civilians or of persons in custody, and in some instances have sought to justify the killings of civilians.[25]

The same report also noted that many Algerians, however, including nonfundamentalists, "suspect that there were other forces carrying out some of the killings, using the climate of violence and mayhem as a cover to settle political and personal scores, to eliminate suspected Islamists within the security forces, or to protect financial interests."[26]

While the chaotic conditions and lack of effective communications in Algeria made it difficult even for professional and experienced international human rights observers to determine the precise identities of the perpetrators of all violent acts in 1992 and 1993, the nature of the victims seemed to indicate that many were targets of the fundamentalist militants. According to HRW, these have included civilian officials and employees from all levels of government, court employees, including prosecutors, judges and clerks, government-appointed imams and ordinary Algerians, including farmers, taxi drivers, shopkeepers, intellectuals and journalists.

Each of these groups appears to have been targeted for specific reasons. The highest casualty rate has been among local officials. Appointed by the government in Algiers to replace FIS officials elected during or appointed after the municipal elections of 1990, who have been incarcerated or forced out of office, some twenty mayors and council members were assassinated in 1992 and 1993. According to HRW, these appointees "had been condemned in an underground FIS communiqué, dated April 19, 1992 and signed by party spokesman-in-hiding Abderrazak Redjam, for 'participating in a plot against the people by taking the place of their elected representatives.'" Referring to the killings, Rabah Kebir, chief FIS spokesman in exile, told HRW in November 1993 that

> [the appointees] were directly notified after they replaced the fired elected people that they should resign from the government because their action was usurpation. Even so, there was no random application of the execution orders against them. Always, the matter was decided after a local study was conducted, and it was determined whether [the appointee] was in fact working to strike at people, that is, informing the police, or facilitating in the work of the security forces in killing people. If he did these things, then he became a target. But if he worked in administrative matters, no.[27]

National government officials have also been targeted, though in lesser numbers due to the higher security presence surrounding them. In March 1993, the minister of vocational education was assassinated in Algiers. Earlier, three members of the National Consultative Council (CNN), a sixty-member advisory body created by the HCE in early 1992 as a substitute for the disbanded APN, were shot to death after underground Islamist publications denounced the CNN as "usurpationist."[28]

In addition, between March and November 1993, some twenty Algerian intellectuals were killed, mostly in and around their homes. These included professors, human rights activists and at least seven journalists. Of the latter, HRW says the attacks were "believed by many to be the work of armed Islamist groups." After receiving several threats against his life beginning in 1991, the anti-Islamist editor of the independent and highly respected French-language daily *el-Watan (The National)*, Omar Belhouchet, was gunned down while driving his children to school in May 1993. While no one has taken responsibility and Belhouchet had had run-ins with the government (he was detained for a week and the paper shut down for ten days in early 1993), most suspected Islamist assassins of the crime.[29]

Most journalists critical of the Islamists have received numerous threats against their lives. They have also altered their work and travel routines, and have asked that their bylines be removed from stories. "Death threats come by fax to a newspaper office and are posted in mosques in my neighborhood," said one Algerian journalist. "After my death threat, I spent two years in hiding, not being able to stroll outdoors, living at friends, neighbors, family, fearing every moment for two years. I couldn't see my own mother. I not only risked getting killed but putting loved ones in danger."[30]

While this journalist had no question in her mind that virtually all the attacks on journalists are the doing of the fundamentalists, human rights organizations say this is often difficult to determine since few murders are accompanied by statements saying who is responsible. Moreover, even when evidence points to fundamentalists, it is difficult to determine which group. By the end of 1992, few in Algeria had any doubts that there were extremely violent militant fundamentalist groups operating around the country, but their relationship to the FIS has remained shadowy. "These are acts of violence of the government because it is not a tradition of the country's Islamists to assassinate foreigners or hijack planes," says Mohammed Seghir, an Islamist scholar unaffiliated with the FIS. "The regime's media machine has convinced the world that it is fighting terrorism. Whenever the Algerian question surfaces, or torture is noticed, the government uses this fear of Islamist autocracy as justification."[31]

But opponents of the fundamentalists have no doubts that the armed groups are part of the FIS. "Some wings of the Islamist movement, with connections to the FIS, seek national reconciliation to win over portions of the army and opposition parties," notes one Algerian journalist.

> This is creating the entertaining illusion of the moderate Islamist. Who can define a moderate fanaticism? These attempts [at reconciliation] failed as soon as the talks reached concrete issues, of the conception of the state, power sharing and denunciation of terrorism. Of course, obviously, [the FIS] cannot disassociate themselves from the armed Islamic groups because of their organic unity and ties. In fact, fundamentalism is a totalitarian movement, which seeks compromise only as a tactic to impose, in insidious fashion, all of its views on everyone and at whatever cost.[32]

Meanwhile, human rights organizations were cautious in making direct connections between the FIS and the armed groups, while the FIS itself issued statements that alternatively indicated a close association among the groups and tried to put some distance between the FIS and the militants. In one communiqué from summer 1993, the FIS said it "vowed to combat not only the regime but also their secularist-communist allies."[33] And indeed a number of union activists and members of the Algerian Communist Party (PAGS) were gunned down in 1992 and 1993, though, as HRW points out, responsibility for the murders has "gone unclaimed, and the motives in many cases remain murky."[34]

Top FIS officials are in fact on record advocating violence against civilians. Anwar Haddam, who won a seat in parliament in the December 1991 elections and represents the FIS in Europe and in Washington, told Agence France-Presse that the murder of psychiatry professor Mahfoud Boucebi in July 1993 was "a sentence and not a crime." Commenting about the killings of intellectuals, Haddam added,

> Who are these so-called intellectuals? Among them are members of the National Consultative Council, which has usurped the place of the people's elected representatives, persons who wrote murderous editorials, and those who, through psychiatry, advised torturers on how to obtain confessions. The Algerian people have chosen as targets only those individuals upon whom the military-security system in Algeria relies. We know them one by one, and they are not innocent people.[35]

In a statement smuggled out of his prison cell in January 1993, Belhadj unequivocally expressed his support for the broadest possible war against the regime. "If I were outside the walls of prison, I would join the ranks of my brothers who fight to rid the people of this brazen junta," he announced. "I swear to you, O Algerians, if I were free I would enlist as a foot soldier under the command of brother *mujahid* Abdelkader Chebouti [leader of the military branch of the FIS, the Armed Islamist Movement (MIA)]."[36]

Around the same time, however, another high FIS official in exile in Sudan told reporters that his organization targeted members of the security forces only and said that the killings of intellectuals and foreigners "could only be the making of the Military Security" or "personal vendettas." He also expressed doubts that a new, more militant organization that has claimed responsibility for numerous assassinations of civilian opponents of the fundamentalists, the Armed Islamic Group (GIA), actually existed and if it did whether it was "infiltrated by the police."[37] In general, HRW announced in its January 1994 report, responsibility for the violence is difficult to ascertain. Pronouncements by FIS leaders are inconsistent; the organization lacks a definitive structure upon which responsibility can be laid; and its current underground status means that most members of the organization do not know what others are doing. But the human rights organization also cautions against accepting government statements at face value. "It is not possible confidently to attribute responsibility on the basis of official press reports or of convictions in the Special Courts," it reported.

> Press reporting on security incidents is not free, and the facts supposedly established in Special Court trials are susceptible to doubt on the grounds that the trials violate standards of fairness and impartiality.[38]

A WAR OF WORDS (1992–95)

The conflict in Algeria is as much a war of words as it is a war of bullets and bombs. The level of political invective reflects both the intensity of the conflict and the extremely divergent perspectives of the combatants. The fundamentalists and their sympathizers say the junta ("I won't say government because according to our Constitution, there is no government," an FIS spokesman said[39]) canceled the election results because it knew it was going to lose. For them, the current regime is illegitimate, undemocratic, foreign-controlled (that is, controlled from Paris), invidiously secular, misleading in its propaganda, economically incompetent, violent, abusive of human rights, unwilling to negotiate and, perhaps most important, out of touch with the essentially Islamic character of Algerian society. The government and its supporters counter that the fundamentalists stole the election, and that they are anti-democratic, under the control of a Muslim "comintern," socially totalitarian, deceptive, economically illiterate, rigid and uncompromising in their negotiating posture and, perhaps most significant, represent a perversion of true Islamic faith.

The following is a selection of issues with arguments made by representatives of the government, the fundamentalists and unaffiliated supporters of both sides:

On the question of elections, that the FIS was indeed winning and that the military refused to allow the electoral process to continue allows the fundamentalists to argue that they should be the rulers of contemporary Algeria. "The military/security establishment, instead of upholding its constitutional duties—to fend off any external threat and protect the sovereignty of the country—played a prominent role [in the cancellation of the elections], turning its machine inward to protect 'the stability of the system,'" says Haddam. The very democratization process of the late 1980s and early 1990s, he adds, was beset with obstacles for the fundamentalists, including "an arsenal of regulations to prevent any opposition from achieving any decisive victory . . . The ruling elite insisted on being outside the democratic process. They refused to be removed through the ballot box no matter how high the cost they may need to inflict upon the population."[40]

Despite its position as the party in power, the government charges that it was robbed in the elections. "Substantial evidence exists that the first round of [the parliamentary] elections," says a release from the Algerian Embassy in Washington, "was marked by wholesale fraud, ballot-box stuffing, double counting of votes, threatening of voters, manipulation of election lists and overall misuse of the system by the FIS, especially in those local governments controlled by the FIS." To which Anissa Benaneur, a supporter of the FLN, adds her personal experience. "I discovered that the FIS had voted for me. From six to eight o'clock in the morning, people at my polling station voted without their ID cards. How can you give legitimate power to a party that cheats?"[41]

Each side also charges that the other is being manipulated by outside forces. The fundamentalists argue that while the French physically left Algeria in 1962, they maintained their control by placing their lackeys, or in more sophisticated formulations their francophile offspring, in charge. This argument is often fused with attacks on the regime's "un-Algerian" secularism and anti-Islamicism. "Under the imposed Marxist rule of Algeria up to the beginning of the eighties, Muslim intellectuals were seen as an ideological danger to socialism and to French culture," notes the pro-FIS Algerian Committee of the Free Activists for Human Dignity and Human Rights.[42] "The actual regime," notes Ali Yahia Abdennour, a lawyer for the FIS, "is the bunch of ex-French officers who are today the generals of the Machiavellian political system."[43]

Meanwhile, opponents of the fundamentalists charge the FIS with running gun-for-drug operations in Europe and being supported by the most repressive Islamic regimes in the Arab world, including Saudi Arabia. Others say that the fundamentalists have "a broader project of building an Islamic empire, the *umma islamiyya*, to counter a hegemonic West which they see as apostate, ungodly, depraved and doomed to hell, even as they use the West for asylum, organizing, and access to media."[44]

Needless to say, each side has also tried to play to the worst fears of the populace, caricaturing the other's position in reductivist terms. On the question of Islam and democracy, the FIS claims the regime is engaged in

an all-out war on Islam itself. "Within this rule [of the FLN before 1992],"
FIS supporters say,

> francophile and communist intellectuals and writers, with no grassroot
> support . . . played an active part in attempting to de-Islamize [sic] Algerian
> society. Under the present rule . . . Muslim intellectuals are eliminated pure
> and simple . . .[45]

The government asserts that a fundamentalist regime would extermi-
nate political pluralism and democracy as well as impose a rigid Islam-based
totalitarian order. After the first round of elections, says Nourredine Yazid
Zerhouni, Algerian ambassador to Washington, "leader after leader of this
fundamentalist movement were [sic] indeed promising nothing short of a
return to the single-party system and to an arbitrary rule." In essence, the
FIS leadership promised to:

- abolish the constitution and the multiparty system
- suspend individual freedom, and particularly freedom of the press
- impose their concept of Islamic law . . . whose devastating and
  oppressive effects have been amply demonstrated in known areas
  of the world
- set up emergency courts and an expeditious judicial procedure
- ban women from the workplace and limit their rights by ques-
  tioning the political, economic, and social gains which they had
  achieved since the war of independence.[46]

On economics, the fundamentalists point to the regime's history of
mismanagement and corruption, while the government says the fundamentalists do not have a clue on how to fix things. Interestingly, both the
fundamentalists and the government appeal to the West, and particularly
to its business and financial communities. Both sides reiterate their commitment to free enterprise, foreign investment and a pro-Western foreign
policy. The regime tries to convince the West that it has shed its socialist
and protectionist economic and trade policies, while the fundamentalists
emphasize the congruity between capitalism and free enterprise and
traditional Islam, even as they continue their attacks on the international
lending institutions that they say are cooperating with the regime to
maintain it in power.

As for the conflict itself, the fundamentalists claim that the government resorted to violence first and that, in response, the opposition had
to defend itself. "This military junta has committed a historical mistake
when it thwarted the democratic process," writes Haddam, "trans-
gressed against the Constitution, confiscated the choice of the people
when it voided the parliamentary elections, dissolved the municipalities
elected a year and a half ago [1990], suppressed and banned the

legitimately winning party, imposed a state of emergency, resorted to brutal and repressive measures and forced the entire country into this regrettable state of war."[47] Indeed, the FIS claims that violence against Muslims dates back to the beginning of the republic.

The government counters the argument by saying that it had to move against the FIS or risk Algerian democracy itself. "The primary reason behind the government's action," says a statement from the Algerian Embassy in Washington, "was to prevent the Islamic Salvation Front from taking advantage of an incipient electoral process and from using terror and violence to turn the country back to a totalitarian, anti-democratic dictatorship, as FIS leaders had openly promised, and as happened in Germany with Hitler fifty years ago."[48] Fatiha Younsi, a high school principal in Algiers and a member of the National Human Rights Watch, adds that the "fanatics [of the FIS] stop at nothing and resort to kinds of violence that amazes and terrorizes those who oppose them." At a 1995 conference on Algerian women, journalist Amal Boumedienne cited case after case of "unspeakable" torture and abuse of women by the GIA, including *muta*, or temporary forced marriage, to Islamic militants.

And, of course, each side claims that the other is the major obstacle to a peaceful settlement of the conflict. The government argues that the Rome signatories, representing all the major opposition parties in Algeria, secular and religious, are demanding sovereignty before negotiations. That is to say, they are demanding that the government concede its power to maintain public order before the opposition will come to the negotiating table. Supporters of the government argue that the Islamists are opportunists and that their cooperation with the secular opposition is a ruse. "The fundamentalists have a dual strategy," says Younsi,

> . . . bloody attacks on civilians to terrorize and paralyze them and to isolate Algeria and close it off the from the world by assaulting foreigners, hijacking airplanes, and calling for a boycott against Algeria even as they condemn the boycott on Iraq. The other strategy seeks to achieve an alliance with other factions, like with the Sant'Edigio [Rome] platform, that is the most obvious proof of it.[48A]

The FIS counters by pointing out that the Rome platform represents parties that received 80 percent of the vote in the 1991 parliamentary elections. "By rejecting this platform," an April 1995 FIS statement read, "and hence by refusing to come to the negotiating table on the terms of the Algerian people, as expressed by its duly elected representatives, the military/security establishment-backed government and its foreign creditors have expressed their desire to prolong the vicious cycle of violence at the expense of not only Algeria's stability but of the entire region. They have exposed themselves in a total shame [sham]!"[49]

Ultimately, all these charges and countercharges are based on the idea that the other side stands in opposition to the basic values of Algerian society. "In post-colonial Algeria," argues Haddam, "the Algerian Muslim people have come to know with full conviction that those in power are nothing more than . . . culturally self-hating elite[s] that care little for the ethical, moral, and civilizational dimensions of Islam." Algeria's UN ambassador, Ramtane Lamamra, sees things differently. "I think Algerians are moderate Muslims, by practice, by education, and by custom," he says. "I don't think there is really an adherence to [the FIS'] political program.

> We have lived with the French for over 100 years, and we have over a million Algerians in France. I think most Algerians are not desirous of militant Islam and they are open to other cultures.[50]

CIVIL CONFLICT TO CIVIL WAR (1994)

The year 1994 began with a threat and ended with a most audacious fulfillment of that threat. In between, the conflict spun out of control. In September 1993, the GIA (which may or may not be directly affiliated with the FIS), an organization often described in the Western press in terms such as "a shadowy guerrilla faction,"[51] issued an ultimatum to the 100,000 foreigners in Algeria: leave by December 1 or die.[52] On December 14, fourteen Bosnian and Croatian nationals (all Christians, according to the Algerian government) were stabbed to death in their quarters near the Croatian-owned power company where they worked. A little over a year later, on Christmas Eve 1994, four armed militants of the GIA hijacked an Air France airbus at the Algiers airport, killing three hostages. Hoping to blow up the jet over Paris, or so some of the passengers claimed, the militants were instead killed at the Marseilles airport by French commandos.

The militants' aims reflected the new international dimensions, as well as the increasing chaos and intensity, of the Algerian conflict. They included a demand that France end its "unconditional political, military and economic aid"[53] to the Algerian regime and pay compensation to the Algerian people for the years of French colonization and colonial war. "France is being sucked deeper into the Algerian civil war," noted *The Economist*, "however much the government may protest its neutrality." And even as the conflict spread across the Mediterranean, it had intensified manyfold back home.[54]

The proliferation of guns and armed groups, as well as the intensified reaction of the security forces, was turning the cities of Algeria into virtual war zones. Some FIS leaders admitted in the winter of 1994 that they were losing control of the armed Islamic groups. "The best organization is no organization," a senior FIS official said. "You now get five or six kids with a few guns who want to help the revolution. Even we don't know who they are."[55] While the government disputed assertions that "liberated zones" were being established in various towns and cities, the *New York Times* reported in January 1994 that the Islamic militants "own the streets after dark [and] have already carved out small enclaves. In the militant stronghold of Blida, 30 miles south of Algiers, the militants run whole neighborhoods and battle the police."[56]

Adding to the carnage was the appearance of anti-Islamic death squads in the large cities. Calling themselves the Organization of Free Algerians (OAL) and the Secret Organization to Safeguard the Algerian Republic, they began reprisal attacks for Islamist slayings in September 1993, but intensified their actions in January 1994.[57]

> Reprisal killings have become so commonplace that neighborhoods where police or security officials are killed now brace themselves for attacks by the paramilitary forces. The death squads often double the number of victims who died at the hands of Islamic militants. If two policemen are shot dead, for example, it is not uncommon to find four bodies dumped by the death squads in the same place the next day. "Every time a policeman is killed here the death squads strike," said a baker in Kouba . . . "We all try to lie low."[58]

Official government forces intensified their raids against militants after the new year, and appeared to be taking the law into their own hands. To take one example, in the town of Larba 30 miles southeast of Algiers, witnesses say they saw soldiers drag five men from their homes and kill them in front of the town hall on January 15. And according to Amnesty International, punishment continues after death as security forces often try to make examples out of those they kill by mutilating the corpses or forbidding neighbors and relatives from collecting the bodies for days. A doctor at a hospital near Larba commented on the five bodies brought in one day.

> When the bodies came in, they were not only riddled with bullets but they were run over by tanks or armored personnel carriers. They didn't even resemble human beings.[59]

The war was taking its toll, not only on the citizenry, but on the government as well. Many of the security forces patrolling the streets wore balaclava hoods (ski masks), so that they could not be targeted for reprisals. The outfits earned them the nickname "ninjas," after the popular Hong Kong martial arts movies. More worrisome for the government was dissent in the ranks. The army was holding together, but many worried that some of the junior officers, tired of serving an illegitimate government and fighting their own people, might begin to side with the militants. "Fifth columnists in the army," noted *The Economist*, "have already been responsible for some of the worst attacks on military installations. Desertions are reported, sometimes of entire units." While trusted regular forces were shouldering most of the burden, the government worried about the conscripts it was calling up as the fighting intensified. "Conscripts are said to be evading the draft, hiding or taking to hills," noted one journalist.

> Their reluctance—they ask why they should sacrifice themselves in defence of a regime that does nothing for them—is fortified by Islamic militants who threaten to kill them to prevent their joining up, and sometimes do so.[60]

In what some called a government show of strength and others a prelude to negotiations, the ruling HCE appointed Defense Minister Liamine Zeroual as president. The appointment, greeted with mixed emotions by most Algerians, followed months of clandestine maneuvering in which the government tried to gain support for its three-year transitional plan leading to presidential elections. This involved open talks with secular opposition parties and secret meetings with FIS officials, both free and imprisoned, who the government hoped to lure to the negotiating table. But a two-day conference at the end of January where the deal was supposed to be ratified was boycotted by everyone except the junta. "The army was left nakedly exposed as the real power in the land," noted one reporter. "The [opposition] parties were not prepared, said their leaders, to lend legitimacy and credibility to a regime set up by the army."[61]

Meanwhile, the Algerian public was losing hope, especially as the war took its toll on the Algerian economy. "The level of cynicism and passive hostility is strikingly high," noted *The Economist*.

> People in the street dismissed the conference as irrelevant to their everyday struggle for survival. "I can't get married because I have nowhere to live and no work," was the answer of one young woman to political questions. Food shortages now mean queues for such staples as semolina, bread and oil. "Nothing will change. It's only talk. It's all disaster. No one asks what we want. We didn't elect the government. Algeria is finished," said a shopkeeper angrily. But the government can probably continue to maintain itself in power through force, with or without popular support.[62]

In March, Zeroual tried to revive negotiations with the FIS and other opposition parties, but his efforts largely failed. There were obstacles both within the regime and without. As *el-Watan* noted, many officers were adamantly opposed to talks with the FIS. "There is a very strong faction within the Army holding that this direction [negotiations] has led nowhere, except to allow the terrorists to gain ground by intimidating the population," editor Omar Belhouchet wrote. "They see the Islamic radicals as a force that is fighting for nothing less than full power, so their only answer is more repression."[63]

While Zeroual and high-ranking generals quickly disputed the report, some officers spoke anonymously to the effect that the FIS was no longer really in control of the armed Islamic militants, so negotiations would be pointless. And indeed, the GIA issued warnings that FIS officials who agreed to talk with the government would be targeted for assassination. Then, on March 12, 1994, the government experienced its worst setback of the war thus far. In a bold daytime raid on the top-security Tazoult prison in eastern Algeria, Islamic militants freed over 1,000 political detainees and drove them away in trucks. The audacity of the raid and the limited number of casualties pointed to collaboration by guards.

While fundamentalist militants were escalating their attacks in the spring of 1994, other sectors of Algerian society were making themselves heard for the first time since the coup and the violence had silenced them. On March 22, tens of thousands of women in Western clothes marched in Algiers to protest against fundamentalist threats. "The boldness of this demonstration—in conditions of such lawlessness that many Algerians are afraid to leave their homes—reflects despair at the ever-worsening violence," noted one reporter. Berbers also marched to protest the slaying of the national secretary of the Berber-dominated Rally for Culture and Democracy party (RCD).

Over the course of 1994, the Berber population increasingly made known its displeasure with both the fundamentalists and the government. "We think Algeria is finished," one Berber university student in Tizi Ouzou said. "We should let the army and the Islamic militants fight it out." And for the most part, the Kabyle region where many Berbers live has escaped the carnage in the rest of the country. In the capital city of Tizi Ouzou people still stroll the streets at night. Still, the Berbers' fears have led to the revival of the intensely nationalistic RCD. As one Berber politician explained, an Islamic republic "would awaken all the old demons" of separatism. Still, few Berbers believe that an independent Kabyle is either realistic or desirable.[64]

As if to answer the women and Berbers, the GIA renewed its warnings and increased its attacks against the army, police, secularist intellectuals, artists, journalists and foreigners. On March 30, 1994, fundamentalists allegedly killed two women, both teenage college students, as they waited for a bus in Algiers. The killings were the first of women specifically for failing to wear the veil in public.

The summer witnessed a dramatic fulfillment of the threat against foreigners. On July 7, seven Italian sailors were found with their throats slit aboard their ship while it was docked in the port of Djedjen, about 200 miles east of Algiers. The ship was carrying grain, Italy's largest export to

Algeria. Italy is also Algeria's largest gas customer. While most attacks on foreigners were directed against the French, with the exception of the killing of the Croats and Bosnians in December 1993, the slaying of the Italians marked a new phase, of assault on Europeans generally. Later in July, two Arab ambassadors were kidnapped in an area the government said was a stronghold of the GIA, but nobody took responsibility for the action. In August, five Frenchmen protecting their national embassy were machine-gunned from a passing car, bringing the total number of foreigners killed to fifty-six since the GIA ultimatum of September 1993.

Autumn 1994 was marked by a series of sputtering talks between the government and the FIS, fundamentalist attacks on a new set of targets, specifically Algeria's economic infrastructure, and several hopeful develop-ments that ultimately proved futile. At the end of August, imprisoned FIS leaders Belhadj and Madani sent two letters to Zeroual that the president described as "an initiative that deserves attention and which merits encour-agement." In the letters, say opposition leaders who received copies of them, the FIS demanded an end to emergency rule and the army's pursuit of militants, as well as a national referendum on the establishment of an Islamic state coupled with early parliamentary elections.

These demands were not new; Zeroual had dismissed similar ones earlier in the year and was expected to do the same this time. But the two sides continued meeting through much of October, despite GIA threats to kill anyone on either side who participated in the talks. In November, however, the government killed the last hopes of a negotiated peace when it refused to attend multilateral talks in Rome. Organized under the aegis of the Vatican's Sant'Edigio community, a group with a record of successful international brokering in places such as Mozambique, the talks were intended to bring all parties to the conflict together, including secular opposition forces, the FIS and the Algerian regime. In his rejection of the invitation, Zeroual argued that "Algerian problems . . . should be treated inside Algeria. All conditions are available in our country to let the different political actors meet in full freedom and discuss the means and the best ways to end the country's crisis."[65] While this reflected the Algerian president's long-standing opposition to outside interference, it also indicated his preference for bilateral talks with the FIS only. The rejection discouraged both Algerians and international observers. As one scholar noted,

> One would think the power apparatus would be aware of its isolation from society, but this seems not to be the case. The ability of the ruling circles . . . to delude themselves on this score never ceases to amaze . . . The current authorities, like their authoritarian counterparts elsewhere in the world, past and present, believe their own rhetoric and view their stage-managed street processions as signs of popular support.[66]

As if to underline the point, the opposition groups took up the Catholic organization's offer and began to meet, even as the regime and the militants engaged in ever more brutal fighting. On December 18, militants blew up power line pylons in the Blida area south of Algiers, cutting off electricity to the capital and the surrounding region. As if to punctuate the new offensive, one of the largest food warehouses in Algiers was blown up and burned to the ground in an attack by forty armed guerrillas. On Christmas Eve, the GIA hijacked the French airbus in Algiers and then on December 28 the GIA took responsibility for the murder of four French and Belgian Catholic priests in the Berber "capital" of Tizi Ouzou. While the GIA claimed it was part of its campaign of "annihilation and physical liquidation of Christian crusaders," many believed it was also a show of force aimed at the largely anti-fundamentalist Berbers.[67] As the year came to a close, Algerian authorities put the number of dead in the conflict at 10,000, though independent sources claimed it was nearer to 25,000.

WAR AND PEACE (1995–1996)

While the government continued to refuse outside aid in negotiating a peace settlement, including French president Mitterrand's February offer of a European Union–sponsored conference, the opposition parties reached an agreement on a plan for transition to democracy in Rome in January 1995 (see Chapter 5). An unlikely statement followed from the GIA. In a January 15 communiqué, the group said it was "ready to stop the war" as long as several conditions were met. First, the government had to release GIA leaders Abdelhak Layada and Ahmen al-Qud. Second, the group insisted that all communist and atheist parties be banned as "enemies of religion" and that the "law of God" be applied to the generals who "have delayed the Islamic plan" for Algeria.[68] No one believed that Zeroual could possibly accept such demands.

Thus, despite the Rome platform, the war in Algeria intensified during the winter of 1995. On January 30, a suicide bombing of police headquarters in Algiers killed 42 and wounded over 250, mostly passersby rather than police. In mid-February, the GIA claimed responsibility for the destruction of three vital bridges in and around Algiers. According to *Africa Report*, over 500 people were being killed weekly in Algeria during February, the most violent month of the war to date. On February 22, the toll climbed dramatically when an alleged escape plan by some of the militants who had organized the breakout at Tazoult almost a year before was discovered by guards who then shot down as many as 200 Islamist inmates at Algeria's highest-security prison, Serkadji, in Algiers. The massacre appalled even those jaded by the routine atrocities of the war. Human rights organizations, including those affiliated with the government, expressed their outrage and demanded an independent investigation into the deaths.

The response by Islamic militants was fast and unforgiving. In a series of attacks, the GIA attacked convoys of security forces with mines planted in roadways. The group also took the war home to those who served in the security forces. On March 17, the fundamentalists set off a bomb in front of a secured apartment building where the families of police were housed. The explosion ripped off the facade but miraculously killed no one.

The randomness and effectiveness of the armed groups, as well as the ruthless efficiency of the government, has created a profound sense of desperation and paranoia in the vast majority of urban Algerians. People refuse to set appointments by phone for fear that security forces, the GIA or anti-Islamic death squads are listening in. "We're just waiting to die," said one pharmacist. "I drove my kids to school and saw children stepping over a body in a pool of blood to get through the door," added an Algiers housewife. Military and police personnel are especially edgy. "They're where you least expect them," said one army major. "They strike when they want to where they want to, and [by] the means they choose." Another officer noted that "fourteen of my military classmates have been assassinated. Someone in the military tipped off the terrorists."[69]

The paranoia was fed by a growing suspicion in Algeria that some of the random acts of violence that appeared to be the work of fundamentalists may in fact have been committed by government forces. One Algerian police officer who fled his job and country told England's *Guardian* newspaper in March 1995 that many Algerians believe the elite squadrons within the security forces may be behind the murder of other police, in order to frame fundamentalists. "Fouad's [his pseudonym] first doubts about the conduct of the civil war surfaced at the funerals of fellow officers," notes the reporter.

> Relatives of slain policemen would tell bewildered colleagues not to touch the coffin, saying: "it wasn't the Islamists who killed him, it was you." The most popular police officers were killed first "as if to shock and disgust people," says Fouad.[70]

He added that he had been called off several chases of suspects and then seen their cars enter military headquarters. "We were fighting the GIA and we realised—we even discussed it with each other—that the spectacular incidents were being staged by the government services" like the assassination of Boudiaf, he notes.[71] The FIS agreed. In May, it cited an Algerian television report of two sisters supposedly murdered by the GIA. "The Algerian TV made a Hollywood movie of the event," noted the FIS statement.

> The two sisters were presented for twenty minutes with their throats [cut] for having refused the temporary marriage with "terrorists" . . . Ali Yahia

Abdennour [an FIS official] conducted a personal investigation. He questioned fifteen families living in the [area]. It emerged . . . that the victims were the sisters of the emir of [the] Mujahadeen in the region. The two sisters used to prepare meals for the Mujahadeen. This was the only reason behind their slaughter by the security services as believed by the fifteen interrogated families.[72]

Whether the government was in fact using *agents provocateurs* or not, the crackdown on the militants was beginning to have an effect by the late spring and summer of 1995. A *New York Times* correspondent described a relatively peaceful Algiers, at least in the daytime. "On these early summer afternoons the most common sight in Algiers . . . is of teen-agers negotiating the hilly streets with their book bags hanging over their shoulders, sidewalk cafes overflowing with domino players, and markets teeming with shoppers," he wrote. "But after the 11:30 P.M. curfew, intermittent shots can be heard as security forces sweep through the neighborhoods looking for suspected terrorist cells." As one Algerian noted, "Normality is a form of resistance." Meanwhile, government officials were announcing that "the tide has turned."[73]

Yet the same obstacles to peace remained and the killing continued. In late May and early June, Zeroual met once more with FIS leaders Belhadj and Madani, ensconced at a government-owned villa in the Algiers area. But the president's continuing rejection of the Rome platform, and the FIS leaders' refusal to bargain separately with the government, doomed the talks once again. On June 3, the two were returned to their cells at an undisclosed prison.

As Independence Day, July 5, approached, many Algerians and outside observers expected Zeroual to make some kind of conciliatory statement that might break the negotiation logjam. Instead, the president delivered a blunt and uncompromising vow to crush the Muslim fundamentalist rebels, though he said the door remained opened to "moderates" who wanted to talk. "It is . . . by maintaining national vigilance without respite, by the firmness of our valiant security forces and the policy of friendly exchange with our errant sons that we will achieve, together, the final eradication of abject terrorism and inadmissible violence from the ranks of our society," he announced. His speech was backed up by an editorial in the army journal dismissing the militants as "traitors and renegades."[74]

Zeroual also said that the government was committed to its transition plan, including a presidential election in November 1995. Those elections provided a shot in the arm for the government. Zeroual easily won, garnering 61 percent of the vote. His nearest challenger, Sheik Mahfoud Nahnah of the moderate Islamist party Hamas, took 25 percent, leaving two secularists with just 14 percent. More significantly, voter turnout was high, with 75 percent of the electorate coming out to vote despite threats by the GIA to "turn polls into graveyards" and a boycott by the Rome signatories, including the FIS, FLN, FFS and other parties.[75] The Organization of African Unity (OAU), which monitored the elections, said, "They took place in a calm atmosphere, in freedom and transparency." But with only 50 monitors nationwide, their verdict was denounced by the FIS, which declared the vote a "sham" and said the real turnout was between 25 and 50 percent.[76] "We don't accept the results of the vote," pronounced Anwar Haddam, an FIS spokesperson in exile, "and we consider that it's still an illegitimate regime."[77]

Still, many Algerians celebrated the results. According to Associated Press, just minutes after Zeroual went on TV to announce the results, "The streets of Algiers reverberated with hundred of rounds of celebratory rifle shots into the sky and the joyous ululation of women." Meanwhile, both sides responded to the election with calls for renewed negotiations, though these efforts have gone nowhere since. For the next six months, the Zeroual regime offered a few inducements and a lot of pressure. It invited one of the FIS' founders to join the cabinet, but one who had much earlier left the party. In May, it announced a constitutional referendum for late 1996 and legislative elections for the first half of 1997, though it offered few details about how either one would be conducted and whether the FIS, or indeed any party, would be permitted to run.

At the same time, it brushed off efforts by France's new president, Jacques Chirac, to arbitrate an agreement between the government and the FIS, continued its harsh crackdown against militants and, in an ominous return to the pre-1989 constitutional era of press censorship, it arrested the editor and suspended publication of *Liberté*, a left-wing Algiers daily, in December 1995, for criticizing a top aide of Zeroual's.

Indeed, the government seems increasingly confident of its position. Besides its election victory, revenues from gas and oil remain unaffected by the conflict. Foreign technicians are housed in armed camps near the fields, and the wide-open spaces of the Sahara and the distance from populated areas make it very difficult for the GIA to attack. In June, the influential *Middle East Economic Survey* announced that "despite the unfavourable political climate in the country, many projects are on their way to completion and that Algeria will be able to develop its oil and gas potential over the next two years."[78] And while oil revenues fed the government, many average Algerians were able to weather the economic crisis by remittances sent back by family members living and working in France.

Not surprisingly, it has been precisely those two economic pillars that the GIA has increasingly targeted. Beginning in July, a wave of bombings and attempted bombings in France, including attacks on the Paris metro, were intended not only to warn France against continued support of the regime, but also to inflame French public opinion against Algerians, in the hope that this might disrupt the flow of funds home. While threats have continued, the bombing campaign came to a halt in late 1995. Earlier in the year, the GIA attacked a gas pipeline that fed Algiers. While this was not a part of the infrastructure of hydrocarbon export, it indicated that the group had found the means to attack this crucial industrial sector. In February 1996, the GIA told oil and gas workers to stop work or it would send hit squads into the desert to murder them. During that same month, the GIA allegedly set off two bombs, one of which killed the editor of the Algiers daily *Le Soir*, a well-known critic of the Islamists.

While the government argues that the conflict is winding down and that the acts of violence are the work of isolated terrorists, a more ominous chapter in the war may have begun. For several years now, a number of Algerian and international experts suspected that the FIS no longer controlled the militants of the GIA, and evidence of this rift continues to mount. As FIS leaders have become more willing to denounce acts of GIA terror, the GIA has carried out its threats to kill FIS leaders who criticize them. In December 1995, two top aides of Madani received a "religious" trial and were then executed by the GIA. While the government hopes that the internecine fighting will tear the Islamist movement apart, GIA bombs continue to go off in the cities, and the Islamic Salvation Army, the FIS' armed wing, is still said to be in control of "large swathes of the country, particularly in the mountainous regions of eastern Algeria."[79]

By 1996, the costs of the war were still mounting. Most outside observers put the total killed at some 60,000, including dozens of judges, hundreds of journalists and intellectuals, over one hundred foreigners and thousands of ordinary Algerians, militants and security force personnel.

In December 1996, Algerian voters overwhelmingly ratified a new constitution. Largely written by the military and the High Council of State, the new charter offers expanded powers to the president and limits those of parliament. It also bans any party "founded on a religious basis." thereby outlawing the FIS. But critics in both Algeria and abroad question the validity of the plebiscite. While the government says that 79 percent of eligible voters went to the polls, casting 75 percent of their votes in favor of the new constitution, independent Algerian journalists say the turnout was more likely between 25 and 50 percent. No independent or international authorities were allowed to observe the election.

THE FUTURE OF ALGERIA

It is not easy to be sanguine about Algeria's short-term future. The government and the opposition are not talking to each other. Indeed, they don't appear to be speaking the same language. The regime does not consider the FIS a responsible political organization that can be entrusted with power. The FIS, along with its secularist allies, views the regime as illegitimate. Thus far, negotiations have produced no significant results, and offers of assistance by outside parties have been rejected outright by the junta in power in Algiers. While some FIS officials have been outspoken in their denunciation of violence, there are serious questions concerning both their sincerity and their capacity to enforce their will on the guerrillas doing the actual fighting. And with each passing day, the war stirs up more bitterness. A sense of helplessness and hopelessness has descended on the Algerian people, particularly young unemployed men, the *hittistes*, who hang out on city streets, holding up the walls. "There are problems with everything," says Abd el-Haq, a self-described *hittiste*.

> Before, I was able to move. I used to visit my family. Today, that's finished, even if there is a religious occasion. You look for work and there isn't any. I have applied at many places. Only the police are hiring. I don't feel like picking up other people's sons or *nahgar* (humiliating people, abusing power). One is no longer living with Muslims . . . Do you want me to tell you the truth? I am living in a foreign country here. I don't have anything, there isn't anything. I don't love Algeria, not at all.[80]

While the FIS asserts that Algeria's problems are essentially moral and ethical ones, most others agree that the economic crisis has been a major cause of the strife, or that it has at least created the atmosphere for acts of political desperation. "We [at *Le Soir d'Algerie*, the *Algeria Evening* newspaper] hired several young jobless men from the neighborhood whom we knew to be FIS sympathizers and possibly even tempted by the terrorism route," explains the paper's editor.

> Now they drive trucks or do other small jobs for us that give them some hope in the future, and their former sympathies are forgotten. They tell us, "We thought it [the FIS] was the only solution for us."[81]

Despite this consensus on the roots of the crisis, or perhaps even because of it, escape from the economic catastrophe that is contemporary Algeria looks far off. That is to say, the only real common ground between the government and the fundamentalists is their economic agenda: increased free trade, liberalization, austerity and privatization. Whether this IMF-sponsored economic formula can or will succeed is not necessarily the point. As the evidence from Eastern Europe and elsewhere indicates, structural adjustment creates tremendous social and political stress in the short term, precisely what Algeria cannot afford. Specifically, structural adjustment appears, at least in the short run, to generate speculation, black marketeering, unemployment and increasing economic disparity between rich and poor, precisely the problems that got Algeria into its current mess in the first place. Nor can Algeria expect much help from its gas and oil sector. True, they will continue to generate needed revenues, but oil and gas prices are not likely to climb in the near future and might drop further if the UN sanctions against Iraq are lifted.

Politically, both the military and the fundamentalists have a sorry record. One side circumvented the democratic process when it appeared it was losing; the other is on record denouncing democracy as contrary to the will of God and alien to the scriptures. Compare these two statements. The first is from Prime Minister Redha Malek; the second from imprisoned FIS leader Ali Belhadj.

> For us, democracy is not a matter of going to the voting booths. That's not democracy. Democracy is a culture, a formation, an organization. If you think democracy consists of going to the voting booths and telling people how to vote . . . it will lead us to catastrophe.[82]

> Among all the reasons for which we reject the democratic dogma, there is the fact that democracy relies on the opinion of the majority . . . As for us, the people of the Sunna, we believe that justice (*haq*) only comes from decisive proofs of the Sharia and not from a multitude of demagogic actors and voices.[83]

On the one side is open contempt for the democratic will of the people; on the other is open contempt for the democratic process itself. The military regime says the people and their political leaders are not ready for a full experiment in democracy yet and need a number of years of transition in which the military will continue to rule. Zeroual himself has said that the Algerian political class has "an infantile ideology."[84] Yet, when given the opportunity to form political and civic organizations in 1989, Algerians showed a remarkable aptitude for associative life, despite almost thirty years of stifling FLN rule.

Meanwhile, FIS leaders evince a similar contempt for the will of the people despite their party's electoral victories. "The ruler is not qualified to modify the law," says Belhadj. "That right belongs neither to the ruler nor to the people, but to scholars who know the rules of Itjihad [free thought] at the same time as the temporal conditions existing in the societies to which they belong."[85] FIS leaders have pronounced their opinion on a number of occasions that liberal democracy is a Western import totally unsuited to a Muslim society. Maybe so, but they have thus far failed to elaborate a concrete and realistic model for how an Islamicized democratic system would operate.

As it is elsewhere, politics in Algeria is often about symbols rather than substance. That is particularly the case concerning the two sides' visions of Algerian society, especially women's place and role in that society. The presence of women in public, and their wearing of the veil, have become heated subjects of debate and sources of violence and retribution. Women have become symbols of Algeria's future social order. The modest Muslim woman, deferring to her father or husband, accepting her God-given role as wife and mother, wearing the veil in public, represents the vision of an Islamic Algeria, just as the bold,

Western-garbed working woman symbolizes a hybrid Algeria, the product of its dual Muslim and French heritage. Real women of both kinds have become targets of violence.

Given the current state of affairs in Algeria, it is difficult to assess public opinion and feeling, especially on social questions. Do most Algerians want an Islamicized society? Would a way out of the current economic morass weaken support for the fundamentalists? Algerian politics has been so polarized since the coup that there seems to be no common ground or room for compromise. The majority of Algerians may very well want a social order grounded in traditional culture, that is to say, Islamicized to some degree. The FIS' electoral victory can be interpreted to say as much. On the other hand, many Algerians clearly want a tolerant society, a modern consumer economy and pluralistic politics. An Algerian intellectual pointed to what he considered proof of that. "When the armed opposition groups took control of whole regions during Ramadan [March–April 1992]," he argues, "there was no popular outpouring such as happened in Iran."[86] And unquestionably the vast majority of Algerians, though by now inured to violence, want an end to it.

Violence does appear to be declining, though threats of violence have not. While the government may see a benefit in the increasing internecine fighting between the FIS and GIA, civilians are as likely to be killed in the crossfire of intra-Islamist violence as they are in fighting between the Islamists and the regime.

With all the difficulties and divisions in contemporary Algeria, the nation and its people are not without some valuable social, political and economic assets. First, experts predict that at current levels Algeria will be able to pump oil for another twenty years and gas for a hundred, long enough for even the longest-term economic development plans to take hold. Second, there is no serious threat to Algeria's territorial integrity, despite some noises being made by Berber nationalists. Unlike the states of the Arab east, Algeria has a strong sense of nationality and, though it means less among the young, a proud anti-imperialist heritage. And despite 130 years of French harassment and thirty years of stifling FLN rule, associative life in Algeria bounced back admirably when given the chance in 1989. Algerians as a whole are relatively well educated, literate and skilled.

Unless the more moderate leaders of the FIS and the regime are being completely disingenuous, both want a return to the democratic process. Of course, whether there can be such a thing as "moderation" among military putschists and religious fundamentalists is another question. Clearly they disagree about what constitutes a fair and workable electoral system. But if there is to be an end to the current conflict, agreement must be reached.

Can Algerians find a way to Islamicize their society while preserving its pluralism? Can the military cede power to the fundamentalists while guaranteeing the rights of political minorities? Can the FIS, or whatever party comes to power, relinquish power if that is the democratic will of the people? Since all sides agree that political peace must precede social and economic restructuring, Algeria's future depends on the answers to these questions.

NOTES

[1] *New York Times*, January 14, 1992, p. A1.

[2] The three civilian members of the HCE included Prime Minister Sid Ahmed Ghozali, Foreign Minister Ladkhdar Ibrahimi and Justice Minister Hamdani Benkhelil. The military members were Defense Minister General Khaled Nezzer, Interior Minister General Larbi Belkhair and Army Chief of Staff General Abdelmalek Guenaizia.

[3] Cited in "Human Rights in Algeria since the Halt of the Electoral Process," *News from Middle East Watch*, February 1992, p. 6.

[4] *Ibid.,* p. 13.

[5] *Ibid.*

[6] *The Economist*, January 18, 1992, p. 42.

[7] Entelis, John. "Islam, Democracy, and the State; The Reemergence of Authoritarian Politics in Algeria" in Ruedy, John, *Islamism and Secularism in North Africa*, New York: St. Martin's Press, 1994, p. 244.

[8] *The Economist*, February 8, 1992, p. 38.

[9] *Ibid.*, February 15, 1992, p. 45.

[10] *Africa Report*, March/April 1992, pp. 16–17.

[11] Cited in "Halt of the Electoral Process," p. 6.

[12] *New York Times*, June 30, 1992, p. A8.

[13] *The Economist*, January 9, 1993, p. 38.

[14] *The Economist* (UK edition), July 18, 1992, p. 48.

[15] *Africa Report*, September/October 1992, p. 53.

[16] *Ibid.*

[17] *The Economist*, February 20, 1993, p. 40.

[18] "Algeria: Deteriorating human rights under the state of emergency," *Amnesty International*, March 1993, p. 9.

[19] *Ibid.*, p. 9.

[20] *Ibid.*, p. 5, 14.

[21] Cited in "Halt of the Electoral Process," pp. 9–10.

[22] Cited in "Deteriorating Human Rights," p. 10.

[23] An important exception was the August 1992 bombing of the Houari Boumédienne Airport in Algiers in which nine persons were killed and over 100 injured. Fifty-five Islamic militants were put on trial the following spring. Thirty-eight received death sentences, though 26 of these were imposed *in absentia*. The rest received sentences ranging from one to 20 years imprison-

ment. Three were acquitted. Human Rights Watch complained of various violations of due process in the case and Algeria's president eventually commuted several death sentences to life imprisonment.

24 Human Rights Watch/Middle East, *Human Rights Abuses in Algeria: No One Is Spared*, New York: Human Rights Watch, January 1994, p. 7.

25 *Ibid.*

26 *Ibid.*, p. 51.

27 *Ibid.*, p. 55.

28 *Ibid.*, p. 56.

29 *Ibid.*, p. 39.

30 Anonymous 1, interview with author, June 23, 1995.

31 Seghir, Mohammed, "Political Islam and Government: Agenda and Method," talk given at Symposium on Political Islam and Women in Algeria, Hunter College, New York, June 23, 1995.

32 Anonymous 2, interview with author, June 23, 1995.

33 FIS National Provisional Executive Bureau (Europe), untitled communiqué, August 25, 1993, unpaginated.

34 HRW, *No One Is Spared*, p. 57.

35 *Ibid.*, p. 58.

36 *Ibid.*, p. 57.

37 *Libération*, December 7, 1993, p. 3.

38 "No One Is Spared," p. 53.

39 Haddam, Anwar, interview with author, August 30, 1995.

40 Haddam, Anwar, "The Algerian Crisis: FIS Perspective," unpublished manuscript, 1994, p. 6.

41 Benameur, Anissa, "Political Islam and Democracy: A Woman's Perspective," talk delivered at Symposium on Political Islam and Women in Algeria, Hunter College, New York, June 23, 1995.

42 Islamic Salvation Front, "Algeria: The Oppressed Intelligence the World Chose to Ignore," in *Tribune of Human Rights in Algeria*, 1994, p. 2.

43 Abdennour, Ali Yahia, "Strangled Human Rights under the Algerian Hidden War," in *Tribune of Human Rights in Algeria*, 1995, p. 1.

44 Younsi, Fatiha, "Socialism and Political Islam in Algeria," talk delivered at Symposium on Political Islam and Women.

45 FIS, "Oppressed Intelligence," p. 2.

46 Zerhouni, Nourredine Yazid, "Algeria: The Struggle for Democracy," unpublished manuscript, 1992, p. 5.

47 Haddam, "Algerian Crisis," p. 6.

48 Embassy of the Republic of Algeria (Washington), "Background Paper on the Algerian Government," unpublished manuscript, no date, p. 3.   48A See footnote 44.

49 Islamic Salvation Front, "Press Conference (Washington)," unpublished transcript, April 26, 1995, p. 1.

50 Lamamra, Ramtane, interview with author, June 21, 1995.

[51] *The Economist*, December 18, 1993, p. 40.

[52] The foreign population in Algeria before the coup included 50,000 citizens holding French and Algerian passports, 25,000 French citizens, and 25,000 persons of other nationalities, largely Spanish and Italian.

[53] Cited in *New York Times*, December 27, 1994, p. A1.

[54] *The Economist* (European edition), January 7, 1995, p. 41.

[55] *New York Times*, January 24, 1994, p. A1.

[56] *Ibid.*

[57] Many inside and outside the government believe the two organizations are, in fact, one, since many of their communiqués are identical.

[58] *New York Times*, January 24, 1994, p. A6.

[59] *Ibid.*, p. A1.

[60] *The Economist*, February 5, 1994, p. 43.

[61] Ibid., January 29, 1994, p. 43.

[62] *Ibid.*

[63] Cited in *Christian Science Monitor*, February 4, 1994, p. 3

[64] *Washington Post*, June 9, 1994, p. 22.

[65] Reuters on-line wire service, C reuters@clarinet.com, November 17, 1994.

[66] Kapil, Arun, "Algeria's Crisis Intensifies: The Search for a 'Civic Pact'" in *Middle East Report*, January–February 1995, p. 4.

[67] *New York Times*, December 29, 1994, p. A10.

[68] *Ibid.*, January 16, 1995, p. A3.

[69] *Time*, March 20, 1995, p. 48.

[70] *The Guardian*, March 9, 1995, p. 8.

[71] *Ibid.*

[72] Abdennour, "Strangled Human Rights," p. 4.

[73] *New York Times*, June 6, 1995, p. A8.

[74] Reuters on-line wire service, C-Reuters@clarinet.com, July 5, 1995.

[75] Reuters on-line wire service, C-Reuters@clarinet.com, November 17, 1996.

[76] Reuters on-line wire service, C-Reuters@clarinet.com, November 18, 1996.

[77] Associated Press on-line wire service, C-AP@clarinet.com, November 17, 1996.

[78] Reuters on-line wire service, C-Reuters@clarinet.com, June 12, 1995.

[79] *The Economist*, February 17, 1996, p. 39.

[80] Verges, Meriem, "'I am living in a foreign country here': A conversation with an Algerian 'Hittiste'" in *Middle East Report*, January-February 1995, p. 16.

[81] *Christian Science Monitor*, May 16, 1994, p. 5.

[82] *Washington Post*, January 26, 1994, p. 1.

[83] Burgat, Francois and Dowell, William, *The Islamic Movement in North Africa*, Austin: Center for Middle Eastern Studies at the University of Texas, 1993, p. 125.

[84] *Washington Post*, January 26, 1994, p. 1.

[85] Burgat, *Islamic Movement*, p. 125.

[86] Kapil, "Algeria's Crisis Intensifies," p. 1.

GLOSSARY

Abbas, Ferhat (Algerian) A nationalist leader of the 1940s through 1960s.

Afghani (Algerian) An Algerian veteran of the anti-Soviet struggle in Afghanistan. Many have become militants in the GIA and MIA (see **Armed Islamic Group, Armed Islamic Movement** and **Islamic Salvation Front**).

Ait Ahmed, Hocine (Berber) Leader of the Berberist Socialist Forces Front party (see Socialist Forces Front).

al-Qadir, Abd (Algerian) Leader of a major rebellion against France in the 1840s, often called the first Algerian nationalist.

Algerian Democratic Movement (MDA) (Algerian) Political party founded by Ahmed Ben Bella after his return from exile in 1989.

Algerian Manifesto for a Democratic Union (UDMA) A nationalist organization founded by Ferhat Abbas in the 1940s (see **Abbas, Ferhat**).

Algerian Peoples Party (PPA) (Algerian) Nationalist party founded by Messali Hadj in the 1930s (see **Hadj, Messali**).

Algiers (Algerian) Algeria's capital.

ALN (Algerian) National Liberation Army of Algeria.

APN (see **National Popular Assembly**).

Armed Islamic Group (GIA) (Algerian) The major force of armed Islamic guerrillas fighting in Algeria today (see **Islamic Salvation Front**).

Armed Islamic Movement (MIA) (Algerian) A small armed Islamic force fighting in Algeria today (see **Armed Islamic Group** and **Islamic Salvation Front**).

assabiyya (Arabic) Tribal loyalties, it has historically been the inverse of the umma (see **umma**).

Atlas Mountains (Algerian) The major mountain ranges that divide the populated coastal regions from the Sahara Desert.

autogestion (French) Self-management. A spontaneous post-revolution peasant and worker movement to give laborers management of the means of production.

Bab el-Oued (Algerian) A working-class neighborhood of Algiers and fundamentalist stronghold.

Badis, Sheikh Ibn (Algerian) The major religio-nationalist figure of the early twentieth century.

barbes (French) Bearded ones, slang for fundamentalist men.

Belhadj, Ali (Algerian) One of the two main leaders of the Islamic Salvation Front (see **Islamic Salvation Front** and **Madani**).

Ben Bella, Ahmed (Algerian) One of the leaders of the War of Independence and Algeria's first president, from 1962 to 1965 (see **chefs historiques** and **War of Independence**).

Benjedid, Chadli (Algerian) Algeria's third president, from 1979 to 1992.

Berber (Greek) The pre-Arab invasion, indigenous people of Algeria (see **Kabyle**).

bidonville (French) Literally "phony-town," it translates as shantytown.

Black October The spontaneous nationwide riots in October 1988.

bled (Arabic) The countryside.

Blida (Algerian) A major fundamentalist stronghold 30 miles south of Algiers.

Boudiaf, Mohammed (Algerian) One of the leaders of Algeria's War of Independence, he was brought back from exile to serve as president after the coup (see **chefs historiques** and **War of Independence**).

boulitique (Algerian) Back-room politics.

Boumédienne, Houari (Algerian) One of the leaders of the War of Independence and Algeria's second president, from 1965 to 1978 (see **chefs historiques** and **War of Independence**).

Bouyali, Moustapha (Algerian) A former FLN commander who led an armed Islamic guerrilla movement against the Algerian government in the mid-1980s.

cadi (Arabic) An Islamic judge.

casbah (Arabic) The old center of Algiers.

chefs historiques (French) The leaders of the Algerian War of Independence (see **Ben Bella, Boudiaf, Boumédienne** and **War of Independence**).

Code de l'Indigénat (French) A set of codes enacted in 1881 that established second-class citizenship for Algerian Muslims.

colons (French) The European colonists who lived and ruled Algeria until 1962 (see **War of Independence**).

Constantine (French) The major city of Algeria's east, also known in Arabic as Qasantina.

CRUA (see **Revolutionary Committee of Unity and Action**).

dinar (Algerian) Algeria's unit of currency. Divided into 100 centimes.

ENA (see **North African Star**).

Evian Agreements The 1962 peace treaty that ended the Algerian War of Independence and established the framework for Algeria's independence (see **War of Independence**).

Family Code of 1984 A fundamentalist-sponsored, *sharia*-based set of codes concerning personal and family behavior (see **sharia**).

FFS (see **Socialist Forces Front**).

FIS (see **Islamic Salvation Front**).

fitna (Arabic) Social divisions and conflict.

FLN   (see **National Liberation Front**).

fundamentalism   (American) A term borrowed from the Christian vocabulary, it signifies a movement to return to Islam's roots and apply the *sharia* to modern society. Scholars often make a distinction between Islamism (known as techno-Islamism in Algeria), which emphasizes the adaptation of the *sharia* to modern society and neo-fundamentalists, who emphasize a strict conformity to the sharia as written. It is also known in Algeria by its French equivalent, "integrisme" (see **sharia**).

GDP   Gross domestic product.

gendarmerie   (French) Algeria's national police.

General Union of Algerian Workers (UGTA)   Algeria's national trade union federation.

GIA   (see **Armed Islamic Group**).

GNP   Gross national product.

Hadj, Messali   (Algerian) Islamic nationalist leader of the 1930s and 1940s (see **Movement for the Triumph of Democratic Liberty**).

Hamas   (Algerian) A moderate Islamic party (no relation to the Hamas of the Israeli-occupied territories).

HCE   (see **High Council of State**).

High Council of State (HCE)   The joint executive that took power after the 1992 coup.

High Security Council   The Algerian joint chiefs of staff, it led the coup of 1992 (see **High Council of State**).

hijab   (Arabic) The veil a Muslim woman is supposed to wear in public.

hittiste   (Algerian) Literally "those who hold up the walls," it refers to young, urban unemployed males.

hogra   (Algerian) Abuse of power.

ijma   (Arabic) The will and consensus of the people.

imam   (Arabic) A religio-political leader of a Muslim community.

intifah   (Arabic) Restructuring. The term applied to Algeria's economic liberalization of the 1980s and 1990s.

Islamic Salvation Front (FIS)   The major fundamentalist party in Algeria.

itjihad   (Arabic) Free interpretation (see **sharia** and **taqlid**).

jahaliyya   (Arabic) The word used to describe pre-Islamic Arab society, it is often used by political Islamists to signify the chaos of secularist Muslim states (see **salafiyya** and **nahda**).

jihad   (Arabic) Holy struggle.

Kabyle   (Berber) The region in Algeria where most Berbers come from (see **Berbers**).

Koran   (Arabic) Islam's holy book.

Madani, Abassi   (Algerian) One of two main leaders of the Islamic Salvation Front (see **Islamic Salvation Front** and **Belhadj**).

Maghrib (Arabic) The Arab West, literally Land of the Setting Sun, it consists of Algeria, Libya, Mauritania, Morocco, Tunisia and the Western Sahara.

Maraboutism (Algerian) A mystical and ecstatic form of popular Islam, related to the sufism of the Middle East.

MDA (see **Algerian Democratic Movement**).

MIA (see **Armed Islamic Movement**).

mission civilatrice (French) Civilizing mission. France's self-imposed duty to Christianize and "civilize" Algeria and its other overseas possessions.

Movement for the Triumph of Democratic Liberty (MTLD) (Algerian) Nationalist party founded by Messali Hajj in the 1940s (see **Hadj, Messali**).

MTLD (see **Movement for the Triumph of Democratic Liberty**).

Muhammad (Arabic) The holy Prophet of Islam.

mullah (Arabic) Local Islamic ministers.

Muslim Brotherhoods (Egyptian and Pakistani) The major fundamentalist movement of the Arab east. It has had a profound impact on Algerian fundamentalist thought (see **fundamentalism**).

nahda (Arabic) Renaissance of Islamic civilization dating from the nineteenth century (see **salafiyya**).

National Charter of 1976 Algeria's second constitution.

National Consultative Council The consultative assembly established by the FLN in 1962.

National Liberation Front (FLN) The revolutionary party that led Algeria's independence struggle and ruled the country from 1962 to 1992 (see **War of Independence**).

National Popular Assembly Algeria's parliament from 1962 to 1992, when it was disbanded after the coup (see **National Consultative Council**).

National Union of Algerian Peasants (UNPA) Government-organized peasants' advocacy group.

ninjas A popular term for the elite security forces. It derives from the all-black outfits and balaclava helmets or ski masks they wear to protect their identity, that cause them to resemble characters in popular Hong Kong martial arts films.

North African Star (Algerian) A nationalist movement of the 1920s begun among Algerian workers in France.

OAS (see **Secret Armed Organization**).

OPEC Organization of Petroleum Exporting Countries.

Oran (Algerian) The major city of Algeria's west.

Organization of Free Algerians A militant organization that attacks Islamic militant groups for their attacks on secular politicians and women who do not wear the veil in public (see **Armed Islamic Group**).

OS (see **Special Organization**).

Ouida clan   (Moroccan) The clan of a city in eastern Morocco that became headquarters for the Algerian Liberation Army during the War of Independence. Boumédienne, who led the forces there, recruited many of his presidential advisors from the clan (see **Boumédienne** and **War of Independence**).

Party of Socialist Revolution   (Algerian) Party founded by Mohammed Boudiaf immediately after independence in 1962 (see **Boudiaf, Mohammed**).

PPA   (see **Algerian Peoples Party**).

PRS   (see **Party of Socialist Revolution**).

Qutb, Sayyid   (Egyptian) The theorist of modern Islamic fundamentalism.

Rally for Culture and Democracy (RCD)   An extreme Berber nationalist party (see **Socialist Forces Front**).

RCD   (see **Rally for Culture and Democracy**).

Revolutionary Committee of Unity and Action   (Algerian) Post World War II nationalist organization and predecessor of the National Liberation Front (see **National Liberation Front**).

Rome platform   The 1995 political program for democratization of Algeria and the end of military rule. All major secular and religious parties were signatories.

salafiyya   (Arabic) A revivalist movement intended to achieve an Islamic renaissance (see **nahda**).

Secret Armed Organization (OAS)   (French) Terrorist organization founded by French *colons* in the last year before Algerian independence (see **colons**).

Serkadji   (Algerian) The major high security prison in Algiers, it was the scene of a prisoner massacre in early 1995.

sharia   (Arabic) A set of legal codes based on the Koran, the life and sayings of the Prophet, and early interpretations by Islamic scholars.

Socialist Forces Front (FFS)   The largest Berber party in Algeria (see **Ait Ahmed**).

Sonatrach   (French) An acronym for Algeria's state-owned oil and gas industry. It stands for National Society for Research, Production, Transport, Transformation and Commercialization of Hydrocarbons.

Special Organization (OS)   (Algerian) Early nationalist guerrilla movement founded by Ahmed Ben Bella in the 1950s (see **Ben Bella, Ahmed**).

sufism   (see **Maraboutism**).

Sunni   (Arabic) The form of Islam practiced in Algeria.

taqlid   (Arabic) Strict adherence to scripture as written (see **sharia** and **itjihad**).

Tizi Ouzou   (Berber) The cultural and political capital of the Kabyle (see **Kabyle**).

trabendo   (Algerian) Black marketeering and smuggling.

UDMA   (see **Algerian Manifesto for a Democratic Union**).

UGTA   (see **General Union of Algerian Workers**).

UNPA (see **National Union of Algerian Peasants**).

ulema (Arabic) State-sanctioned Islamic scholar.

umma (Arabic) The Islamic community.

War of Independence Algeria's successful liberation struggle against France, from 1954 to 1962.

westoxification (Iranian) A term used by fundamentalists to describe the poisoning of Muslim society by cultural imports from the West (see **fundamentalism**).

zakat (Arabic) *Sharia*-sanctioned tax, often used to support the poor (see **sharia**).

Zeroual, Liamine (Algerian) Former Defense Minister appointed president by the High Council of State in 1994 (see **High Council of State**).

BIBLIOGRAPHY

Addi, Lahouari, *L'Algérie et la démocratie: pouvoir du politique dans l'Algérie contemporaine*, Paris: Éditions la découverte, 1994.

Ageron, Charles-Robert, *Modern Algeria: A History from 1830 to the Present*, Trenton, N.J.: Africa World Press, 1991.

Arkoun, Mohammed, "Algeria" in Hunter, Shireen, *The Politics of Islamic Revivalism: Diversity and Unity*, Bloomington: Indiana University Press, 1988.

*Barakat, Halim, *The Arab World: Society, Culture, and State*, Berkeley: University of California Press, 1993.

Bennoune, Mahfoud, *The Making of Contemporary Algeria, 1830–1987: Colonial Upheavals and Post-Independence Development*, New York: Cambridge University Press, 1988.

*Burgat, Francois and Dowell, William, *The Islamic Movement in North Africa*, Austin: Center for Middle Eastern Studies at the University of Texas, 1993.

Duvignaud, Jean, *Change at Shebika: Report from a North African Village*, New York: Vintage, 1970

El-Kenz, Ali, *Algerian Reflections on Arab Crises*, Austin, Tex.: Center for Middle Eastern Studies, 1991.

Entelis, John and Naylor, Phillip (eds.), *State and Society in Algeria*, Boulder, Colo.: Westview Press, 1992.

Entelis, John, *Algeria: The Revolution Institutionalized*, Boulder, Colo.: Westview Press, 1986.

Esposito, John, *The Islamic Threat: Myth or Reality?*, New York: Oxford University Press, 1992.

Fanon, Frantz, *A Dying Colonialism*, New York: Grove Press, 1965.

Fanon, Frantz, *The Wretched of the Earth*, New York: Grove Press, 1963.

Fox, Robert, *The Inner Sea: The Mediterranean and its People*, New York: Alfred Knopf, 1993.

Gerber, Haim, *Islam, Guerrilla War, and Revolution: A Study in Comparative Social History*, Boulder, Colo.: Lynne Rienner Publishers, 1988.

Horne, Alistair, *A Savage War of Peace: Algeria, 1954–1962*, New York: Penguin, 1987.

Hourani, Albert, *A History of the Arab Peoples*, New York: Warner Books, 1991.

*Kelsay, John, *Islam and War: A Study in Comparative Ethics*, Louisville, Ky.: Westminster/John Knox Press, 1993.

*Kepel, Gilles, *The Revenge of God: The Resurgence of Islam, Christianity and Judaism in the Modern World*, University Park: Pennsylvania State University Press, 1994.

Knauss, Peter, *The Persistence of Patriarchy: Class, Gender, and Ideology in Twentieth Century Algeria*, New York: Praeger, 1987.

*Lazreg, Marnia, "The Kabylie-Berber Cultural Movement in Algeria" in Schwab, Peter and Pollis, Adamantia, *Toward a Human Rights Framework*, New York: Praeger, 1982.

*Lazreg, Marnia. *The Eloquence of Silence: Algerian Women in Question*, New York: Routledge, 1994.

Les Temps Moderne, January–February 1995.

Mansfield, Peter, *The Arabs*, New York: Penguin, 1992.

Middle East Report, January–February 1995.

Ottaway, David and Marina, *Algeria: The Politics of a Socialist Revolution*, Berkeley: University of California Press, 1970.

*Reporters sans frontières, *Le drame algerién: un peuple en otage*, Paris: Éditions la découverte, 1994.

Richards, Alan, and Waterbury, John, *A Political Economy of the Middle East: State, Class, and Economic Development*, Boulder, Colo.: Westview Press, 1990.

*Roy, Olivier, *The Failure of Political Islam*, Cambridge, Mass.: Harvard University Press, 1994.

*Ruedy, John, *Islamism and Secularism in North Africa*, New York: St. Martin's Press, 1994.

*Ruedy, John, *Modern Algeria: The Origins and Development of a Nation*, Bloomington: Indiana University Press, 1992.

Sivan, Emmanuel, and Friedman, Menachem (eds.), *Religious Radicalism and Politics in the Middle East*, Albany: State University of New York Press, 1990.

*Tlemcani, Rachid, *State and Revolution in Algeria*, Boulder, Colo.: Westview Press, 1986.

Van Sivers, Peter, "National Integration and Traditional Rural Organisation in Algeria, 1970–1980: Background for Islamic Traditionalism?" in Arjomand, Said Amir, *From Nationalism to Revolutionary Islam*, Albany: State University of New York Press, 1984.

Zartman, I. William, "The Military in the Politics of Succession" in Harbeson, John (ed.), *The Military in African Politics*, New York: Praeger, 1987.

---

* Especially recommended.

INDEX

Entries are filed letter by letter.
Page references followed by "g" indicate glossary.